828 S645t
ne A.

ENTERED JUL - 9 1998

A Tale of Two Towns

A Tale of Two Towns
A Mining and a Farming Community in the 1890s

Duane A. Smith

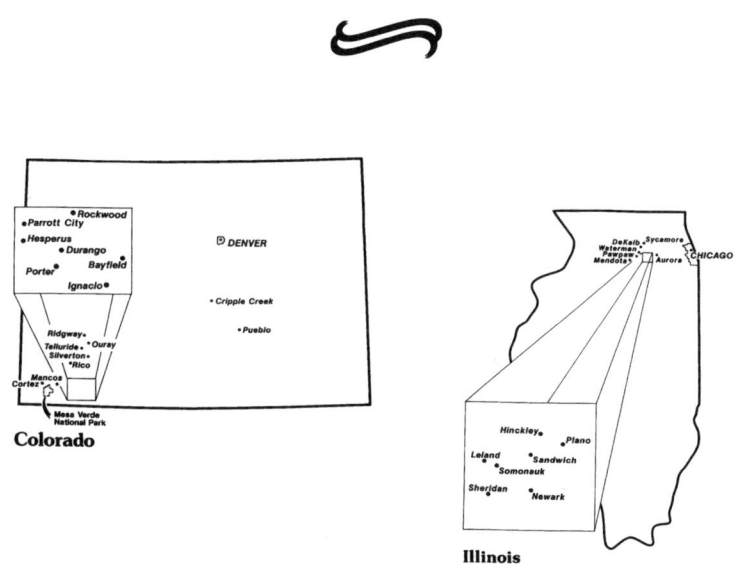

University Press of Colorado

© 1997 by the University Press of Colorado
Published by the University Press of Colorado
P.O. Box 849
Niwot, Colorado 80544
Tel. (303) 530-5337

All Rights reserved. Printed in the United States of America

The University Press of Colorado is a cooperative publishing enterprise supported, in part, by Adams State College, Colorado State University, Fort Lewis College, Mesa State College, Metropolitan State College of Denver, University of Colorado, University of Northern Colorado, University of Southern Colorado, and Western State College of Colorado.

Library of Congress Cataloging-in-Publication Data

Smith, Duane A.
 A tale of two towns: a mining and a farming community in the 1890's / Duane A. Smith.
   p.   cm.
  Includes bibliographical references and index.
  ISBN 0-87081-395-1 (casebound : alk. paper)
  1. Sandwich (Ill.)—History. 2. Durango (Colo.)—History.
3. Sandwich (Ill.)—Social life and customs. 4. Durango (Colo.)—Social life and customs.
5. Agriculture—Illinois—Sandwich—History—20th century. 6. Mineral industries—Colorado—Durango—History—20th century. I. Title
F549.S358S65   1997
977.3'28- -dc21   97-21784
                                                                      CIP

The paper used in this publication meets the minimum requirements of the American National Standard for Information Sciences—Permanence of Paper for Printed Library Materials. ANSI Z39.48-1948

10 9 8 7 6 5 4 3 2 1

```
977.328 S645t

Smith, Duane A.

A tale of two towns
```

Dedicated to
Beverly Johnson
Agnes Henning
Florence Devine
May Sebby
Marjorie Smith Hash

CONTENTS

Preface ix
Prologue xiii

1. The Most Brilliant Future 1
2. The Men and Women Merely Players 17
3. Front Page Headlines 29
4. Best of Times, Worst of Times 43
    Photographic Essay: The Towns 65
5. The Boys Got What They Wanted 75
6. Two-for-a-Quarter Statesmen 89
7. School Marms and Printers' Devils 105
8. No Better Place in America to Live 121
    Photographic Essay: The People 133
9. Old-Time Religion 151
10. This Is Woman's Opportunity 167
11. Joy in Mudville 191
12. Friendship, Love, and Truth 205
13. The Good Old Days 221

Epilogue: After the Ball 245
Essay on Sources 253
Index 255

PREFACE

What is about to unfold is the story of two small towns—Sandwich, Illinois, and Durango, Colorado—towns like those many Americans remember from their youth; towns that gave residents a sense of place, a sense of home; towns where people had time to talk to you, knew when you were sick, and missed you if you failed to show up in church on Sunday; towns with schools within walking distance, alleys behind homes, and vacant lots for games and youthful adventures.

Sandwich and Durango represented a way of life in the United States that reached its peak between the 1870s and World War II. They represented a nation that epitomized the credo of the late House Speaker "Tip" O'Neill's father: "Do the best you can for your neighbor. Never forget from where you come." In those two generations, the United States, as author Richard Critchfield wrote, "went from country to city, farm to factory, horse to car, kitchen surgery to scientific medicine, fundamentalism to Darwinism, tent meeting to Hollywood movie."

The two towns, Sandwich and Durango, were, respectively, a farming community and a mining community. They were selected for this study partly because I have always been fascinated by the similarities and differences between two communities with such diverse and yet hauntingly similar economic backgrounds and histories. They were also chosen because of my deep roots in both. As Abraham Lincoln said in his farewell to his Springfield friends in February 1861, before he boarded the train for Washington, D.C., "To this place, and the kindness of these people, I owe everything. Here I have lived a quarter of a century, and have passed from a young to an old man. To you dear friends, I owe all that I have, all that I am."

The worlds of agricultural and mining towns have long intrigued me—the worlds of Laura Ingalls Wilder's Walnut Grove and Mark Twain's Virginia City (however different in size and temperament they might have

PREFACE

been). Although Western urban history has made great progress in the past generation and has come into its own as a field of study, comparison studies of ordinary mining and farming communities remain extremely rare. No doubt, the limited sources available and other research problems may have caused scholars to consider other urban subjects, but the potential rewards are great in small-town America, where a large percentage of Americans lived.

Tale of Two Towns answers a variety of questions about this genre of community. For example:

> Was there something innately distinctive about Western small-town urbanization compared with Eastern?
> Might there be a common, bonding national culture found in both mining and farming communities?
> Which cultural characteristics did settlers carry with them when migrating west?
> Did outside influences affect the two towns differently?
> What impact did regionalism have on each town?
> Would a visitor notice differences between Sandwich and Durango, strolling down their respective Main Streets or getting to know their residents' lifestyles?

The people of these communities were, in the words of historian Bruce Catton, "average folks whose lives tell a quiet story of ambition gently trailing off into obscurity." A century ago these people had lives of their own. The years since have blended those lives together in the mists of history.

The decade of the 1890s was chosen because Sandwich and Durango were comparable in size during those years; because it was a watershed era for both; and because in that decade, as Oliver Wendell Holmes, Jr., said of an earlier generation, Americans' "hearts were touched by fire"—they experienced the depression that followed the panic of 1893, as well as the election of 1896, the Spanish-American War, and the stirring of reform. The world crashed in on previously insular towns like Durango and Sandwich. Change was at hand. Perhaps these towns and their inhabitants failed to be touched to the depth that Holmes said his Civil War generation had been; nonetheless, the 1890s signaled a watershed in U.S. history, an end and a beginning.

PREFACE

The story of these two hometowns reflects that of thousands of similar late nineteenth-century communities scattered across the continent. The towns and their people embody a generation of Americans poised between a rural, inward-looking America and an urban, worldly America of a new and challenging century. They tell us much about ourselves and offer a fleeting look at the American soul.

No historian researches and writes in isolation. Many people need to be thanked, not the least of whom are the people of the 1890s, who hardly expected to share their lives with me. In addition, Roger Peterson, Barbara Hoffman, and Gary Moss helped a complete stranger find photographs of Sandwich, and librarian Joanne Johnson aided in a variety of ways, as did my mother and father, both natives of Sandwich. W. Dean Holdeman motivated me to get started, and Dorothy Hecathorn shared her historical resources and love of local history. Sandwich City Clerk Barbara Olson contributed material, and Cindy Ditzler of the Regional History Center at Northern Illinois University, and the staff of the Illinois State Historical Library, were most helpful.

Robert McDaniel and Charles DiFerdinando of the La Plata County Historical Society contributed their expertise, Shane Voss gave his time and enthusiasm, and Catherine Conrad contributed her knowledge of the collections of the Center of Southwest Studies at Fort Lewis College. The staffs of the Fort Lewis and Durango Public Libraries provided assistance in a multitude of ways, and Durango City Clerk Linda Yeager allowed my access to city records. My wife, Gay, even in her illness, prodded me along; an author could not ask for a more attentive and loving editor.

This book is affectionately dedicated to the teachers of my first four years as a student in the W. W. Woodbury School in Sandwich. They influenced and shaped my life more than I realized at the time, and to each I owe an enormous debt of thanks and gratitude. Even today I can almost taste the graham crackers and milk I got every morning. I remember purchasing defense stamps, and I hold a tender spot in my heart for Dick, Jane, Sally, Puff, and Spot, not to mention rhythm bands and my promotion to a "bluebird" in music class. My cousin Marge Smith could run faster, hit a ball harder, and generally do better than all of us in those years; I enhanced my skills just trying to keep pace with her. No one has been of greater help in bringing this book to publication than she. She did much of the legwork in Illinois and found photographs that helped bring the 1890s back to life.

PROLOGUE

*Sell the cookstove if necessary and come.
You must see the Fair.*

—Hamlin Garland

Come! Come to the fair! What fair? Why, the colossal, unbelievable 1893 World's Columbian Exposition. Host city Chicago had never seen its like before, nor had the whole country, perhaps the world. Among the millions of people who traveled to Chicago that summer were awed Durango and Sandwich tourists.

On Tuesday morning, August 22, an observant, excited Sandwich teacher Nellie Forsythe took the 8:30 train for the "White City" sixty miles away. The thirty-year-old woman spent the next five days there, while visiting her aunt in Douglas Park. Despite a setback returning home one evening — "I had quite an experience getting on the wrong train, but we finally got there"—she had a wonderful time sightseeing (Forsythe diary, Aug. 22–27).

On the fair's Illinois Day (Aug. 24), she told her diary, "All we saw was an immense crowd." But she persisted and before going home on the midnight train two days later, found time to see " 'America' the grandest historical spectacle of the time. It was magnificent surely." Relaxing at home the next day, she concluded, "My mind is in a whirl. Such sights I have seen. I am resting all day." Another excited visitor could only recommend, "Sell the cookstove if necessary and come. You *must* see the Fair."

Sandwich Free Press editor William Deacon confessed on June 22, "Your feet will give out long before your eyes are satisfied." He, too, gushed over what he saw, tired or not: "It is the supreme culminating effort of the nineteenth century to place before this generation the best of all lines of human progress."

Sandwich and Durango both participated in the 1893 World's Columbian Exposition, better known as the Chicago World's Fair. When

xiii

PROLOGUE

Congress passed an act in 1890 providing for an exhibition, the intent had been to celebrate the four hundredth anniversary of Columbus's arrival. Keen rivalry for the honor and profit of staging the fair slowed preparations, and Chicago was not selected as the site until too late for an 1892 opening. A preliminary dedication and parade took place on October 21, 1892, and then a terrible winter slowed construction. *Sandwich Argus* editor Miles Castle seemed a little skeptical at first, thinking that the fair might not debut, even in 1893. After visiting the unfinished site in July 1892, he felt they would have to hurry, and he truthfully believed it could not be done (*Argus*, July 16, 1892). That was not his main concern, however: "Another thing struck us which was that there is a vast sum of money expended foolishly to say the least, especially in view of the fact that these immense and costly buildings have to be removed as soon as the exhibition is over." Castle's concern misfired. The fair opened on May 1, 1893—which was really almost a miracle—and Sandwichites went in large numbers to see it.

It seemed then to be an ill-omened time to open such a celebration, amid the devastating economic crash of 1893. Despite such an inauspicious beginning, the fair proved a rousing success, the triumph and the coming of age of the United States and Chicago.

It became the most famous fair ever held on U.S. soil. No fair before or since captured the national imagination quite so completely. In half a year, the exposition drew twenty-seven million people to its 633 acres and two hundred buildings. One guidebook estimated that to see everything "quickly" would take "three weeks of walking" (*A Week at the Fair*, 17, 35). Even conscientious Nellie could not have seen the whole fair. Exhibits arrived from around the world (seventy-seven countries), none quite so controversial as the belly dancer, Little Egypt, the epitome of 1893 daring. Defenders and critics seriously debated whether the customs of Cairo should be "faithfully reproduced or the morals of the public faithfully protected"! For whatever reason, crowds flocked to the show.

Thrills and wonders, the fair had them all. Nothing seemed more thrilling than that first-of-its-kind mechanical wonder, the 264-foot-high Ferris wheel, a surefire excuse for nationalist chest-beating, on which a twenty-five-minute ride cost fifty cents (Patton, "Great Chicago Fair," 42). The midway captivated many, but so did the various state, industrial, and international buildings. Not to be overlooked, women offered a Woman's Building

PROLOGUE

designed by architect Sophia Hayden and overseen by a Fair Board of Lady Managers. Contemporary descriptions used such words as "vision, dream and enchantment" to describe the fair.

The Chicago World's Fair introduced visitors to Shredded Wheat cereal, pancake mix, Juicy Fruit gum, zippers, fiberglass, and the first demonstration of long-distance telephone service between Chicago and New York City (Patton, "Great Chicago Fair," 42). Souvenir postcards, commemorative stamps, cotton candy, and an elevated electric train running around the fair's perimeter were other firsts. Visitors gawked at private Pullman cars, while nudity in art shocked many (*A Week at the Fair*). They were amazed by Edison's Kinetoscope (the forerunner of motion-picture photography), huge industrial machines, new uses for metals, and the Palace of Electricity (Patton, "Great Chicago Fair," 28–44). Souvenirs carried home included Heinz's green plastic pickles and other free treats from businesses. One Sandwich couple brought cotton candy home on the train for friends to sample. At home, they placed it in a dish, only to find nothing but sugar and water the next morning![1]

The fair was bigger and grander than any before it and provided a dry run for mass-marketing, packaging, and advertising techniques of the twentieth century. It stimulated piano sales and popularized the syncopated melodies that became ragtime. Chicago and its rural hinterland sent the most visitors; others came from throughout the country and the world. Most of the visitors were more than a "little overwhelmed" by what they saw.

But the fair proved more than all that. Determined to have a world's fair that outshone any in history, Chicagoans included a galaxy of cultural attractions, among them a World's Congress of Historians and Historical Students. Young University of Wisconsin professor Frederick Jackson Turner traveled down from Madison to participate. Despite declining an invitation to visit that symbol of the popular "wild" West, the Buffalo Bill show, Turner's address on the evening of July 12 shaped the course of Western history for the next century. Not satisfied with the West that Buffalo Bill portrayed, Turner argued that the westward-moving U.S. frontier was a unique historical phenomenon that allowed a special interpretation of, and contribution to, the development of U.S. society.

Whether any Durangoans or Sandwichites relinquished other attractions to avail themselves of the opportunity to hear about "The Significance of

xv

PROLOGUE

the Frontier in American History" will never be known. After an intolerably hot day at the fair, probably none did.[2]

More likely they took in "Buffalo Bill's world-renowned Wild West Show," which set up business right across from the Sixty-second Street entrance to the fair. That was the West they wanted to see, the real West, not a scholarly, interpreted one. One 1893 book about the fair said, "Colonel Cody has outdone himself in his efforts to make the exhibition outshine all its previous brilliant successes" (*A Week at the Fair*, 246). Probably fewer frequented the "home" operated by the famous evangelists Dwight Moody and Ira Sankey. Constant services would "strive to win the erring from their ways, and spur on the virtuous to further works of righteousness." The services may have been needed, but people did not go to the fair for a heavenly purpose!

This wonder of wonders unfolded right in Sandwich's backyard. Sandwich was close enough by train, so that people from farther out could stay with friends in Sandwich and go from there for a day's outing at the fair. They could catch the 4:25 a.m. train (special round trip for $2.70; children five to twelve, half price) and return home at a "sensible time of day" (*Sandwich Free Press*, April 20, 1893). When "misrepresentations and misstatements" about the exposition swirled around upstate Illinois, the *Free Press* (April 13, 1893) printed a letter from the fair's president, Harlow Higinbotham, hoping to clear the air. The admission charge of fifty cents covered everything except a few attractions, he noted; the grounds contained an "abundance" of free drinking water and fifteen hundred "absolutely free toilet rooms and closets"; and the fair provided "ample provisions for seating without charge."

The Illinois Building, with its 152-foot-high dome, contained Sandwich exhibits. A rare assortment of Indian relics from druggist Ira Converse's collection occupied a "prominent place." Elsewhere visitors could see equipment from the two local manufacturing companies, and the windmills and cultivators of one of the firms, the Enterprise Company, won awards (*Free Press*, Nov. 2, 1893). Sandwich benefited from the fair in a variety of ways—promotion, advertisement, and visitors. Sandwich residents, like Nellie, also benefited from the enjoyment of attending the fair itself.

Durango was too far away to benefit so instantly. The "Spanish Renaissance–style," twin-towered Colorado Building contained an exhibit of La

PROLOGUE

Plata County's resources, from coal to grains. Although adventuresome Durangoans did visit the fair, even with a special rate on the Burlington Railroad, it cost twenty-three dollars round trip from Denver to Chicago (*Durango Herald*, Oct. 22, 1893). That, plus other expenses, proved too heavy a burden for most Durangoans, who were facing the worst depression the town and state had ever seen.[3]

For Sandwich, nearness and immediate promotion did not translate into long-range advantages. Durango, despite being over one thousand miles from the fair, benefited much more in the long run. The reason was the "amazing, stupendous" Cliff Dwellers exhibit, one of those that cost an extra twenty-five cents admission and ten cents for a catalog (*A Week at the Fair*, 102–04). At the south end of the grounds, snuggled between the Anthropological Building and the Old Times Distillery Company that showed the "process of distilling sour-mash whisky," loomed Durango's future. Here, within a replica of "Battle Rock Mountain," sat a reproduction of "the wondrous and long-deserted cliff dwellings of the Mancos Cañon," one-tenth the size of the originals. Considerately, "mummies" were displayed in a separate room, so the fastidious or delicate would not have to view them. The fair's Mesa Verde publicity gave Durango a tremendous tourist boost that grew in the following years. The little village of Mancos might be physically nearer the ruins, but Durango sprinted far ahead in promoting itself as the "gateway."

Let us visit the 1890s world of Durango and Sandwich with eyes and minds as open and enthusiastic as Nellie Forsythe's. Although the two towns might not loom as important as their larger "neighbors," Denver and Chicago, in the saga of U.S. history, they represent small-town America and thus a much more typical window into their era. They are not insignificant, unimportant, out-of-the-way towns; rather, they symbolize the heart and soul of a nation in the throes of change.

The people whom Nellie knew and the Durangoans who walked and worked in their own town were ordinary Americans with a story to tell. Their dreams and hopes, their successes and failures, reveal much about them and late nineteenth-century America. No great leaders emerged from either community. Most of these people lived the quiet life of middle-class America, hoping to make a living and give their children more opportunity than they themselves had. Even a century later, making their acquaintance will help reveal to us how and why the United States arrived where it is.

PROLOGUE

Come now, meet these people in the pages ahead with Nellie's enthusiasm, her adventuresome nature, and her inquisitiveness. Some of the people you meet will play only cameo roles, others will dominate their communities. Share their workday, their recreation, their politics, and their aspirations.

Maybe if Fred Turner had studied these people and their communities more carefully, he would not so confidently have stated, "Each frontier did indeed furnish a new field of opportunity, a gate of escape from the bondage of the past; and freshness, and confidence, and scorn of older society, impatience of its restraints and its ideas, and indifference to its lessons, have accompanied the frontier."

Durangoans worked hard to recreate the world they had left back East—its society, customs, image, and lifestyle. So had Sandwich, a generation before, patterned itself after the Eastern communities that most of its residents once called home. The bonds of the national culture of the United States proved far stronger than the peculiarities of place and time.

Come back then to another age, neither far away from us nor in a strange country. As Mark Twain observed, "There was never yet an uninteresting life. Such a thing is an impossibility. Inside of the dullest exterior there is a drama, a comedy, and a tragedy."

NOTES

1. Nellie Forsythe diary, Aug. 22–27, 1893, Regional History Center, Northern Illinois University. For a general background, see the following works: *A Week at the Fair* (Chicago: Rand, McNally & Co., 1893). Julian Ralph, *Harper's Chicago and the World's Fair* (New York: Harper & Brothers, 1893), 1, 161–62, 235–36. Paul Patton, "The Great Chicago Fair, a Wonder of Wonders," *Smithsonian* (June 1993), 38, 40, 42–44, 46, 48. William Cronon, *Nature's Metropolis* (New York: W. W. Norton & Co., 1991), 341, 368. Dean Andrea Oppenneimer, "Revisiting the White City," *Historic Preservation* (March–April 1993), 42, 44, 46. Jessie Heckman Hirschl, "The Great White City," *American Heritage* (Oct. 1960), 9–19, 75.
2. Ray Allen Billington, *Frederick Jackson Turner* (New York: Oxford University Press, 1973), 124–31. Ray Allen Billington (ed.), *Frontier and Section* (Englewood Cliffs, N.J.: Prentice-Hall, 1961), 37–62.
3. *A Week at the Fair*, 203, 204, 246. *Sandwich Argus*, July 16, 1892. *Sandwich Free Press*, April 13, April 20, May 4, May 18, May 25, June 22, June 29, Oct. 26, Nov. 2, 1893. *Durango Great Southwest*, Aug. 2, 1892. Durango Board of Trade Minutes, Dec. 12, 1892. *Durango Herald*, Oct. 22, 1893.

A Tale of Two Towns

1

THE MOST BRILLIANT FUTURE

> *Darling, I am growing old,*
> *Silver threads among the gold.*
> —"Silver Threads Among the Gold" (1873)

As Charles Dickens described the era preceding the French Revolution in the opening of *A Tale of Two Cities*, "It was the best of times, it was the worst of times." What is about to unfold is the story of two U.S. towns that were similar in some ways and very different in others. One, Sandwich, was an agricultural community on the prairies of northern Illinois at an elevation of 667 feet; the second, Durango, was a mining community at 6,512 feet, nestled near mountains ringing the Animas River Valley of southwestern Colorado. In a long-ago decade, they were more alike than different; it was a decade in which they both experienced the best of times and the worst of times.

Those times were the decade that ended the nineteenth century, the 1890s, labeled in lore and legend as the Gay Nineties, a misnomer if ever there was one. A United States beset by one upheaval after another hardly appears to have qualified as gay. The Transforming Nineties would have been a better, if less catchy, title, because the United States that emerged in 1900 was not the same as the one of 1890.

National events collided with Sandwich and Durango, two rural towns that did not receive much notice outside their local areas.[1] These communities reflected the era, its trials and tribulations, its accomplishments, and its personality. What is about to unfold tells us much about them, their time and place, and more than a little about ourselves.

The 1890s came near the end of the Victorian Era, which was named for the British queen who had ascended to the throne back in 1837 and would rule past the new century's dawning. Victoria's sense of duty, her decorum, and her strict moral code influenced life and society in both

A TALE OF TWO TOWNS

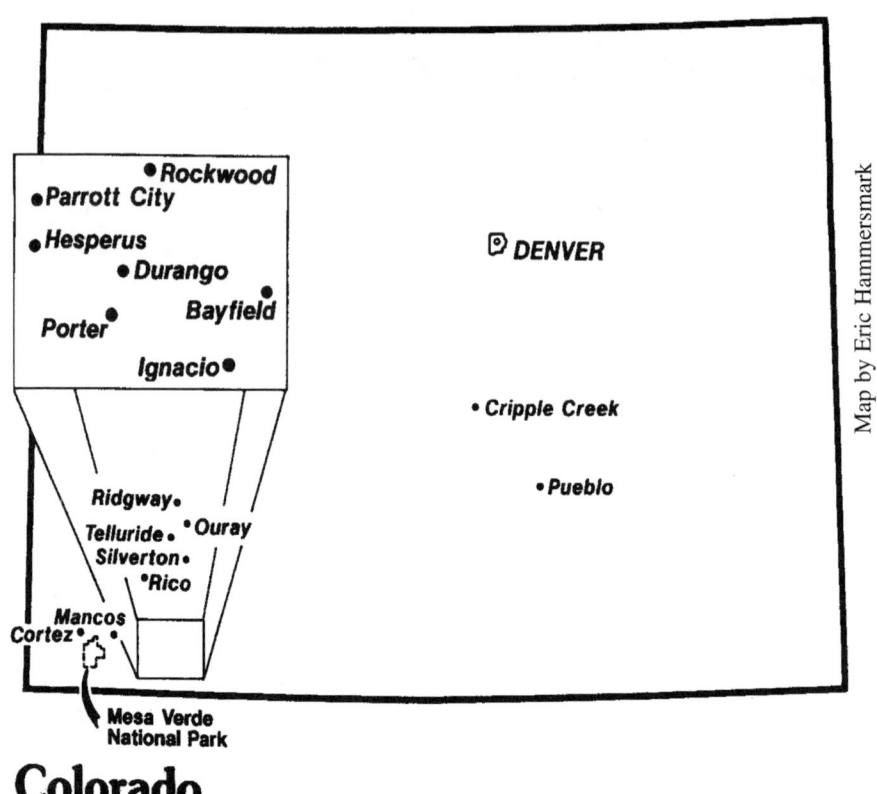

England and the United States to a degree unequaled since then. Her name was attached to the era's architecture and to its culture, even as U.S. xenophobes died a thousand deaths. Victorian culture created a bond between the Midwestern farm town and the Rocky Mountain mining town. The dominant middle class in both communities believed in the work ethic, law and order, domesticity, education, and morality and indulged in conspicuous consumption. Residents of both towns could have exchanged places and adjusted readily.

The story, however, really begins many decades earlier in Illinois, before the rolling drums of the Civil War called the country to arms and

THE MOST BRILLIANT FUTURE

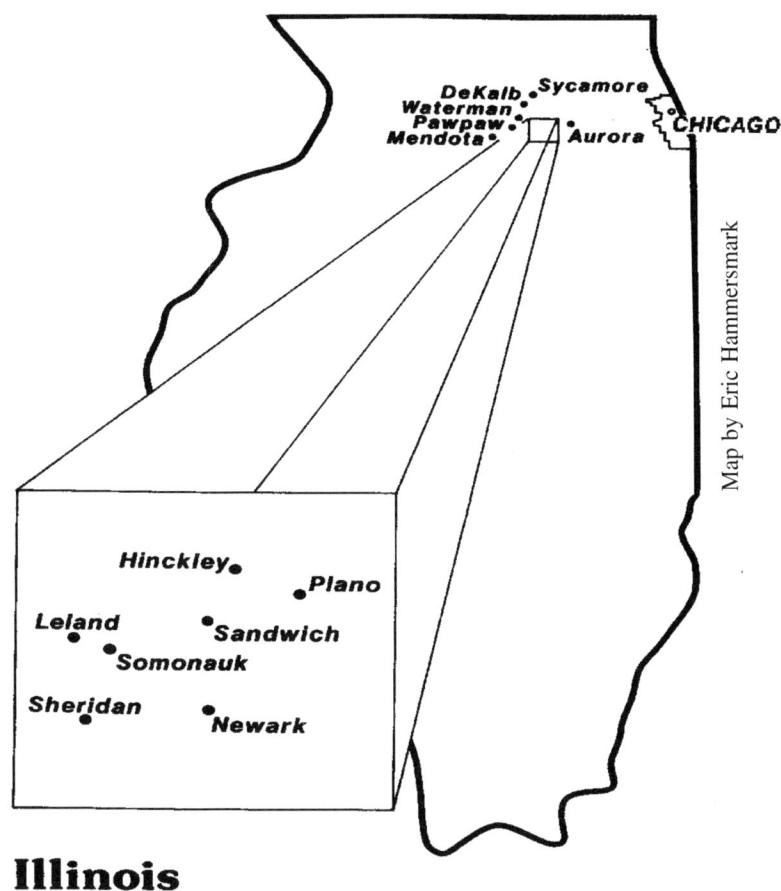

Illinois

Abraham Lincoln left Springfield for Washington, D.C. White settlement at that time crept along the rivers and streams, as pioneers largely avoided the prairies, convinced that land without trees was infertile. Northern Illinois was the home of the Potawatomi Indians, who suffered the misfortune of being in the way of the onrushing frontier. Gradually, the Potawatomi ceded their lands and, by the 1840s, most of them had moved across the Mississippi River.

The newcomers seized the opportunity to mine lead in the Galena region and avail themselves of the commercial opportunities of Chicago. They also quickly realized that the potential for this open prairie lay in farming. A recent arrival, Irish Methodist minister James Shaw, put his finger on the future when he said, "Illinois is the paradise of farmers. There is no country where the soil is so rich, or more easily worked, or more productive" (Shaw, *Twelve Years*, 79).

Northern Illinois was endowed with that soil in abundance, and in the 1830s and 1840s settlers came in increasing numbers. Political organizations followed quickly after them. De Kalb County, named for the Revolutionary War hero Johan Kalb (Baron de Kalb), was carved out of this domain on March 4, 1837. The process of opening the rich land sounds relatively easy today, but the pioneers struggled mightily. Farming was a physically demanding, labor-intensive occupation, which initially promised slow growth and small returns. In addition, the settlers in De Kalb County, as in the rest of Illinois, suffered from the ague, a malarial fever that debilitated its victims in a recurring cycle of chills, fever, and sweating. Hard, tedious work, small returns, and ill health—no wonder many men risked the rush to California's golden Sierra Nevadas in 1849. A few never came back, some returned with the means to launch a business or purchase more farmland, and almost all had the adventure of their lives.[2]

What the early settlers needed most was better transportation; stage and wagon travel proved slow and cumbersome, and it was hindered by the weather. Better transportation came in the form of the railroad, the wonder of the age. It automatically brought rural and urban areas closer together, lowered travel costs, and reduced time spent moving people and freight. Railroad lines could break radically with geographical contours, following the straightest possible route between markets, and could carry more people and goods than any other means of land transport. Trains customarily were unaffected by weather conditions. No longer would rural communities be islands of isolation.

The other key to Illinois development, Chicago, already dominated the region. As James Shaw noted, "No city in the United States, or the world, has risen so fast, or increased so rapidly." Yet Chicago also needed railroads to reach its potential, to tap its highly profitable hinterland. They came during a frenzy of railroad building in the 1850s. Chicago emerged as a railroad hub, a "gateway metropolis," tied by iron rails to a vast hinterland and limited only by the ambitions of its merchants and railroad barons.

THE MOST BRILLIANT FUTURE

The railroad that eventually became the Chicago, Burlington and Quincy reached Aurora in 1850 and Mendota three years later. On the way, it passed the future site of Sandwich. Along its route, hamlets sprouted like dandelions; two of them, Plano and Somonauk, bracketed the site of Sandwich. A nineteenth-century settlement could be confident of a bright future, if it secured railroad connections. Without the iron rails, its future looked bleak. The railroad constituted the fastest, cheapest, and safest year-round form of transportation, and it easily supplanted the stage, the horse, and walking as the most comfortable. The editor of the *Monmouth (Ill.) Atlas* (March 30, 1855) understood all this: "The Railroad is putting new life and activity into everybody. Business is going ahead rapidly. . . . All kinds of produce can now be turned into cash at high prices, and if farmers do not get rich it will certainly be their own fault. . . . The 'good time' which has been so long on its way, may with truth be said to have come. Let those who can do so enjoy it, as best they may."

The farmers who opened the land between Plano and Somonauk and north three miles to Freeland Corners had long been isolated. Crops yielded little profit after the sixty-mile trip by wagon to the Chicago markets. Despite the prospects of the region, the promised land of the "Garden of the Lord" had not yet yielded its riches.

All this would change with the coming of the railroad, which might not be able to cure the ague but did promise a solution to most of the other isolation-related problems. Illinois nearly doubled its urban population in the 1850s, and, in the case of Sandwich, a few prairie settlers perceived the opportunity to make their own small contributions to the state's economic progress.[3] Before the railroad could effect all its benefits, however, there had to be a convenient shipping point for farmers.

The CB&Q provided shipping outlets at Plano and Somonauk, leaving the farmers in between with what they considered an unfair transportation handicap. Consequently, in the fall of 1853, these farmers, and the residents of Newark, six miles south of the railroad, pushed for another station. The railroad responded by putting in a flag station—the train would stop when flagged by passengers and when mail or freight stood waiting. That was a start, but Newark, a thriving village at the time, wanted more. Its residents contrived a plan to get their demands met. They established a carriage line, which transported passengers to the railroad daily. Everyone who could raise the funds was encouraged to take a trip by rail. As a result, the CB&Q was convinced of the need to establish a regular stop, Newark Station, in 1855.

Almon Gage, who owned the land where the station was established, promptly offered free land to all who would settle there. Soon a hotel, blacksmith shop, and store arose and, according to Mrs. Mary E. Lewis, who arrived in 1854, a "little red school house and Baptist church." Residents of the fledgling settlement did not cotton to the idea of being the "tail to Newark's kite" (*Sandwich Free Press*, July 23, 1896). Boston native and lawyer (Sandwich's first), Stephen B. Stinson, an 1856 arrival, remembered that the name Newark Station "did not quite suit the enterprising people who had secured the station, and they cast about for a name to please them better" (*Sandwich Argus*, June 9, 1897). Gage modestly refused to name it Almon, so they looked elsewhere. The honor of selecting a new name was finally accorded to Democratic Congressman John Wentworth, who had helped secure the station. Having been born in Sandwich, New Hampshire, the soon-to-be Chicago mayor named it after his hometown.

Businessmen who would play historic roles in the development of Sandwich quickly established themselves in 1854–56: hardware man George Kleinsmid, banker and lumberman Miles Castle, manufacturer Augustus Adams, and merchants and bankers George and James Culver. Sandwich's destiny would be guided by its businesspeople, who invested more than many other settlers in its future and wanted their town to become a community in which people would want to settle and invest. Realizing that something more was needed to distinguish Sandwich from its neighbors, they looked to industry.

Fifty-year-old inventor Augustus Adams built a small factory in 1856 to manufacture agricultural implements. Adams's story, one that involved "pulling himself up by his bootstraps" from humble beginnings, symbolized the kind of boost a move to the west could give an individual. Stories like his became legendary, though the west did not always guarantee success—far from it. Eleven years later, Adams merged his company with a stock association, which became the Sandwich Manufacturing Company. The latter was soon joined by the Enterprise Company, giving the town a pair of industries to supplement agriculture as its economic foundation.

This farsightedness eventually made Sandwich a banking, business, and industrial center. The town gained an advantage over nearby rivals such as Somonauk, Plano, Hinckley, and Newark, which were all small farming villages with a culture and an agricultural base similar to those of Sandwich.

Sandwich gained a newspaper, something every infant community wanted in order to promote itself and enhance local pride. The *People's Press* debuted on September 10, 1857. In the second issue, the paper described Sandwich as "a stirring business village":

> Besides the railroad buildings, Sandwich has three churches—Baptist, Methodist and Congregational. The Presbyterians worship in a large school-room, but are preparing to build a church.
>
> A large and commodious two-story building erected for an academy, and occupied as such for two years, is now used for a district school . . . besides which there is a small private school.
>
> The people of Sandwich and vicinity must be a reading people, if we judge of them by the amount of reading matter received at the postoffice.
>
> There is one stream grist and flouring mill, one iron foundry, machine shop and planing mill, two lumber yards. . . . There are 11 stores, all doing a good and some a heavy business, two blacksmith shops, two wagon shops, one livery stable, one bakery, one hotel, two merchant tailors, two shoe shops, one jeweler, 20 or 30 carpenters and joiners.

In other words, Sandwich had everything a progressive, prosperous village with a promising future should have—churches, schools, businesses, industry, and an intelligent citizenry. Unfortunately, the *People's Press* suffered the fate of many a pioneering newspaper. After six months, it ceased publication and, as one writer quaintly described its fate, the "editor and publisher, having got deeply in debt, left the country, without bidding his friends and patrons an affectionate good-bye" (*Portrait and Biographical Album*, 795).

With perhaps the exception of the newspaper's publisher, Sandwich's founding fathers had planned well. The town's growth was slow and steady, typical of a farming community. The census taker in 1860 counted 952 people. That total embraced nearly an equal split between men and women, and all of them were white. No "free colored" were enumerated. Notwithstanding its youth, Sandwich already played a role in a national drama. One branch of the Underground Railroad passed nearby. Over this route, escaping slaves hurried on their way to Canada and freedom.

Sandwich experienced some of the same troubles that afflicted other new communities: jealous neighbors (Somonauk, in particular), overblown expectations, and the financial panic of 1857 and subsequent national depression, which hurt both the railroad and the young towns along its route. That bane of all new towns, fire, struck in 1864, causing heavy losses. Nevertheless, the young community rebounded and rebuilt with stone and brick. Its faith in the future remained steady. Just how confident were its pioneers? Stinson and some others had already been planting trees—elm, maple, ash, and cherry—to beautify the town and disprove the 1850s contention that forest trees would not grow well in prairie soil. As Stinson wrote in 1896, "From the first, great pains have been taken in planting of trees along our streets and the beauty and comfort resulting from this fact are often spoken of by those visiting the town" (*Free Press*, Nov. 5, 1896).[4]

The news of the shelling of Fort Sumter in April 1861 marked the watershed of Sandwich's early history. Energized, patriotic Sandwich folks raised two infantry companies within two weeks, and "the ladies met at the different churches and prepared quaint, home made uniforms for these brave boys" (Gross, *Past and Present*, 1:311–12). Miles Castle claimed that Sandwich had the "honor of having the first uniformed company" mustered in the state; other towns undoubtedly challenged that claim. Nearly two hundred Sandwich men served in the Tenth and Thirteenth Illinois Infantries, the Eighth Illinois Cavalry, the 105th U.S. Infantry, and other regiments (*Portrait and Biographical Album*, 881). Those who returned would never forget the experience of their youth. In the words of fellow veteran Oliver Wendell Holmes, Jr., "It was given to us to learn at the outset that life is a profound and passionate thing."

Sandwich would not forget those years either, for the Civil War brought renewed prosperity to railroad, town, farm, and state. This prosperity made Sandwich the largest community in the southern part of De Kalb County. For several years, Sandwichites harbored the grandiose idea of capturing the county seat from Sycamore. The issue came to a head in the spring of 1867. Alas for Sandwich—in the end, all the meetings and speeches led to nothing.

THE MOST BRILLIANT FUTURE

By 1870, Sandwich's fourth newspaper, the *Gazette* (established in 1865), could proudly list among the town's businesses four general merchants, four grocers, two lumber yards, and two hardware stores, as well as six churches and a graded school (*Free Press*, May 21, 1891). The population, meanwhile, had nearly doubled to 1,844. The town also evidenced a strong leaning toward temperance. Castle remembered that the owner of the first saloon was threatened and ultimately forced to close his establishment after a "long and bitter contest." Afterward, the struggle continued relentlessly. An 1885 writer summarized the result: "The license party has generally been successful, and there have usually been from two to four licensed saloons" (Gross, *Past and Present*, 1:311). The saloon owners paid a stiff price for the right to sell liquor, the license fee being five hundred dollars per year.

Originally platted in 1854, Sandwich was incorporated as a village in 1860 and adopted a city organization by vote in November 1872. The picture painted by census takers in 1880 was typical of a northern Illinois farming community. The population in the previous decade had increased by slightly more than five hundred people. In De Kalb County, Sandwich now ranked second only to Sycamore. The population remained white and Anglo-Saxon, with the native-born outnumbering the foreign-born by more than four to one. The British Isles, Germany, and the Scandinavian countries sent almost all of the foreign contingent. The twenty-five-year-old community had secured a solid place in its county and dominated the surrounding towns, although a rival loomed within five miles in every direction. Mature and prosperous, Sandwich anticipated an even more promising future.[5]

At this same time, out in southwestern Colorado, another railroad, the Denver & Rio Grande, was founding a new community. On September 13, 1880, farmers started the fall harvest in the fields around Sandwich, when the first survey stake was being driven for the new town of Durango, named after the town in Mexico that the railroad hoped to reach one day.

In truth, there never should have been a Durango. Two miles north of it, the six-year-old farming village of Animas City had suffered the deadly consequences of misreading history. Its population grew at the same pace Sandwich's did, though to a smaller degree, reaching 286 people in 1880. Local ranchers and farmers had only one market, the San Juan miners to the north, who lived high in the mountainous headwaters of the Animas River. Animas City had been established where it stood because of the relatively long growing season (one hundred days) in its part of the Animas Valley and because the Animas River flowed nearby. Without a reliable water supply, settlement in southwestern Colorado proved a decided gamble.

In 1879, the D&RG sent surveyors through the Animas Valley to mark out a route into the San Juan Mountains, which held those inviting mining districts. The railroad offered to make Animas City its hub in southwestern Colorado, but in so doing demanded that certain terms be met. Animas City's council refused to submit, so the railroad threatened to establish its own community somewhere farther south along the Animas River. The council did not yield; indeed, it scoffed at the railroad's effrontery. The Denver & Rio Grande did not bluff. When its tracks reached the area, it founded Durango, and its trains never stopped at Animas City, dooming the bypassed village to oblivion.

Railroads thus gave birth to both Sandwich and Durango and shaped their early histories. The railroads brought the world to the towns, unlocked the door to prosperity, reduced travel time and costs, and tied the towns to the wholesale markets of Chicago and Denver. Just as each town had its own economic hinterland, so too was each a part of a larger hinterland wrapped by those iron rails. This economic network influenced daily life in subtle and dramatic ways. For example, in 1883 the United States adopted standard time, thanks to the railroads' efforts, with four time zones. Sandwich was placed in the Central Zone, Durango in the Mountain Zone. The homogeneity, regimentation, and standardization that increasingly characterized Victorian America had taken a giant leap forward.

The comparison of early Durango and Sandwich does not end with their railroad heritage. Politically, they were both Republican. De Kalb County and northern Illinois were strongholds of the Grand Old Party, and Colorado had voted Republican since the state's birth in 1876. The GOP's conservative, business, patriotic, and middle-class platforms appealed to the voters in these towns. Businessmen charted the course of development in Sandwich and Durango, more often behind the scenes than out in front. Protestantism dominated each town, while middle-class, Victorian American values strongly shaped the man and woman on the street.[6]

Like Sandwich, Durango also suffered a major fire. On July 1, 1889, a disastrous conflagration swept away seven blocks, over a half million dollars' worth of property. With optimism as endemic in Durango as it was in Sandwich, the town rebuilt and became better than before.

The contrasts between the two towns, however, are striking. Unlike Sandwich, and unlike most other Western towns, Durango was a planned community. D&RG president William Jackson Palmer platted towns along his railroad to increase company profits. Durango and Colorado Springs were classic examples of Palmer's carefully crafted strategy to utilize the sites for business districts and homes, and to do so in such a way as to enhance what today would be called "quality of life."

Durango's economic influence stretched fifty miles north to Silverton, Colorado, the same distance south to Farmington, New Mexico, west as far as one cared to go, and over a hundred miles east to the San Luis Valley. Durango's population immediately soared. By Christmas 1880, an estimated 2,500 people lived there, though because the railroad construction crews wintered in town, this figure may have been temporarily inflated. The state census takers in 1885 counted 2,254 people. Without question, the pace of Durango's development surpassed anything Sandwich and most other farming towns ever experienced. Within six months, Durango boasted 6 hotels, 3 groceries, 10 restaurants, 4 hardware stores, 20 saloons, 2 bakeries, and a total of 134 businesses.

Unlike Sandwich, Durango had no nearby large rival like Chicago—or even a lesser one, such as Aurora, Illinois. Denver lay a day and a half away by train, and no challengers threatened nearby. With no serious rivals, Durango, the largest community at that time on Colorado's Western Slope (the largely unsettled forty percent of the state beyond the Continental Divide), exhibited glowing prospects.

The D&RG had come for more reasons than to tap the San Juan silver mines and to start a new community. It opened up nearby coal mines, which provided fuel for its engines and a profitable product to transport. Denver & Rio Grande leadership also established, across the river from Durango, the San Juan & New York Smelter (later renamed the San Juan Smelter), which seemed destined to become one of the largest smelters in the region. The railroad also commenced transporting tourists into the mountain-fringed valley and the mining regions beyond. In the same month that Durango was established, the U.S. Army, because of tension with the neighboring Utes, was busy constructing Fort Lewis fourteen miles to the southwest. The fort was a source of business that local merchants, ranchers, and farmers did not hesitate to tap. After some political infighting, Durango also wrested the county seat from the declining mining camp of Parrott City, which lay west of Durango at the mouth of La Plata Canyon. Thus was generated for Durango an economic versatility unknown to Sandwich.

Agricultural development remained limited by the fact that two miles south of Durango sat the Ute Indian reservation, a vast land running across the entire southern boundary of southwestern Colorado. The remaining county land could be farmed only if water became available, a condition that would limit its agricultural production through the next century. Farmers near the rivers could irrigate easily, but on the surrounding mesas, water would come at a premium.[7]

Durango obviously did not have nearly as rich an agricultural hinterland as Sandwich did, but this lack was more than compensated for by Durango's greater versatility. Like the leaders of Sandwich, Durango's merchants charted their town's destiny. These early leaders included banker Alfred P. Camp, entrepreneur Thomas Graden, mine owner and smelterman John Porter, and druggist and mine owner Charles Newman. Like their counterparts in Sandwich, they hoped to make Durango a place where tourists would come, investors would invest, and settlers would stay.

Durango's city government was organized in May 1881, after a brief lawless period during which the size of this "metropolis of the San Juans" overwhelmed La Plata County law enforcement. The town of "churches, homes, and schools" tried to model itself after the middle-class Victorian communities from which most of its founders had emigrated. Most of these founders were Midwestern Anglo-Saxons, but they also included a sprinkling of northern Europeans. The Chinese constituted the largest non-European ethnic group; they numbered fewer than fifty.

By 1890, Durango had a population of 2,726 and Sandwich 2,516. Sandwich had added only a few hundred people during the past decade, but that was better than many of its neighbors, which had lost population. Only the town of De Kalb, thanks to the barbed wire industry, had sprinted ahead and finally passed Sandwich to become number two in population, behind Sycamore.

Sandwich's stagnation was not hard to explain. Agriculture was changing rapidly, thanks to new machines, seeds, fertilizers, and a host of new inventions. It had become less labor-intensive than ever before. The average farmer could farm more acres and produce more per acre than his grandfather. This revolution had been going on for several generations. The attraction of the cities further accelerated this transformation; the plentiful, paying jobs there drew the young from dawn-to-dusk farms and small market towns. At the same time, crop and animal prices fell as Western competition flooded the markets. At this early date, the future of the small family farm was already a matter of serious concern.

Although in 1890 farming still prevailed as Illinois's number one industry, in the last thirty years of the nineteenth century there was a steady drop in the farm population. Sandwich faced a problem whose long-range implications the town had not even begun to perceive or understand.[8]

Although the populations of the two towns were of similar size, other aspects differed markedly. For example, males outnumbered females in Durango throughout the 1880s. The gap later narrowed, but men still represented fifty-nine percent of the 1890 population. Durango also contained more foreign-born and African American residents, though fewer than fifty African Americans lived there at the time.

Agricultural statistics reveal important differences between the older farming county in Illinois and the upstart Colorado newcomer. In 1890, De Kalb County produced $2.8 million in farm products and had land and improvements valued at $20 million. La Plata County, in sharp contrast, produced only $222,000 in farm products, with land and improvements valued at $2.8 million. No more clearly was the disparity shown than in De Kalb's 3.4 million bushels of corn versus La Plata's 4,585 bushels, or De Kalb's 113,000 bushels of apples compared with La Plata's 213 bushels. De Kalb had eight times as many cattle as La Plata. The same ratio applied to property valuation, taxes, and all agricultural census statistics. The older, more established county overshadowed the younger one in all areas except irrigated acreage.[9]

Sandwich and Durango stood at the threshold of a new decade on January 1, 1890. The *Durango Herald* saluted the occasion and unknowingly spoke for each town when it stated, "Nothing can possibly keep her back." In sentiments that papers in both communities echoed, the editor concluded, "Durango has the most brilliant future before her of any town in the state, outside of Denver and Pueblo." Both Sandwich and Durango cast off on a ten-year adventure with confidence and faith.

NOTES

1. Urban history has come into its own in the past generation. Works such as Robert Dykstra's *The Cattle Towns* (1970), Carl Abbott's *The Metropolitan Frontier* (1993), Gunther Barth's *Instant Cities* (1975), Lionel Frost's *The New Urban Frontier* (1991), Lawrence Larson's *The Urban West as the End of the Frontier* (1978), Richard Francaviglia's *Main Street Revisited* (1996), and Bradford Luckingham's *The Urban Southwest* (1982), present research on Western towns with similar economic bases or compare larger cities. David Hamer's *New Towns in the New World* (1990) is a comparative study of nineteenth-century urban settlement in the West, the Canadian West, Australia, and New Zealand. All of these volumes have been most helpful, although not directly related to this study.

    Because many readers do not check sources, or are perhaps annoyed by a plethora of notes, the use of notes has been kept to a minimum in this volume. The notes are to provide scholars with the names of the sources utilized. The sources appear in the order in which they were utilized in the section under discussion, except that, within each note, all citations from the same newspaper are placed together in the order they appear in the text.

2. Richard V. Francaviglia, "Victorian Bonanzas," *Journal of the West* (Jan. 1994), 54, 55. James Shaw, *Twelve Years in America* (Chicago: Poe & Hitchcock, 1867), 79. Thomas Ford, *History of Illinois* (Chicago: S. C. Griggs, 1854), 100–03, 446. John Clayton, *The Illinois Fact Book* (Carbondale: Southern Illinois University Press, 1970), 30. Eliza W. Farnham, *Life in Prairie Land* (New York: Harper & Brothers, 1846), 347. Lewis M. Gross, *Past and Present of DeKalb County, Illinois* (Chicago: Pioneer Publishing Co., 1907), 1:42, 86. R. Carlyle Buley, *The Old Northwest* (Indianapolis: Indiana Historical Society, 1950), 2:55, 117.

3. William Cronon, *Nature's Metropolis* (New York: W. W. Norton & Co., 1991), 74–78, 325, 377, 385. Richard J. Jensen, *Illinois* (New York: W. W. Norton & Co., 1978), 76. Richard C. Overton, *Burlington Route* (New York: Alfred A. Knopf, 1965), 3–5, 18–20, 23, 32–33, 39, 41–43, and the *Monmouth Atlas*, quoted on page 42 in Overton. Shaw, *Twelve Years*, 29–30. William Ferguson, quoted in Robert P. Sutton, *The Prairie State* (Grand Rapids, Mich.: William B. Ferdmans, 1976), 351. Gross, *Past and Present*, 1:303. *Sandwich*

Argus, June 19, 1897. Robert P. Howard, *Illinois* (Grand Rapids, Mich.: William B. Ferdmans, 1972), 267.

4. Gross, *Past and Present*, 1:93, 107, 115, 162–63, 303–06, 319–20. *Sandwich Free Press*, July 23 and Nov. 5, 1896. *Argus*, Jan. 11, 1879; Jan. 11, 1896; June 19, 1897. *Portrait and Biographical Album of DeKalb County, Illinois* (Chicago: Chapman Brothers, 1885), 795, 870–71. Richard Critchfield, *Trees, Why Do You Wait?* (Washington: Island Press, 1991), 12, 25, 29–30. *Population of the United States in 1860* (Washington: Government Printing Office, 1864), 90. Overton, *Burlington Route*, 47, 50–51, 64–66. No early records mention that Sandwich was named after Sandwich, Massachusetts.

5. *Argus*, Jan. 11, 1879. Gross, *Past and Present*, 1:106–07, 113, 115, 194–97, 259–60, 285, 307–08, 311–13. *Sandwich Gazette*, quoted in the *Free Press*, May 21, 1891. *Statistics of the Population of the United States Tenth Census* (Washington: Government Printing Office, 1883), 44, 56–57, 133, 387, 431, 504, 820. Jensen, *Illinois*, 77–78. *Portrait and Biographical Album*, 795–96, 873, 880–81.

6. Cronon, *Nature's Metropolis*, 79, 97, 279–82, 326, 332–33, 369. Thomas J. Schlereth, *Victorian America* (New York: HarperCollins, 1991), 30–31. John H. Keiser, *Building for the Centuries* (Urbana: University of Illinois Press, 1977), 72, 74, 111. Jensen, *Illinois*, 73.

7. Sources for Animas City and Durango: *Durango Record*, Jan. 29, 1881, and *Durango Herald*, Jan. 1, 1890. Duane A. Smith, *Rocky Mountain Boom Town* (Niwot: University Press of Colorado, 1992). Duane A. Smith, *Durango Diary* (Durango: *Durango Herald*, 1996).

8. *Population of the United States 11th Census* (Washington: Government Printing Office, 1895), 103–04, 108, 408, 541. *Free Press*, July 23, 1890. Allan G. Bogue, *From Prairie to Corn Belt* (Chicago: University of Chicago Press, 1963), 149, 157, 160, 163–66, 169, 185, 195, 202–03. Fred Kohlmeyer, "Illinois Agriculture in Retrospect," in *Illinois: Its History & Legacy* (St. Louis: River City Publishers, 1984), 1, 4–9. Keiser, *Building for the Centuries*, 116.

9. *Statistics of Agriculture* (Washington: Government Printing Office, 1894), 100, 126, 134, 205, 279, 283. *Free Press*, July 23, 1890. *Wealth, Debt, and Taxation* (Washington: Government Printing Office, 1895), 21, 25, 605, 610. *Compendium of the Eleventh Census: Population* (Washington: Government Printing Office, 1892), 478, 516, 525, 529, 541, 588, 668–69.

2

THE MEN AND WOMEN MERELY PLAYERS

Many the hopes that have vanished,
After the ball.
—"After the Ball" (1892)

No song was more popular in the 1890s than "After the Ball." Popular among the Victorians, who reveled in such tearjerkers, this haunting melody has continued to appeal to the public to this day. It stands as one of the greatest hits in the history of U.S. popular music. The 1890s have retained a mystique that makes them as romantic as the song.

The story about to unfold revolves around the people who first heard and sang this lilting song, ordinary people from all walks of life. It is a tale of now-forgotten average folks, "might-have-beens and used-to-be's," whose lives portray an unpretentious era of unfulfilled aspirations gently trailing off into obscurity. No historical work chronicles their lives; their stories are largely confined to their own communities. In the words of Charles Dickens, "Trifles make the sum of life" (*David Copperfield*). Before the curtain goes up, the cast must be introduced because, as Shakespeare wrote in *As You Like It*,

> All the world's a stage,
> And all the men and women merely players:
> They have their exits and their entrances."

These residents inhabited two towns in the side eddies of mainstream America, far from the action on Wall Street, in capitol corridors, or on large industrial assembly lines. For them and their families, life centered around Main Street and its immediate vicinity. Here they awakened each morning to their individual joys and sorrows, their frustrations and successes. The drama of their lives was enacted far from the bright lights of fame and fortune.

The 1900 census provides an impersonal, quantitative portrait of the two towns. Sandwich and Durango consisted overwhelmingly of white, northern European Americans. Over ninety-nine percent of all Sandwichites and ninety-five percent of all Durangoans matched that description. By 1900, only one African American family lived in Durango. In Sandwich, there were two African American families and two single African Americans. Immigrants from Germany, England, Ireland, Scotland, and Wales far outnumbered all others. Immigrants made up approximately ten percent of the total population of each town. Some recent arrivals also came from Canada, Norway, Sweden, and, in Sandwich at least, Russia. The new wave of emigration from southern and eastern Europe had little or no impact on either community—Sandwich had no southern or eastern Europeans, and Durango had fewer than a dozen Italians and Austrians, who worked in the smelter and in the coal mines.

The overwhelmingly European American nature of the population limited the social and ethnic variety of the two communities. Only Durango contained a small ethnic neighborhood, a Hispanic area beyond Railroad Street and along the Animas River. Almost all of the Hispanics came from New Mexico and Colorado, not Mexico. In both towns there existed, to be sure, right neighborhoods to live in and a right and wrong side of town.

Both towns mirrored the racial and ethnic makeup of their respective counties, with one exception. No Utes were reported to be living in Durango, even though their neighboring reservation made them the largest ethnic group in La Plata County. Just as the Potawatomi formerly occupied the land that became Sandwich, the Utes had once held the land of Durango. But the Utes ceded the land in 1873. In 1900, men still slightly outnumbered women in Durango, a fact that reflected male dominance in agriculture and mining.

If the census enumerators got honest answers from their respondents, there was no illiteracy problem in either town. Far less than one percent of the people of each town admitted that they could neither read nor write. Foreign- and native-born residents split that small number about evenly. An interesting contrast appeared regarding home ownership. Sixty-six percent of Sandwichites owned their homes, while sixty-four percent of Durangoans rented theirs. These figures reflect the longer existence and greater stability of Sandwich. In neither community was there evidence of a marked economic or social distinction between those who owned and those who rented.

Very few families were headed by women in Sandwich, and the women who headed families were usually widows. Durango had more women heads of household, many of whom had mining husbands working elsewhere. Families headed by women still made up fewer than one percent of all families in Sandwich and Durango. Working wives were a rarity in both towns. Widows and unmarried sisters generally shared housing with members of their families.

Durango contained a much wider cross section of the United States, hosting residents from all regions of the country. Almost all of the residents, however, came from the Midwest. Illinois ranked as one of the leading contributors. In Sandwich, only one person, a child, was born in Colorado, and less than one percent of all others came from the former Confederate states. These statistics provide some insights into the nature of the people, but they do not tell the whole story.[1]

A walk through each community led to encounters with a fascinating mosaic of people. Durango carpenter Ogle Monteith and his family emigrated from Scotland in 1882. Married twenty-five years, he and his wife, Christina, had sixteen children, only four of whom were still living. Unlike many of their neighbors, they had purchased their home but were still paying off the mortgage. Englishman William Gill and New Mexican Anton Salazar mined coal. Both had been married fourteen years. Because of the dangers involved in their occupation, many miners, whether they mined coal or hard rock, never married.

Married three years, railroad conductor James Henry and his wife, Allie, lived with their two-year-old son, Willie, in a rented house. They had come originally from Iowa and Illinois. Ida and George Goodman owned their home debt-free and had one child, who was fifteen years old. George and his boarder, Harry Baumer, were housepainters and paperhangers. Sandwich had a Goodman, too—German immigrant and merchant Gus Goodman, whose general store was one of the town's popular establishments.

New Yorker George Dommick and New Mexican Martin Valdez both worked at Durango's smelter, and their wives, Belle and Matilde, each gave birth to seven children. Six of the Dommicks' children, and five of the Valdezs', were still living. Matilde Valdez, a Coloradan, could neither read nor write. Teamster Ramon Blanco and his wife, Pacifica, owned their own home, while newlyweds Lucindo and Lucia Aragon rented their first house. Lucindo hoped to earn enough at the smelter to eventually purchase a home.

In Sandwich, Carl Johnson, who emigrated from Sweden in 1860, labored as a blacksmith. Carl owned his home free and clear, and he and his wife, Ida, were the parents of two children. His brother Nelson, a laborer, lived with them. Large families were common in Sandwich, too. Josephine Kisel and her day-laborer husband, William, had eight children, six of them living. Married twenty-five years, Englishman Alfred Hall and his wife, Testa, had fourteen children, of whom nine survived. This baker rented his home and had come to the United States in 1888. Illinois-born housepainter Arthur Barrows owned the home where he and his wife, Elizabeth, and their daughter, Lois, lived. Harriet and Charles Frost had three children, two of whom still lived at home. They also had a live-in "servant," a success story for a factory laborer.[2]

A servant would have seemed less unusual in the home of a merchant or a professional person. Durango bankers Alfred Camp and William Vaile and Sandwich bankers Frederick Mosher and Miles Castle could afford to provide such luxuries for their wives Estelle, Julia, Elizabeth, and Freelove. So, too, could others of their economic status.

Julia and William Vaile had no children, in contrast to Elizabeth and Frederick Mosher's five. These U.S.-born couples ranked as members of their communities' upper classes. Both men were Civil War veterans, and Mosher was quite a prominent local hero. The "very somber" Mosher, who walked to the bank every day, moved to Sandwich after a wartime career that included incarceration by the Confederates as a prisoner of war and involvement in a series of major battles, including almost all of those during Grant's 1864–65 campaign. Vaile, described as "a gentleman and fine bank officer," was also considered "quite a character." When the First National Bank closed for the day, he would gather up any "short checks" on the saloons and go out to obtain the money, taking "time to stop and have a drink for himself." A conservative nineteenth-century banker normally shunned saloons, but this was a "working" trip!

Some of Durango's business and professional men rented their homes. Among them were businessman Robert Sloan, lawyer Richard McCloud, and merchant Ike Kruschke. Others, like Alfred Camp and carriage manufacturer Harry Jackson, owned theirs.

Ike Kruschke, a German-born Durango pioneer, had immigrated in 1866, married his wife, Hattie, in 1867, and become one of Durango's leading merchants in the town's first decade. Of the Kruschkes' three children, two were living. Their father sponsored one of the local baseball clubs. The energetic, Massachusetts-born Charles Newman had parlayed money earned from his chain of six Colorado drugstores into successful mining investments. He and his wife, Marian, were pillars of the Episcopal church. Highly respected merchant Charles Corlinsky and his wife, Annie, came to Sandwich from Russian Poland and adapted well to their new home. They and their two children lived in their own home, thanks to the success of their dry goods store.

Mary and Joseph Dyas owned and operated the well-known Sandwich House hotel and also held the town record for the length of a marriage: fifty-three years. The eleven children of hardware man George Kleinsmid and his wife, Louise, kept George busy hustling up business in Sandwich. Almost everyone in Sandwich knew popular, "sharp as a tack" Ed Ledoyt, whose booming voice could easily be heard a block away. A "rabid" Republican, Ed served several terms as postmaster.

Among the professional people, successful lawyer John Blee was one of Sandwich's few Democrats. A graduate of the University of Michigan, he had also been a newspaper editor. Prominent socially, Blee and his wife, Ellen, were the parents of twins. Dr. Charles Winne, also a graduate of the University of Michigan, settled in Sandwich after serving in the Civil War, and he eventually opened a drug store. His son-in-law, Ira Converse, joined him in the business; both men held several township and city offices. In 1897, Dr. Sherman Culver married English-born nurse Louise Lockwood, who, when the decade ended, was studying to receive her medical degree and taking care of their son. Durango doctor William Wycoff and his wife, Maria, recent arrivals from Indiana, also had one child.

William and "sweet" Nellie Forsythe Woodbury had been the subjects of one of Sandwich's more romantic stories of the decade. She was a teacher and he a principal and then a superintendent. They recorded their daily experiences in diaries, two of the few that have survived. Durango druggist George Tiffany, a "sincere, outspoken" man, married Lillian Mayers in 1894. They had one son. Tiffany's neighbors, attorney and author Richard McCloud and his wife, Ellen, had one daughter, as did attorney Reese

McCloskey and his wife, Mabel. Among the various groups in Durango and Sandwich, the professional class produced the smallest families.

Ex-slave Hope Turner lived two houses down the street from Miles Castle in Sandwich. A widower, this laborer owned his home and seemed well received within the community. So did Baker Fletcher, an African American who listed no occupation; he and his wife, Mary, were parents of four children. Durango's only African American family, that of Jennie and George Barnett, had five children. Sadly, six others had died. George worked as a janitor. Although there were too few African Americans in Sandwich and Durango to allow many generalizations, there is little doubt that blacks found themselves locked into menial, lower-paying jobs.

Women heading households were relegated to similar positions. In Sandwich, Mary Fluelling supported her son as a dressmaker, while Durango's Capitola Conway earned a living for herself and her daughter as a laundress. Both women were divorced, as was dining-room girl Louise Morgan of Durango, who had four children, ages three to ten. Irish widow Mary Porter of Durango listed no occupation, but her two oldest daughters listed theirs as dining-room girls. Nine of Mary's fourteen children were living, seven of them at home. In Sandwich, Bathsheba Hummel's husband had died while returning from the California gold rush, and one of her sons died in the war. She overcame both tragedies, raising three other children with "her loom" and buying a home as well. Of the other women, only Louise Morgan owned her home. To all appearances two of these five families, the Porters and Conways, faced some trying times.

A few families lived in the two communities and farmed nearby. In Sandwich, Connecticut-born Daniel Sweeney supported seven of his children as a farmer. Daniel and his wife Corhrise's six other offspring had already ventured out on their own. Durangoan James Conway and his wife, Mary, had eight children. While children helped carry out the tasks necessary to keep a farm going, not all farm families had as many as the Sweeneys and Conways. Lifelong Republican Bert Bark and his wife, Grace, lived north of Sandwich with two children, Marium Reinette and Hurdman. Bert was hailed as one of the more "prosperous" farmers and stockbreeders of De Kalb County.

Durango had something that Sandwich would not tolerate—a red-light district. Durango's permissiveness was one of the major factors that differentiated it from Sandwich. Both men and women ran businesses in the red-light district.

In both towns, the saloon keepers teetered between the status of acceptable and unacceptable businessmen. One of Durango's saloon keepers, English immigrant George Isgar, along with his Canadian-born wife, Helen, maintained a middle-class home with two children. Less welcome in Durango was gambler Forrest Mays, who rented a home for his wife and two children. Questionable occupation notwithstanding, he could afford a house servant for his wife, Harriet. Durango's legendary madam, Bessie Rivers, the "land lady of a sporting house," employed four women: Georgie Smith, Mattie Shefler, and Nellie Boynton—"boarders" who listed themselves as married—and May Deibel, who was single. These women were in their twenties or early thirties. Of the seventeen women who enumerated their occupations as "sport," "boarder," "landlady," or "inmate," seven listed themselves as married, one as divorced, three as widowed, and six as single. All were born in the United States, most coming from the Midwest or Colorado.

Sandwichites would have spurned these female "unfortunates" as outcasts from Victorian society. Durango proved more tolerant; their commerce was, after all, good for all local businesses. Even so, it was understood that they were not to mix with the "acceptable" women or appear in residential areas, particularly on the showpiece Boulevard.

Victorians exhibited some strong racial biases and stereotyping, which emerged in a variety of ways. The following comment in the *Sandwich Free Press* (Aug. 11, 1898) about a watermelon feast enjoyed by Sandwich's Odd Fellows gave evidence, though unintentionally, of that stereotyping: "No band of pickaninnies ever got outside of more melons than the feasters and still they called for more." The *Durango Great Southwest* (Aug. 3, 1892) displayed a similar attitude when it commented that, if "the colored people of the south" knew what sort of watermelon country Durango was, there would be a "general exodus and consequently a sable cloud hanging over us." Nellie Forsythe's matter-of-fact remark in her diary, while visiting the World's Fair, seems typical: "Aug. 25 Darkies' day. Saw a good many of them at the Fair."

African Americans were always referred to similarly in news stories. When the Fletcher family gave a concert, joined by a few other blacks, the *Sandwich Argus* (May 7 and 14, 1892) hailed the "colored singers of

Sandwich." The duets sung by the twins, Floy and Flossie, earned special mention, but the paper criticized the small house, which it said was "much smaller than the merit of the entertainment deserved." A later announcement in the *Argus* (June 5, 1892) of a program at the Methodist church, entitled "Jubilee Singing," pointed out that the songs would be rendered "as they only can be by the colored people." Police notes referred to "colored" prostitutes and involvement in criminal or riotous activity by men or women of "color," making a point of labeling them as such. The term *nigger* was used privately but not in the public press.

Occasionally, the public and press derived amusement at the expense of African Americans. When the Durango "colored club" endorsed one 1894 candidate for city attorney and its "ladies auxiliary" supported his rival, the *Durango Herald* (April 3) could not suppress a journalistic chuckle. In 1894 enough blacks lived in town to imitate the social and political aspirations of their white neighbors. The depression, better opportunities elsewhere, and a desire to associate with more of their own race apparently caused almost all of them to leave Durango by 1900.

The entrenched enmity toward African Americans that was emerging in some larger Northern cities in the 1890s had not yet reached these rural towns. Quite the contrary, at least in the case of the Fletchers, who were roundly supported in the press for their musical efforts.[3]

Matters of race rumbled around the two communities like distant thunder, but there had been no overtly hostile encounters involving ethnic minorities. Nevertheless, even here there arose strong hints of what might be coming. The labor violence at Pittsburgh's Homestead plant (1892) and elsewhere generated comments against "wholesale foreign immigration" (*Durango Herald,* July 6, 1894). "Good citizen" foreigners were one thing, "bloodthirsty mobs" quite another. Interracial marriage evoked the worst of middle-class Victorian fears and bigotry. The *Durango Herald*, on October 28, 1898, featured an article about a young New York widow marrying a black man. It carried the headline "Gone With a Coon." Not to pick on Durango, but the same newspaper reported on July 30, 1892, the visit of an "Italian colony," with a tame bear and monkey, in these words: "They are fair types of the Italian Lazaroni, lazy, dirty and mendicant. The bear is the cleanest animal in the crowd." Finally, during the depression, after a "colony of Japs" visited town, the *Durango Daily Southwest* (Aug. 2, 1893) expressed gratitude that they had left "none of their tribe behind." During this same time, racism toward Hispanics stayed muted, except in references to such things as the "huts and hovels" of "Mexican town." The reference was apparently to "Mexican Flats," located just south of Durango, along the Animas River. Its location said much about attitudes and degree of acceptance; even so, the Hispanics in Durango appear to have been accepted or rejected on an individual, not an ethnic, basis.

Both Sandwich and Durango had small Jewish communities, whose members included several prominent merchants. As far as can be ascertained, no discrimination against Jews on religious or racial grounds occurred. Jews were accepted on their individual merits and played prominent roles within the mercantile world. Neither town had a synagogue nor, it appears, enough Jewish males—ten—to celebrate a seder at Passover. For the high holy days, such as Yom Kippur or Passover, they would have had to worship in nearby synagogues in Chicago and Aurora in Illinois, or in Denver.

Neither community contained a large Chinese contingent, a logical circumstance in Sandwich. Toi Gee, "our Chinaman," did live in Sandwich and ran a laundry there during the first half of the decade. What eventually happened to him has been lost to history. Laundryman Ho Lee may have taken his place. Lee, a thirty-seven-year-old bachelor, was the only Chinese the census enumerator, Benjamin Kellogg, could find in 1900.

In Durango, an interesting omission occurred when the 1900 census taker, Anna Hammond, ignored or somehow overlooked the town's Chinese. More Chinese lived there than in Sandwich—a total of twenty-seven by a federally mandated count in 1894. They operated restaurants, laundries, and at least one store that sold "Chinese and Japanese goods." Though not segregated residentially, their businesses were clustered around Tenth and Main, extending west into the red-light district. The Chinese worked hard and generally stayed out of the news but received some bad press because of opium. Durango fought an ongoing battle against Chinese opium dens. According to the *Herald* (May 9 and 10, 1894), a raid in 1894 corralled one man and three women, all white "dope fiends," plus six pipes, lamps, "dope," and other paraphernalia. Without question, some Chinese were still in town in 1900, but the census returns give no evidence of their presence.[4]

The residents of Sandwich and Durango were not unlike those of neighboring communities or their fellow Victorians throughout the country. They had time to greet their neighbors on the street and to worry about them if they missed lodge or church meetings. This was small-town America. Through the "best of times and the worst of times," they persevered, hoping for a better today than yesterday and dreaming about an even better tomorrow.

NOTES

1. These figures are based on the original returns for the census of 1900. Unfortunately, the 1890 census results were lost in a fire. In Sandwich, 1,400 people were sampled out of a total population of 2,520. In Durango, 1,700 people were sampled out of a total of 3,317. I made a quick visual check of the remainder of the census to be sure some significant trend was not overlooked. *Population* (Washington: United States Census Office, 1901), volume 1.
2. Lewis M. Gross, *Past and Present of DeKalb County, Illinois* (Chicago: Pioneer Publishing Co., 1907), 2 volumes. Richard McCloud, *Durango As It Is* (Durango: Durango Board of Trade, 1892). John G. Canfield, *Mines and Mining Men of Colorado* (Denver: Carson, Hurst & Harper, 1893). Sarah Platt Decker Chapter of the D.A.R., *Pioneers of the San Juan Country*, 4 volumes (Colorado Springs: Out West Printing, 1942 and 1946; Durango: Durango Printing Co., 1952; Denver: Big Mountain Press, 1961).
3. Nellie Forsythe and William Woodbury diaries, Regional History Center, Northern Illinois University. *Sandwich Free Press*, July 13, 1893; Aug. 1, 1898. *Durango Great Southwest*, Aug. 3, 1892. *Sandwich Argus*, May 7, May 14, 1892; June 5, 1897. *Durango Herald*, May 3, 1894; Oct. 28, 1898. Lewis O. Saum, *The Popular Mood of America, 1860–1900* (Lincoln: University of Nebraska Press, 1990), 197. Ila Smith and Stanley Smith, interviews by author, Aug. 30–31, 1989.
4. *Herald*, July 30, 1892; March 18, April 3, May 9, May 10, July 6, 1894; Oct. 28, 1898; March 2, 1899. *Durango Daily Southwest*, Aug. 2, 1893. *Free Press*, March 19, 1890; Oct. 4, 1894. McCloud, *Durango*, 74. Maps of Durango and Sandwich published during the 1890s and early 1900s by the Sanborn Map Company of New York.

3
FRONT PAGE HEADLINES

There'll be a hot time in the old town tonight.
—"A Hot Time in the Old Town Tonight" (1886)

In the watershed decade of 1890s, events occurred that would, in some respects, affect the country for decades to come. The events may have had an immediate and direct impact on Durango and Sandwich, or they may have been noticed only briefly in passing. Neither community constituted an island unto itself, and the outside world intruded into each with increasing frequency, particularly as news-gathering became easier, thanks to national wire services.

Nothing impacted the two communities more than the financial panic of 1893 and the subsequent depression. The United States, in all its history, had never witnessed economic woes quite this perilous or devastating. The depression touched farm and town alike, Westerner and Easterner, businessman and laborer, and housewife and schoolteacher. Before the depression ran its course, its ramifications set the stage for major changes in the United States. Sandwich recovered first, after about four years; Durango still suffered as the decade neared its end. To make matters worse, both towns had been enjoying prosperous times in the early nineties.

There had been signs for months that a violent financial storm might be brewing before it hit in May 1893. The causes were international and national—excessive speculation and expansion, declining agricultural prices, an unfavorable balance of trade, overcapitalization of businesses, and a drying up of credit. These factors silently stole up on the country, but the emotional event that put the United States over the brink was the nation's gold reserve falling below $100 million. Americans had deemed the government solvent, as long as the gold reserve remained above that figure. In April 1893, it slipped below. This unleashed fear, followed by panic and a cascading economic crash; in what seemed the twinkling of an eye, a brutal depression drearily settled over the country. Before six months had passed, eight thousand businesses and four hundred banks failed. One hundred fifty-six railroads eventually went into bankruptcy. The South and West were harder hit than the Midwest and East; that led to great political unrest and agitation, which merged into the rhetoric of the Populist Party and the Free Silver movement.

Colorado and Durango were devastated, mainly because of the collapse of the price of silver. As the country's number one silver producing state, Colorado watched with horror as the price plummeted by half, tumbling into the forty-cents-per-ounce range before rebounding into the low sixties. Overproduction, declining international markets, a scarcity of industrial uses, and the repeal of the Sherman Silver Purchase Act caused the collapse. Coloradans chose, however, to believe in a conspiracy theory. Eastern and European bankers and creditors, they thought, were out to ruin the state, its people, and its chief industry. To them, the threatened repeal of the 1890 Sherman Act, which guaranteed government purchase of fifty-four million ounces of silver per year (the nation's estimated annual production) proved their contention. To Eastern businessmen and the Republican Party, this pork-barrel legislation gravely undermined business confidence at best and was the major cause of the crash at worst. Why? Because the silver certificates issued by the government could be redeemed for gold; such action, critics charged, drained the Treasury. The *Sandwich Free Press* (July 6, 1893), for example, believed that the Sherman Act was "undoubtedly a factor in our troubles."

President Grover Cleveland called a special session of Congress, and after a riotous three-month debate, Congress repealed it. The depression did not end, and Western silver states and the Populist Party cried foul. The "heartless" repeal sharpened their suffering, and increasingly angry Coloradans lashed out. And they did in fact suffer. Their cries were not rhetoric for rhetoric's sake.

A survey conducted by the Colorado Bureau of Labor Statistics found that in the state between July 1 and August 31, 1893, 45,084 persons lost their jobs, 435 mines closed, and 377 businesses failed. Four hundred Durangoans were thrown out of work and 15 businesses closed. Durango's situation, the report concluded, was "gloomy." If that seemed bad, the story from the major community in Durango's economic hinterland, Silverton (population 1,154, plus miners in nearby mines), proved worse—10 mines closed, 3 businesses failed, and 1,000 people were out of work: Silverton's general feeling was "dark." Then, there was Rico (population 1,134), which the Rio Grande Southern had just brought into Durango's orbit. The crash hit few towns harder than Rico, where 30 mines shut down, 22 businesses failed, and 1,000 people left town. Rico's situation was reported as "hopeless."

An unidentified Durangoan commented, "Of course we have suffered severely, but not so extensively as in other portions of the state" (*Effects*, 33). With eternal Western optimism, this individual believed "the worst of the crisis is past and hereafter there will be a steady, gradual improvement in all lines of business." Such an improvement would not happen for years. Though bombastic editor Dave Day initially waxed optimistic in the midst of collapse, pointing out that one of "the surest indexes" had not slumped—none of the large gambling houses had closed its doors—he eventually advised his readers, "By jogging along with paying strict attention to business, the people of Durango will establish for it a reputation which will enhance all values when capitalists again are ready for investment in this state" (*Durango Solid Muldoon,* July 21, 1893).[1]

Raw statistics tell only part of the story. The Rio Grande Southern, built in 1890–91 from Durango to Ridgway, went into receivership, the smelter closed, the company that published the *Durango Great Southwest* failed, Henry Strater lost his hotel, a construction boom collapsed, and the jobs-wanted column in the newspaper lengthened weekly. Ernest Amy reported to stockholders of the smelter company, "At no time in the history of the Company, have we been compelled to face so many unforeseen difficulties in the way of conducting successful operations." Perhaps Frank Burke wrote a fitting summary of the period in his suicide note: "Good bye all friends. Times too hard. The Boys can have a wake. Born in '58 Baltimore, Md. What I owe now I'll owe forever."

Sandwich's situation became neither as drastic nor as dramatic as Durango's. The newspapers cataloged the hard times without editorial comment, generally promoting the idea that "the scare seems over," or the "outlook is surely brightening" (*Sandwich Argus,* July 1 and Aug. 5, 1893). The community did not avoid troubles, however. In March 1894, the Grand Army of the Republic (GAR) needed to replenish its Relief Fund by sponsoring a program by the Blackhawk Minstrels of Aurora. Other local relief groups asked for such items as surplus clothing. The *Sandwich Argus* (April 7, 1894) observed that the "stagnation of business and low prices" had resulted in demands for a "return to the old conditions and a protective tariff." Interestingly, people in both communities enjoyed "hard times" parties and "poverty socials."[2]

Although the *Durango Daily Southwest* pleaded for public work projects in July 1893, and the *Sandwich Argus* initially supported Coxey's Army of unemployed, as it marched on Washington in the spring of 1894 to demand government help, there did not appear to be general support for such radical moves. The public instead seemed to support the commonly held idea that the federal government should stay solvent and let the business community pull the country out of the depression. As far as can be discovered, no one from either town marched with Jacob Coxey.

Sandwich, in the next few years, furnished mixed signals about the depression's impact. In 1894, the town built two schoolhouses, in 1895, home and business construction appeared strong, and, in 1896, the CB&Q complimented the "little city" for its "business interests and activity . . . [having] been better maintained through the depressed times since 1893 than [those of] any other town along their line" (*Argus*, Sept. 19, 1896). Neither of the town's banks closed, and so it avoided one of the plagues of the era. Yet the *Argus* (Sept. 19, 1896) observed that, although sales might be up, "collecting pay [was] a slow process." In May of the next year, Castle still talked of a "despondent time," even though recovery continued.

In its January 1, 1895, special issue, the *Durango Herald* summarized the previous year "with all its distress, trouble and disappointments." Not discouraged, Durango had met "distress with fortitude and disappointment with renewed energy." Fortunately for the town, its three banks—First National, Smelter National, and Colorado State—had remained solvent, preventing further panic, and the smelter eventually reopened. Still, the difficulties did not end. On June 17, 1897, the *Herald* commented that no individual in La Plata County who was engaged in any "business, industry or labor is not today struggling under depressed conditions." A year and a half later, business was "slowly picking up a little."

In the volatile, speculative business world of Durango, some of the town's venturesome merchants had been mortgaged to the hilt when the depression struck. Their businesses closed their doors as the economy collapsed, some to reopen later under new management or under the same owners, who were now refinanced and hopefully more worldly wise. The town survived the depression, but the boom days of its first twelve years faded into memory. The businessmen and businesswomen had learned a lesson; Durango's business community had emerged much more conservative and was willing to accept the fact that the boom mining days in its hinterland had ended. Unlimited growth and sky's-the-limit dreams were replaced by a declining role for mining and a slowly growing role for agriculture. Durango emerged from the depression more like Sandwich, both towns relying on agriculture to underpin their economic "empire."

Sandwich had been fortunate. It had not suffered as much as Durango and, indeed, if the papers can be trusted, local businesses and manufacturing companies weathered the storm remarkably well. Among the major employers, only the Enterprise Company closed. That closing came in 1897, though the company soon reopened. Business had slowed, but failures had not come. The conservative nature of the local business and banking leadership paid off handsomely. Unemployment occurred, but according to the *Argus* on September 19, 1896, "Little distress [resulted] from want of employment." Farm prices had declined, but that problem was softened by the fact that local farmers had not been deeply in debt and were able to retrench successfully. For both towns, the 1893 crash and depression would not soon be forgotten.[3]

The Pullman strike in the spring of 1894 was by far the most significant labor trouble during the depression. Eugene Debs and his American Railway Union joined striking workers against the Pullman Company at the company town of Pullman outside Chicago. On June 26, Debs ordered a boycott of all Pullman cars, and his men obeyed by removing them from trains and leaving them on sidetracks. The railroads promptly fired the union members. This led to a general railroad strike that in the midst of the depression further damaged the struggling national economy. Bitter unemployed workers poured out their frustrations and hatred in acts of violence that nearly paralyzed rail traffic between Chicago and the West.

The owners asked for federal help after Illinois governor John P. Altgeld ordered state troops to preserve law and order but not to break the strike on the railroads' behalf. Finally, on July 4, President Grover Cleveland intervened. He sent in the army to guard the mails and, conveniently, mail cars appeared on most trains. A "blanket injunction" against the union and its strike followed. It resulted in Debs and other leaders being cited for contempt and being thrown in jail. This episode established the precedent of using federal troops to break a strike. Washington's involvement on behalf of business had never been so blatant. To critics, this all appeared to prove the allegation that a corrupt alliance existed between business and government to suppress the people's liberties.

The strike hit Sandwich quickly. The freight blockade, as the *Sandwich Free Press* noted on July 12, made a lot of "business for the express company." The editor thought that because of such a wholesale increase in business, express charges should be lowered. He whistled in the dark with that wish. The paper also criticized both sides. It called Debs an anarchist, supported by "disreputable democratic politicians." Nevertheless, it turned against the "brutal, selfish men like the Pullmans and Carnegies," who controlled vast interests and, from a safe distance, cut wages. The GAR predictably passed a resolution endorsing and approving Cleveland's "firm, manly and patriotic course" (*Free Press,* July 19, 1894).

Durango also faced train stoppages. On July 4, the Durango Herald saw a consolation: plenty to eat existed "in this section," unlike in some Eastern cities that faced food shortages. "And another thing—our outside creditors cannot reach us—for a few days." The strike soon passed, and creditors knocked on the door, but for conservatives in both communities, these events provided another example of the violent, anarchistic, and un-American nature of labor unions. The conservatives would not forget. The news coverage had been sensational, making things seem worse than they actually were, but the strike in some ways matched the conservatives' worst fears.[4]

On a more upbeat note, the Klondike gold rush of 1897–98 offered one more frontier opportunity for those "poor man's diggings." In Sandwich and Durango, the gold rush did not receive much attention outside of syndicated articles and a *Herald* "Klondyke" column in August 1897. (The paper soon learned the correct spelling!) Overall, the newspapers presented straightforward accounts of the harsh weather, the long journey, and the other problems encountered by those who went.

Rather interestingly, and hardly accidentally, Durango newspapers expanded their coverage of local mining districts, stressing the great opportunities in the La Plata and Needles districts and even offering good words for a rival, booming Cripple Creek.

Apparently, few people in either Durango or Sandwich stampeded to the Yukon, or if they did go, they did not send back letters the newspapers published. Frank Gallotti and Wesley Helm left Durango, for example, then disappeared from view. Others planned to go in the spring of 1898, but whatever happened to their plans failed to make the news. More might have gone, and the Klondike news might have remained in the headlines, if it had not been for an even more electrifying matter.

Mounting trouble with Spain over Cuba seized the headlines once reserved for Alaska. Long a troublesome remnant of Spain's shrinking empire, Cuba gave Madrid nothing but misery. A revolt broke out in 1895 that quickly gained the attention of some Americans, especially the New York City press, which exploited it for all the tragic struggle it seemed to be worth. Readers in Sandwich and Durango followed the exploits of the Cuban "patriots," who were struggling for their independence, and read of the "brutality" of General Valeriano Weyler, better known as "Butcher" Weyler, the governor general of Cuba. The scorched earth, guerrilla war between the two factions gave rise to an endless variety of articles, propaganda, and sensationalistic journalism.

By 1897, Americans' emotions boiled over, and U.S. money was being lost in destroyed sugar plantations and other investments. More than a few Americans donated money to the Cuban cause, and some even launched filibustering expeditions to get supplies and arms to Cuba. Sympathy for the insurgents rose like a July thermometer. Officially, the United States remained neutral, but with the public, it was another matter. Following William McKinley's 1896 election, the United States started to take a more active role in pressuring Spain to stop some of its actions, particularly the herding of Cubans into "concentration" camps. Even when Spain made some concessions, Washington kept pressing for more. Independence appeared to be the only answer from the U.S. point of view. No Spanish government, or at least none that hoped to stay in power, dared surrender Cuba. Spanish public opinion would not have tolerated losing the last remnant of Spain's once imperial New World glory.

The predictable resulted. By New Year's Day, 1898, the United States teetered on the threshold of war while still seeking a solution to the Cuban mess. Not many Sandwichites and Durangoans seemed very concerned about the prospect of warfare. Diplomacy did not interest most of them, nor did the possibility of conflict appear terrifying. The horrors of the Civil War had receded into a glorious memory of an epic struggle characterized more by romance than by dread. A new generation of young men wanted their chance at "manhood," a chance to brag about their exploits.

Newspapers in both towns provided excellent coverage of the 1898 Cuban situation. They even published photographs, a first for an ongoing event. The papers had more drawings than photos, but readers received good visual coverage to supplement excellent, if biased, reporting. The readers further received assurances that the United States stood militarily prepared: those photos of modern naval warships reassured everyone that Spain could never attack the U.S. mainland.

The turning point in U.S. involvement came in February. First, the U.S. press obtained a letter criticizing President McKinley that was written by the Spanish ambassador, Enrique Dupuy de Lôme. Americans might say what they would about the president, but a despised Spaniard was held accountable. That the private letter had been stolen from the mail mattered not.

Before Spain could make amends, the situation exploded. "SHIP BLOWN UP," "GREAT LOSS OF LIFE," "SUSPECT THE SPANIARDS," screamed *Sandwich Argus* headlines of February 26. The battleship Maine had been sunk in Havana harbor, the victim of a "secret infernal machine." Two hundred sixty officers and other men lost their lives. Vengeance! cried the war hawks: "Many Americans would wipe the Spanish off the earth." Like the editors of other papers, the *Argus*'s Miles Castle kept hammering with one inflammatory headline after another. For example, on March 5, the headline "DOGS OF WAR GROWL" introduced a discussion aimed at proving that a conflict with Spain was "inevitable." Miles boiled over at McKinley, because he hesitated to go to war. Americans "thrilled" for war (April 5), but they did not stop to consider who stood to gain the most from the sinking of the Maine:

> The Argus wants war, as its editor thinks there are many things worse, among them the insults that have been borne so meekly. (April 2)

> War would be welcomed to establish our record as a people ready to protect national interests and national honor. . . . for we must give the Dons a good drubbing before we quit. They need it—and we need to do it. (April 9)

The *Durango Herald* proved to be only slightly calmer. War, it said on April 13, was "always to be regretted" but often "is a christian act," when "it serves to redeem and relieve long suffering people." The *Herald*, Castle, and other war hawks got their wish, and there was no question that they completely dominated both communities' public forums. However, before war was declared on April 21, Durango found itself mightily embarrassed.

As patriots throughout the country chanted, "Remember the Maine, to hell with Spain," a national wire service, on March 20, reported that Durango had hung and burned an effigy of President McKinley. How unpatriotic! That was bad enough, but the story did not end there. Following the burning, there were heated speeches, in which the orators suggested that people should "subscribe and reimburse Spain" for explosives used to sink the Maine (*Herald*, April 18). Within a few minutes, the listeners subscribed one hundred dollars. Further mortification! It all turned out to have been a hoax sent over the Associated Press wire by newspaperman Walter Davis. Apparently he was trying to embarrass the rival *Herald*, but it completely backfired. Unmourned, he and his family left town in July. Unfortunately, no copies of Davis's paper remain. Apparently known as the *Uplift* (the *Herald* would not deign to call it by name), it did not survive the aftermath. On July 2, the *Herald* summarized all that could be said about the mess: "Our people are not ninnies and naturally resented being misrepresented."[5]

When the United States finally declared war, Durango did all it could to make amends: volunteers flocked to the colors, and locals cheered patriotic speeches. So did Sandwichites. "To Arms! To Arms!" proclaimed the *Sandwich Free Press* on April 28. The Stars and Stripes, the paper said, "flew from every Sandwich flagstaff and in many a window." The *Free Press* declared that people were "thoroughly disgusted with Spanish barbarity and cruelty" and would rejoice to see its "blood-thirsty, treacherous rag" banished "forever" from waters near our shores. To their amazement, the first battle occurred in the Philippines, where Admiral George Dewey's fleet, following Dewey's celebrated order, "You may fire when ready, Gridley," steamed into Manila Bay and blew the Spanish Pacific fleet out of the water. The battle, if it can be called that, lived up to Americans' fondest expectations. Not a single U.S. ship was damaged, and the only casualties were eight sailors who were slightly wounded.

"Blazing sky-rockets, colored lights and booming cannon" celebrated the "brave commander's great achievement." A "victory unparalleled in naval warfare," proclaimed the *Durango Herald* (May 9), which, to enhance war fever, also published the lyrics and scores of patriotic American music. A few letters from boys who marched off to glory and ended up in camps far from the battlefield made the war more personal. But the exploits of Theodore Roosevelt and his Rough Riders, "Teddy's Terrors," added a dash of romance and heroism. Almost before Americans realized it, the "Splendid Little War" came to an end in August. Spain had far declined since its glory days and was an obviously weak opponent.

The GAR thought it all magnificent. So did other Sandwichites and Durangoans in the glorious afterglow. The *Sandwich Argus* became briefly upset when the secretary of war said no women nurses would be permitted to minister to the sick or wounded. The paper declared on April 30, "The order is barbaric and contrary to the usages of all civilized nations." A few people complained about increased taxes, but the struggle was so short that it hardly mattered.[6]

The amazingly brief war, America's "coming out party," slipped into history. The United States had gained a colonial empire stretching from the Far East to the West Indies, and had emerged a fledgling world power. Most Sandwich and Durango people burst with pride; a few harbored concerns about just what had happened. Miles Castle reflected these reactions in an editorial on December 3, in which he reviewed the just completed peace negotiations. With pride, he wrote, "This places us in the very front rank among nations, both in territory, wealth and power. It gives us a vast field for enterprise, and makes our President the most powerful ruler among nations, during his four years rule." However, he feared the changes that had taken place so quickly and, seemingly, so innocently. "This settlement gives us a series of long and severe wars, for we will have to civilize the heathen of those distant countries by the sword and musket, the most efficient missionary agents the world has known."

Concerns aside, particularly such civilizing methods, Miles felt confident that all would turn out well. "It was God's plan and in Dewey he chose a fitting instrument. Now we must watch and wait."

One did not have to watch and wait long. Reports of the sordid efforts to "civilize our little brown brother" in the Philippines soon started to surface. It became a full-scale brutal campaign that would take more lives, time, and money than did the war itself. On July 1, 1899, Castle advised his readers, "We complain about the Philippine war, the loss of men and money, but we have become a great nation and must take a hand in civilizing the savage nations with cannon—one of God's methods for evangelization of the heathen." The White Man's Burden did not seem so romantic now, but Miles did not waver from his view that stern measures had to be taken against these "savages."

Americans were in too much of a hurry to do the very things Castle wanted to accomplish, including sending over Theodore Roosevelt and his Rough Riders! "Isn't Teddy a grand fellow, Americans admire a fighter," said the *Sandwich Argus* on July 1, 1898. The stage was set for the twentieth century, the international problems were at hand, and the "bully" leader was ready to take center stage.[7]

A slowly dawning awareness of problems at home existed as well, the concerns that motivated the soon-to-commence Progressive Era. The apprehensions of the Populists did not die, even though their political party did after the 1896 campaign. The growing power of big businesses, the "trusts," as they became known, typified by banker J. P. Morgan, oil man John D. Rockefeller, and steel baron Andrew Carnegie, did not wane. Their power and wealth had become worrisome. The contrasting plight of labor, according to Miles Castle (Jan. 14, 1899), symbolized a "mighty unrest" that underlay the nation's prosperity and "must ere long cause a vast upheaval." The rights of the common people seemed threatened by political bosses, concentration of wealth, and Wall Street bankers. Maybe the Populists had been right when they said "All power to the people." Reality surfaced close to home with such issues as unfair electricity rates, railroads with too much power, and the declining political power of rural voters.

Of the old and the new, it can be said that the old still held sway, but the new knocked on the door. Durangoans and Sandwichites glimpsed, ever so fleetingly, what lay ahead for them, their towns, and their country. In this time of renewed prosperity, new international recognition and national vigor, few stopped to ponder. In the few short years of a decade, these Victorians unexpectedly helped set the nation's course for the next century. Whether the news appeared on the front page or, as was more likely, on the inside pages, the future had arrived for the perceptive to see and contemplate—the king is dead, long live the king! As the popular song said,

> And when the verse is through, in the chorus all join in.
> There'll be a hot time in the old town tonight.

NOTES

1. *Sandwich Free Press*, July 6, 1893. *Effects of Demonetization of Silver . . . August 31, 1893* (Denver: Smith-Brooks, 1893), 7, 11, 13, 22, 33. *Durango Solid Muldoon*, July 21, 1893.
2. Annual Report of the San Juan Smelting and Mining Company (1893–94), 1, 5–6. *Durango Daily Southwest*, July 16, Aug. 22, 1893. *Durango Herald*, Aug. 24, Sept. 26, Sept. 27, Oct. 20, Oct. 21, Nov. 9, Dec. 23, Dec. 31, 1893; May 19, 1894. *Solid Muldoon*, July 21, 1893. John H. Keiser, *Building for the Centuries* (Urbana: University of Illinois Press, 1977), 5. *Sandwich Argus*, July 1, July 22, Aug. 5, Aug. 12, Aug. 26, Sept. 9, 1893; Jan. 20, March 10, April 7, May 12, 1894. *Free Press*, Oct. 26, Nov. 2, Nov. 9, Dec. 14, 1893.
3. *Argus*, April 21, April 28, May 12, Nov. 17, 1894; April 20, 1895; Jan. 4, Sept. 19, 1896; May 8, 1897. *Durango Southwest*, July 16, 1893. *Free Press*, July 18, 1895. *Herald*, Jan. 1, 1895; June 17, Nov. 18, 1897. *Denver Times*, Dec. 2, 1898.
4. *Free Press*, July 12, July 19, July 26, 1894. *Herald*, July 4, 1894.
5. *Durango Weekly Herald*, July–Sept. 1897. *Argus*, May–Aug. 1897 and April 1898. *Free Press*, Feb.–April 1898. *Durango Evening Herald*, March 29, March 31, April 13, April 15, April 18, July 2, 1898.
6. *Evening Herald*, April 21, April 22, June 6, July 6, 1898. *Free Press*, April 28, May 12, May 19, May 26, July 7, 1898. *Argus*, April 30, 1898. Stuart McConnell, *Glorious Contentment: The Grand Army of the Republic* (Chapel Hill: University of North Carolina Press, 1992), 232–34. *Herald*, May 3, May 4, May 7, May 9, May 10, June 16, June 17, June 21, 1898.
7. Nell Irvin Painter, *Standing at Armageddon* (New York: W. W. Norton & Co., 1987), 141–42. *Argus*, Dec. 3, 1898; July 1, 1899. *Free Press*, Feb. 9, 1899.

4

BEST OF TIMES, WORST OF TIMES

For I've worked eight hours this day,
And I think I've earned my pay.
— "I've Worked Eight Hours This Day" (1893)

Main Street (officially Main Avenue in Durango) was the heart and soul of these two towns. Along it the visitor saw the best of the Victorian world and also could sample the worst. In both communities, Main ran north and south. In Sandwich it formed, with Railroad Street, an intersection that served as the commercial, professional, industrial, and governmental hub of the city. In Durango, Main paralleled Second Avenue, which included the La Plata County courthouse, and the two streets served as the town's hub with one exception—the smelter lay across the river.

On Main, in both towns, stood the brick-and-stone business district, the best hotels, the railroad depot (which in Sandwich was actually a block east on Center), banks, and a few stray saloons and billiard parlors. One of Durango's two red-light districts cuddled up at the south end of Main, the other was partly on the nine hundred block's west side and curled west across the tracks. Homes spread out along Main, beyond the business center of both towns, and nestled all around the street. In Sandwich, everyone lived within walking distance of downtown. A Durangoan's walk would have become a little longer as the town expanded northward, but the pride of the community, its trolley, erased the stroll for only a nickel.

Victorian architecture helped provide a cultural link between the two communities and between the mountains and the heartland, in general. The permanent masonry buildings, in Italianate style with a variety of detailing, had become less elaborate by the late 1890s, but they clearly exhibited their owners' faith in the urban middle-class work ethic and in their town's future. Not incidentally, the buildings also displayed their owners'

A TALE OF TWO TOWNS

Durango 1890s

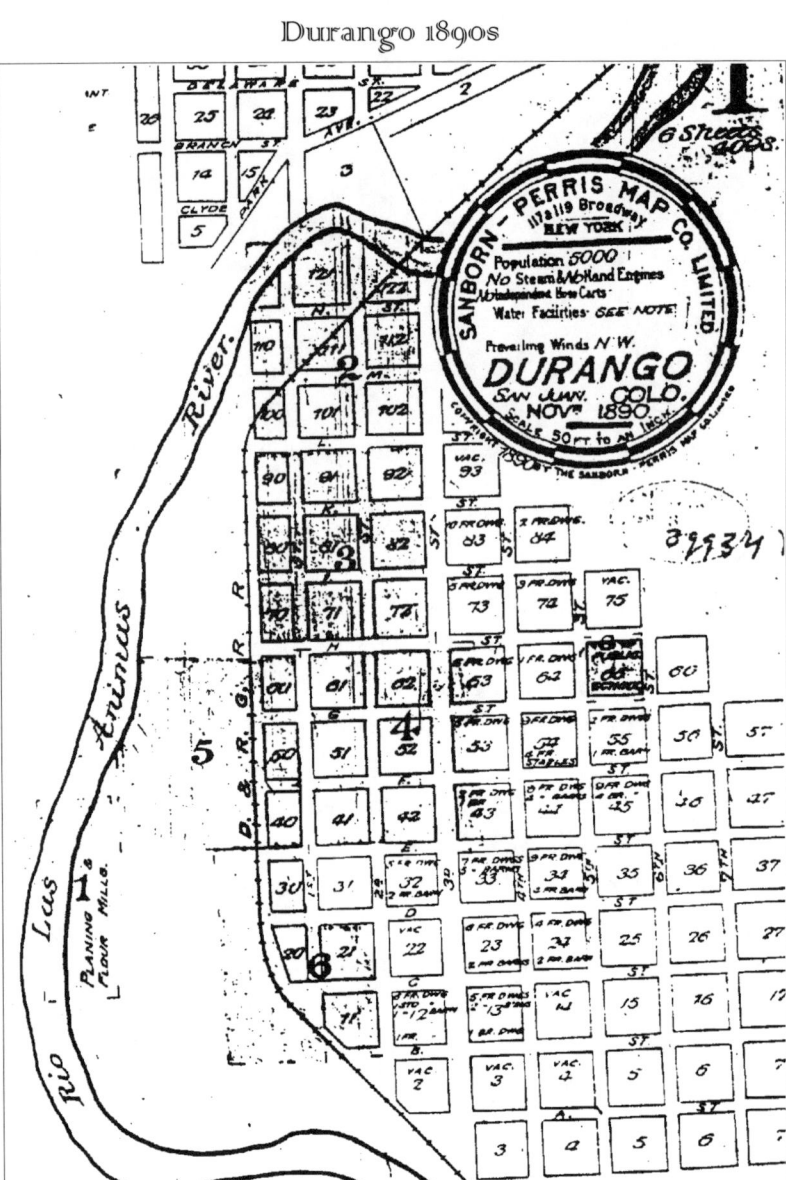

materialistic success and belief in a "rational world view." Whether the buildings were single storefronts with one entrance or commercial blocks with several entrances, they presented the community image that their businesspeople desired. Lined like troops standing for inspection in the center of town, these buildings told much about the Victorian world.

BEST OF TIMES, WORST OF TIMES

Sandwich 1890s

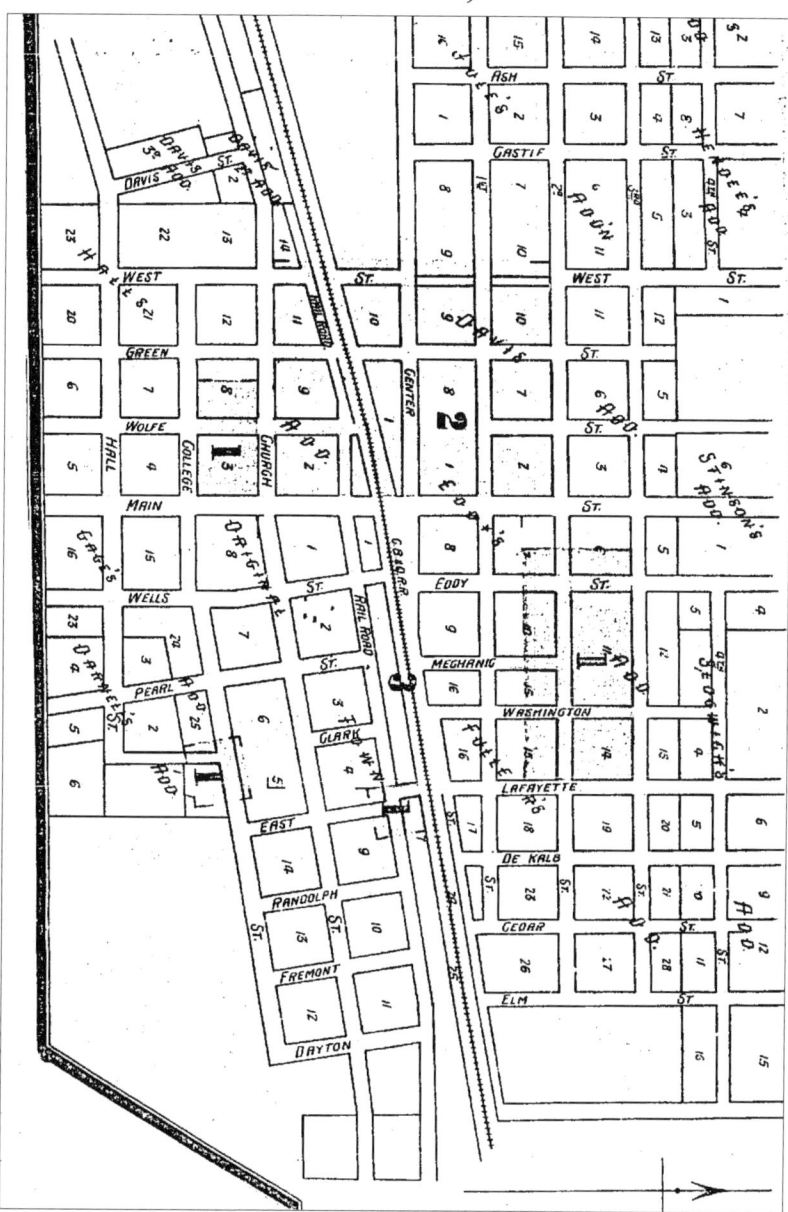

    Railroad tracks helped define each community. Running east and west in Sandwich, they separated the town into sections, Main being the only principal thoroughfare that ran the community's whole length. Durango's Main extended all the way to Animas City and was the only connecting link between the two towns. It paralleled the railroad tracks as they stretched north toward the San Juan Mountains. In Sandwich, the railroad divided the streets, which had different names on the two sides of the tracks. This was not true in Durango, although West Second and Third were separated from East Second and Third by the river, railroad, and Main.

Sandwich's street namers showed much more originality than Durango's. In Durango, the unimaginative Denver & Rio Grande management caused the problem initially. They simply settled on numbers, designating the routes running east and west as streets and those running north and south as avenues. This lackluster naming system was also applied to new streets added later. The same thing happened in other D&RG towns. Sandwich had shown more originality, although it refrained from having any avenues. As Sandwich moved north (where, in the 1890s, most of the residential development occurred), it started a pattern of naming east-and-west streets by number and north-and-south streets by name. At least no one ended up on the corner of Fifth Street and Fifth Avenue!

In the classic U.S. style of town design, Sandwich and Durango were laid out in a grid pattern in which streets intersect at right angles. Sandwich looked like hundreds of other Midwestern checkerboard prairie towns with a slight variation along Center, Railroad, Church, and College Streets because of the CB&Q tracks not running true to the compass. Durango in the 1890s formed a perfect grid that was fit into the contours of a river valley and its benches.

The size of residential lots was much more generous in Sandwich than in Durango. Sandwich laid out lots "one chain wide" (sixty-six feet) by two chains deep. In Durango, on the other hand, the Denver & Rio Grande's original survey laid out twenty-foot-wide frontage lots (150 feet deep), forcing many people to buy two or three to accommodate their homes. This proved typical of the West, where homes were crowded together in the "wide-open spaces," though the practice did at least provide some shelter from winter storms. Durango had more alleys behind residential and commercial blocks, thereby providing more ease of access and a bit more privacy.

In the Victorian world of Sandwich and Durango, the merchants, newspaper editors, and bankers shaped their communities. Bankers Miles Castle (Sandwich), Westel Sedgwick (Sandwich), and Alfred Camp (Durango), newspaper editors Miles Castle and David Day (Durango), hotel men Henry Strater (Durango) and Joseph Dyas (Sandwich), merchants Tom Graden (Durango), Isaac Kruschke (Durango), George Kleinsmid (Sandwich), Enos Doan (Sandwich), and Charles Winne (Sandwich), and industrialists J. Phelps Adams (Sandwich), John Porter (Durango), and Ernest Amy (Durango) worked behind the scenes—occasionally running for elective office—to make their communities vital players in their regions. To be sure, they wanted to generate a profit. But to do so they had to entice more business, investment, and people looking for a place to live and prosper. To achieve these goals, they had to be concerned about the quality of life and about stability. Not transient, these individuals had come to stay. They invested more and had more to gain; without them neither community would have succeeded as well as it did.[1]

Durango and Sandwich boasted strong professional communities. Doctors, dentists, and veterinarians aided people and animals. Durango did not have a veterinary surgeon and dentist like Sandwich's Dr. Bint C. Powell, who promised that "all diseases of the domesticated animals would be scientifically treated." Sandwich actually had two such specialists. Durango, in 1892, had four dentists, eleven physicians (including two women), and fourteen lawyers; five years later their respective numbers were three, ten, and twelve. In 1899, five doctors, one dentist, and three lawyers made up Sandwich's professional community. Lawyers found more business in Durango, where contested mining cases occupied much of their time and tapped mine owners' pockets. Real estate agents hustled their trade, again with greater prospects in newer Durango, where more land and opportunity remained available. The same was true for engineers and architects. Durango had a few of each; Sandwich had only two engineers.

The two towns also boasted conservative, strong banks, and, providentially, reality matched the boast. All the banks weathered the crash of 1893 and the depression years, in no small measure preventing these down years from becoming much worse in Sandwich and Durango. Miles Castle and his Sandwich Bank had been in business since 1856; his partner, Civil War veteran Fred Mosher, joined in 1866 and together they followed a "safe, conservative" banking policy that allowed them to weather two depressions. The same can be said about former Sandwich mayor Westel Sedgwick and his sons, who together purchased the nine-year-old Culver Brothers Bank in 1884. Sedgwick was a renaissance individual. He graduated from Chicago's Rush Medical College and, after coming to Sandwich in 1857, studied law. He was admitted to the bar in 1862 at the age of thirty-five. Former surveyor and miner Alfred Camp could not match Sedgwick's versatility, but his First National Bank in Durango marched on the same conservative path as did the Sandwich banks. So did the younger Colorado State Bank (founded in 1887) and the Smelter National Bank (founded in 1892). All three Durango banks included more outside investors than did those in Sandwich, reflecting Durango's greater investment possibilities. No bank scandals or failures marred the decade in either town, an enviable record for those days.

Because both towns aspired to be dominant commercial communities, they offered a variety of businesses to attract customers. Those mainstays of any new community, blacksmiths, rooming houses, and general merchants, had evolved into more specialized businesses, such as grocery, hardware, shoe, furniture, dry goods, jewelry, clothing, millinery, photography, lumber and paint, cigar and tobacco, farm supply, mining supply, and variety stores, as well as newsdealers, hotels, restaurants, mail and hauling services, laundry services, barber shops, bakeries, coal dealers, and even bit and two-bit saloons to cater to the less or more discerning customer. General stores continued in business, and the blacksmith still provided his service, though he might also offer a livery and feed stable and rent buggies and carriages. Customers had plenty of businesses to select from as they strolled down Main in either town.

Of these businesses, saloons and billiard parlors, plus Durango's gambling dens and houses of prostitution, were the only ones that might be termed unacceptable. Expensive licenses and efforts to remove or segregate these businesses reflected their pariah status. After a long fight, Sandwich went dry and closed its saloons. Durango, on the other hand, gradually prevented its saloons from intermingling with other, acceptable businesses by "zoning" them into two districts.

Both towns contained strong industrial components. In Sandwich, the Sandwich Manufacturing Company and the Enterprise Company fronted Main on the north side of the railroad tracks. Each company had a spur line for receiving and shipping. As the *Sandwich Free Press* proudly boasted on September 3, 1891, Sandwich's industrial names were carried "on products from Plymouth Rock to the Golden Gate," and it might have added that they were transported to Europe and Central and South America, too. The larger of the two companies, Sandwich Manufacturing, employed up to 250 to 300 men at peak periods. The Enterprise Company fluctuated in the 75- to 100-employee range. Both companies produced farm machinery. Sandwich Manufacturing made mowers, corn shellers, harvesters, and binders. The Enterprise Company made windmills, pumps, and cultivators.

Organized in 1867, the Sandwich Manufacturing Company, under the careful, sensible leadership of Augustus Adams and his two sons, Henry and J. Phelps, boasted a long record of dividend payments, which initially were as high as twelve percent but, by the 1890s, had fallen to four percent. Most of the dividends went to Sandwich people and nearby residents who had invested in stock over the years. The company's large plant sat on two city blocks west of Main, along Center Street. It shared one of the blocks, the Hummel Block, with the YMCA and the *Sandwich Free Press*. Otherwise, the two blocks were all manufacturing. The company pumped thousands of dollars into the local economy. For example, in 1891, it had a weekly payroll of nearly thirty-five hundred dollars. During peak periods, men in some departments worked a ten- to twelve-hour shift. The 1890s depression slowed the company down but did not stop the payment of dividends or close the establishment. The company's salesmen scurried throughout the Midwest and took long trips to Central and South America. They sold their products worldwide. With a solid reputation and popular products, the Sandwich Manufacturing Company proved a decided asset to its community.

It definitely helped popularize Sandwich. The company exhibited its "handsome machines" at the World's Fair in Chicago and at the 1898 Trans-Mississippi Exposition in Omaha. One of the company's greatest publicity stunts involved a CB&Q train of thirty-nine cars carrying 810 of the extremely popular "clean sweep" hay loaders. The Clean Sweep Special, with "gaily decorated" banners, steamed west from Sandwich in May 1899, stopping at towns along the route. "The largest train ever taken out on any road loaded with one kind of machinery" was, understandably, followed with great interest in Sandwich (*Free Press*, April 20, May 4, and May 11, 1899). What the *Free Press* cheered in 1891 remained true throughout the decade: "It is a credit to the town, county and state and not only citizens of Sandwich benefited by its location here, but every farmer in this vicinity whose property is enhanced in value."[2]

Right across Main sat the smaller Enterprise Company. Organized in 1868 by bankers Castle and Sedgwick and other locals, it made its fame with pumps and windmills and also manufactured corn and cotton cultivators and planters, and tanks and tank heaters. The windmills ("seven different styles") proved especially popular on the Great Plains, where pumping water became essential for farmers and ranchers. The company's "traveling men," or "drummers," canvassed the Midwest and beyond.

The blowing of the Enterprise whistle at 5:30 in the morning grew into a Sandwich tradition that urged everyone to be up and going. Its brick-and-stone buildings covered nearly two blocks, sharing the end of the block facing Center and the CB&Q tracks with the Sandwich House hotel and a number of stores. The 1890s depression and "fierce competition" temporarily got the best of the company. Farmers had little money for new purchases and only slowly made payments on old debts. In desperation, the firm sold its line of corn shellers to the John Deere Company in 1897, but that did not prove to be enough. Later that year, the Enterprise Company closed, a victim of $187,000 in judgments won by creditors. Rumors circulated that inside creditors were trying to "absorb company assets" worth $344,000 (*Sandwich Argus*, July 10, 1897). If so, the plot failed. Put in the hands of an assignee, the company reopened and by April 1898 was reported to be "doing a big business."[3]

Durango's major industry was the San Juan Smelter, followed by coal mines that arched around the town to the southwest. At its peak, the smelter employed three hundred men, with a monthly payroll of thirty thousand dollars. The company left its mark on Durango in many ways. A brown smoke cloud gushed from its stacks and covered Durango like an umbrella. Citizens loved this sign of prosperity, and photographers worked to catch the sight on film. The noise of the company's stamps crushing ore resounded up and down the canyons and could be heard miles away. The mineral and chemical particles floating out of the smelter settled on Smelter Mountain, killing the vegetation there, and with help from an unfavorable wind, might change a Monday-morning load of wash from "white as the wind driven snow" to brownish or grayish. Still the smelter represented jobs, taxes, and local purchases. There were no complaints.

The fate of the smelter paralleled that of the community in the hard-luck 1890s, years of boom and bust. The decade opened with high hopes and improvements at the plant that doubled its ore-working capacity to two hundred tons daily. The building of the Rio Grande Southern to tap the Rico and Telluride mining districts also promised better days ahead. Dave Day could hardly contain himself. He wrote in the *Durango Solid Muldoon* (Jan. 1, 1893) that the whistle of the new railroad's first locomotive "sounded the note" that gave Durangoans "new energies" and added to the conviction that nature had "marked this for the site of a great city."

Day's literary flights aside, competition from larger Denver and Pueblo smelters, and the fact that the San Juan Smelter chronically ran short of working capital, threatened to negate any benefits the railroad might bring to Durango. It did not help when falling silver prices decreased Silverton's ore output and that of every other San Juan district, leaving the smelter in short supply. Then the owners discovered that an auditor had "systematically defrauded" the firm. Overcoming all this, the firm was reported to be "doing splendidly" by the end of 1892.

The building of the rival Standard Smelter a half mile south threatened the older smelter's new prosperity with a disastrous smelter war, even though the existence of two smelters moved town booster Richard McCloud to rhapsody. According to him, Durango was the Smelter City "because God so ordained it" by placing coal and ores of "almost inexhaustible quantity" all around it (McCloud, *Durango*, 11). The crash and depression ended those dreams. The Standard Smelter failed and was absorbed by its rival, which then closed for six months. The San Juan Smelter reopened in January 1894 and limped along until a larger smelter from Denver, the Omaha & Grant Smelting Company, leased it. The larger company purchased the San Juan Smelter in 1895. Omaha & Grant promptly began renovating the plant, but a fire set the company back. After the smelter was rebuilt, it finally became what its founders had envisioned—the dominant smelter in southwestern Colorado.[4]

Durangoans and Sandwichites had been reading about consolidation and the emergence of trusts in U.S. business. Now Durango had witnessed it. In 1898, Omaha & Grant merged into a smelter trust that eventually became the gigantic, monopolistic American Smelting and Refining Company.

Instinctively mistrusting conglomerates, Durangoans warily eyed developments across the river. Before long, the smelter trust was accused of being secretive and impersonal and of interfering in local politics. Dave Day and his *Democrat* took repeated swipes at the "combine." Still, the community could do nothing. Like it or not, modern industrial organization and attitudes had reached the Animas Valley.

Then Durango witnessed another of the new industrial-age repercussions—labor strife. On June 1, 1899, the community was hit by a bitter smelter strike over demands for an eight-hour day at the same pay as was previously received for a ten- or twelve-hour day. Starting in Durango, the strike eventually spread throughout the state, paralyzing the entire Colorado smelting industry. The month-old Durango Mine and Smeltermen's Union Number 58 of the Western Federation of Miners took on the trust, which stood rock-solid against the union. Peaceful at first, amid Durango pleas for good feelings, the strike dragged on into August, with one Durango scab worker killed and bitter feelings generated toward the union. Meanwhile, hard-rock (gold and silver) and coal mines closed, railroad shipments declined, and local businesses suffered. Somehow, "be of good cheer" statements rang hollow. Despite local efforts to settle the dispute, the matter was resolved beyond southwestern Colorado. The beaten union conceded, and work resumed.

Durango would not forget this trauma, nor really understand why the community had gained the image of being such a violent labor town. That the blame might be laid on a mysterious outside group called "professional labor agitators" did little good, except to give momentary comfort. Durangoans of all walks of life emerged from the strike dogmatically antiunion, and they remained so for a long time. One might expect that only the elite and middle classes would come out of this experience opposed to unions, but union organizers would not find Durango to be fertile ground in the generations that followed. Many of the workers in the smelter were farmers looking for extra pay. They had no interest in unions and hated the disruption that the strike brought to their lives. The regular workers saw no benefit from the disturbance. All they saw were lost wages. Even the coal miners, despite attempts by the United Mine Workers to organize them, stayed nonunion throughout the statewide coal troubles of 1903 to 1914.

As the *Durango Herald* expressed it on August 23, 1899, "The people of Durango have been long suffering but maybe they will be given a rest—when judgment day arrives. The smelting industry has made Durango what it is. It will continue to bring good cheer to the entire southwest." The smelter and mines resumed normal operations, ore shipments increased, business improved, and what had once seemed like a "low ebb" passed into history amid glowing expectations for the new century.[5]

The smelter relied heavily on Durango's other important local industry, coal mining. That industry dominated two satellite communities—Porter and Hesperus. Although Durango never became a major coal-mining district compared to Colorado's southern coal field or Pennsylvania's large districts, it did provide fuel for the entire southwestern Colorado region. In 1896, La Plata County produced 99,166 tons of coal, ranking eighth among sixteen Colorado coal-producing counties. The mines were mostly small operations. For example, in 1897–98, the six leading producers employed a total of only 164 miners.

The bituminous, or soft, coal produced by La Plata County mines provided fuel for the D&RG and the Rio Grande Southern. It was also shipped in large quantities to nearby towns and hard-rock mines. Small amounts of coal were treated by heat in the twenty-eight coke ovens that lay west of the smelter. This process, besides adding another generous measure of smoke and gases to the atmosphere, produced coke that burned with an intense heat. The smelter and the town's blacksmiths used most of the product.

The railroads made coal mining profitable. The D&RG people owned several mines, including the largest, which was operated by the Porter Fuel Company. The construction of the Rio Grande Southern's tracks made possible the opening of both the Hesperus and Porter mines. Coal was a major reason Durangoans pushed for a southern railroad outlet; they wished to tap the Pacific Coast and Mexican markets. That dream died aborning. The railroad was never built.

The Porter Fuel Company, organized in 1890, reflected the vicissitudes of the industry. Mining engineer John Porter, who had come to Durango with D&RG president William Jackson Palmer and organized the smelter, promoted coal and organized his namesake company. Its main operations revolved around the little camps of Porter, which was a couple miles southwest of Durango in Wild Cat Canyon, and Hesperus, which lay sixteen miles west of Durango. According to the *Herald* (Jan. 8, 1897), the Porter Fuel Company "turns more money loose each month than any other agency" except the smelter. With a reputation for the "finest quality, free burning" coal sold locally, Porter Fuel shipped to Silverton, Rico, and Telluride, and east as far as the San Luis Valley. The depression severely cut into its business, and then a strong revival was staggered by the 1899 smelter strike that closed the mines and idled over one hundred coal miners. Union coal miners had struck anyway, in sympathy with the smelter workers, and demanded higher wages. The company responded by simply shutting down. According to the *Herald* (Aug. 18, 1899), the miners returned to the "same liberal wages paid prior to the strike" and "no discrimination [was] shown" against "those who went on strike."

Labor unrest always lurked near the surface in coal mining. Several wildcat strikes hit Durango's mines over such issues as increased pay per ton and working conditions. Perilous working conditions throughout the industry caused repeated management-labor conflicts. La Plata County coal mining proved no different. It was extremely dangerous. Miners in the unstable mines worried about slabs of rock falling at any time. But gas was potentially more hazardous. The smallest spark might set off an explosion. Ventilation problems hounded local mines, which the state inspector rated as "not very good [most of them fell in this category] to fairly good." Miners faced these conditions to mine coal at forty or fifty cents per ton, and that included cleaning and delivering the coal at the mine's portal. And it was not a 2,000-pound ton, either. The company weighed each car and demanded a long ton of 2,200 pounds. Timbering and all other "dead" work was done on the miners' own time, which did nothing to promote safety or concern for anything except digging.

Accidents claimed the lives of coal miners year after year, even in these small mines. A roof cave-in crushed Antonio Susio and Thomas Barnes in 1893, and Otto Johnson and Theodore Peters were killed by falling rocks in 1898—only names now, but heartaches then. Fortunately, no disastrous explosions occurred. Miners lived in the small semicompany towns of Hesperus (population 200 in 1897) and Porter (population 144 in 1895), near the mines, or in the south end of Durango, close to nearby mines. They worked in a dark, dangerous, difficult world. Few people worried about them unless the coal did not arrive on time. Their work was vital to the local economy.[6]

Agricultural machinery, smelting, and coal mining—these were Sandwich's and Durango's major industries. There existed, however, in and about the towns, other smaller concerns. In that era, when local manufacturing still held a place in the economy, some of these industries flourished. Durango's Harry Jackson and Sandwich's Gus Walter and J. Kehl & Sons manufactured "fine" carriages, buggies, and wagons. In Durango, entrepreneur Thomas Graden, another of Palmer's boys, owned flour and lumber mills and also the Graden Mercantile Company, the town's only "department" store. Lumbering continued to be an important Durango industry, as it had been since 1880. Local sawmills shipped eight hundred carloads of lumber in 1897. West of Sandwich, Louis Dieterich's tile works produced "1st class drain tile" and bricks (*Free Press*, June 11, 1891) but, by 1897, was not running. The Eureka Flouring Mill, "capacity seventy-five barrels per day," provided a market for local farmers and supplied "a large territory around Sandwich" (*Free Press*, Sept. 3, 1891). Graves' Nursery, near Sandwich, became one of the few businesses with enterprises beyond the hinterland of the two towns. It owned nurseries in Iowa and Missouri.

Oak Ridge Cemetery contained many monuments carved by the Sandwich Marble and Granite Works. The Durango Iron Works produced products for the living. Durango had two brick companies, and in Sandwich, Thomas Emerson manufactured cigars. The Sandwich Creamery twice won the Illinois Dairymen's Grand Sweepstake Award for its butter, and its product always received "top market price," according to the proud *Free Press* (May 21, 1891) and *Argus* (Dec. 15, 1894). Durango was equally proud of its Smelter City Brewing Association, which, besides brewing beer, made "artificial ice" machines that produced ice for homes and businesses. The association failed, however, to achieve its goal of driving "eastern beer out of the market" (*Durango Great Southwest*, Dec. 25, 1893). Dave Day expressed the hopes of the association, when he wrote in the *Solid Muldoon* (Jan. 1, 1893), "[It] will not be long before the thousands of dollars annually sent East for beer will remain at home, where it belongs."[7]

Durango never drove Milwaukee and St. Louis beers out of the field. Schlitz, Pabst, and Anheuser-Busch finally triumphed. The same fate awaited all the local industries. Big brand names, lower-priced products, promotion, and outside competition would be too strong in the decades ahead.

Beyond the urban centers of Durango and Sandwich stretched their agricultural hinterlands. Town and country were tied together and relied on each other for continued prosperity. Local merchants depended on farmers coming to town on Saturdays, especially in Sandwich, where the town provided markets and a shipping point. Flour mills and a creamery offered the farmers a cash market, and Sandwich's grain elevator meant a buyer or possible storage for grains. Farm wives brought in their butter and eggs to trade for what they needed. An "excellent butter maker" would find her product in demand and sold only to a store's "special" customers. When the farmer suffered, Sandwich suffered. The same kind of relationship existed in Durango, but not to the same extent. In Durango, ranchers and farmers were important, but mining was more so.

At least one merchant innovatively reached out to promote his business, joining the onrushing advertising revolution. Sandwich merchant Roy Warner, famous at Christmastime for a basement "full of toys," became one of the first to advertise in rural areas. To promote his "department" store, five different departments on several floors, he placed signs along the roads leading to Sandwich. They read "3 miles to Warner's" and then "1 mile to Warner's." Farm families could not miss them as they drove into town.

Merchants gave out "tin money" or tokens as change to entice customers to come back. Farm wives, for example, would receive an extra two cents a pound for butter or eggs, if they accepted a store's tokens. A few stores would accept competitors' trade tokens, but most would not. Credit remained a fact of life for the merchants, even with the problems it could cause. Home delivery also was something the customers favored. Considering the market that was available, merchants had to play all their cards carefully.

Durango's and Sandwich's merchants and industrialists did not find life all profit and progress. After two grocery stores closed in February 1898, the *Sandwich Free Press* (Feb. 23, 1899) was moved to admit, "The competition is too great in Sandwich in this line, making the income rather small." During the 1893 panic and early months of the depression, the banks were especially vulnerable to "runs" and repeatedly assured customers and depositors that all was well.

In an era that relied on customers being offered at least monthly credit, collections in depressed times—and not infrequently in good times—gave merchants headaches. In the *Free Press* on July 2, 1896, hardware man George Kleinsmid admonished his "friends and patrons," "I would like to give a polite invitation to call and settle last year's account as I need money badly and would like to balance my books for the year."

Competition also drove business hours, and Sandwich merchants, at least, tried to arrange voluntary agreements to close at 8:00 p.m. during the fall and winter, except Mondays and Saturdays and the holiday season. Durango considered closing all businesses on Sundays, but, unfortunately, business owners could not agree on the matter, and the subject was dropped. Sometimes agreements succeeded, sometimes they did not. In any case, businesspeople worked long hours. One belief that unified them all was that townspeople should patronize local merchants and not Sears, Wards, or outside stores: "The home merchant is the man who helps pay for the streets you walk upon, for the school in which your children, or perhaps you, were educated; he helps to keep up the church in which you worship" (*Free Press*, Aug. 18, 1898). They had a case; outside firms were already making inroads and local money was leaving the two communities.[8]

These merchants were not tight-fisted, nose-to-the-grindstone individuals, who did not look beyond their ledgers and profits. They generally were community minded and community spirited. Sandwich merchants, joined by their Plano and Somonauk counterparts, went so far as to sponsor a merchants' picnic for their clerks, customers, friends, and families. The picnickers were taken by a special train to Glen Park, near Sheridan, for a July outing in 1898 and 1899. The twin purposes of the picnic—to provide "rest from the cares of business" and to promote "a more fraternal feeling, [removing] caste distinctions and petty jealousies" (*Free Press*, July 21, 1898)—showed an awareness of things beyond the store. Twenty-five hundred people reportedly took advantage of the picnic, baseball games, swimming races, and other attractions of the park.

For their own good, and not incidentally for that of their communities—it is hard sometimes to see where the one stopped and the other started—they also promoted a variety of other activities and projects. The telephone was changing the United States by the 1890s, ending isolation, speeding business, replacing afternoon "card calling," and, in a score of different ways, influencing the life and times. Durango started out with private lines but, by 1894, had a telephone exchange with over seventy subscribers. Sandwich moved a little slower, but the city council granted a franchise in 1898, and soon poles and wires crisscrossed the skyline.

Durango had electricity and arc lights before the decade opened, being one of the first Colorado cities to grant a franchise (1887) for the new power and light source. Sandwich again marched a step behind. However, by the fall of 1890, the town council listened to companies explain the wonderful benefits of their power plants and systems. A couple of years passed before a consensus developed. Some people feared unknown consequences, such as cost, and worried about "electrocution" from a switch or a light. Did electricity cause freckles? Those in favor argued for the benefits of the "light without heat, without smell and without trouble" (*Sandwich Argus*, April 17, 1894). Simply not having to clean lamp chimneys seemed a big enough benefit for some proponents.

Amid all the turmoil of 1893, the year proved in one respect magical: petitions supporting electric lights moved the council to order the equipment needed to provide electric power. By the summer of 1894, Sandwichites basked in arc lights on street corners, and some homes and businesses had plugged in, giving the town "quite a metropolis appearance" (*Free Press*, Aug. 30, 1894). Electrification proved a rousing success. Within a year, many of the expenses for "the second to none in the state" light plant had been financed by fees. Of course, there were some complaints, such as "What's the matter with the arc light on the corner of Main and Somonauk?" It should be properly operating, complained the *Free Press* on May 19, 1898. The benefits far outweighed the usual trial-and-error troubles: "The advantage of possessing well-lighted streets can hardly be overestimated, and the installation of the plant will add greatly to the prosperity of the town. Property values will be increased, and the added attractiveness of the town will tend to draw to it new residents" (*Argus*, March 3, 1894). Businesspeople had no reason to complain. The phone and electric light helped them in a host of ways, not the least of which were easier customer contact and less danger of fire from stored kerosene and lighted lamps.[9]

Electricity allowed Durango to go "modern" and to remedy a mistake. An 1891 experiment with a horse-drawn streetcar line running down Main Avenue faltered. According to the *Durango Weekly Tribune* (May 18, 1891), people objected to the "obstructing" of the street, and trolley crews compounded matters by being abusive, insulting, and "invariably" pulling away from the depot before all passengers boarded. Within a short time, lack of business gave the line a well-deserved final run. John Porter, Thomas Graden, and other businessmen, plus the D&RG's Durango Land and Coal Company, rescued the idea.

The new Durango Railway and Realty Company, which owned land between Durango and Animas City, electrified the trolley for ease of transportation. Durangoans beamed with pride when the "wide and roomy" electric streetcars arrived, furnished "with every facility for killing dogs known," the most modern "nickel in the slot" device, and the "latest and best heating apparatus." "Bully for Durango and rapid transit!" shouted the *Great Southwest* on January 2, 1893. Initially, the cars ran from the depot to the Brookside subdivision and, eventually, they served that "fashionable suburb," Animas City. "In fact," said the *Great Southwest,* "Denver, Chicago nor other cities can boast of any finer service from track to trolleys."

Arc lights, electricity, telephones, and, for Durango, a trolley, marked truly progressive cities. Durango and Sandwich offered more than that, however. They also had some outstanding brick-and-stone business blocks. In 1894, a Sandwich pioneer and prominent businessman, sixty-two-year-old Abram A. Marcy, built the two-story Marcy Block on Main just south of the CB&Q tracks. According to the *Sandwich Free Press* (Jan. 24, 1895), it contained stores on the first floor and offices, three "elegant suites," and three flats on the second floor. The block was hailed as Sandwich's most "magnificent building." Marcy, who had come to Sandwich in 1854, did not get to enjoy his triumph very long because he died of heart failure in 1897.

Charles Newman built a similar structure for Durango, completing his three-story block on Main in 1892–93. A man of "unfailing sagacity, indefatigable industry," druggist and mine investor Newman served in the Colorado Senate. He was one of the few movers and shakers of Durango to run for public office at the state level. The Newman Block was the crown jewel of the rebuilding efforts that took place after the disastrous 1889 fire. In 1892–93, the last Durango building boom of the nineteenth century included the construction of the First National Bank, a courthouse, a high school, another business block, and many homes.[10]

All this would not have been possible without the hundreds of members of the "tin [or lunch] bucket brigade," the workers in skilled and unskilled trades, including both men and women and, in a few cases, children. They worked the hard, physical jobs. Subject to a foreman's or a supervisor's whims and to economic downturns, most worked a six-day week of fifty to sixty hours. In some businesses and industries, like coal mining, they faced seasonal unemployment.

A TALE OF TWO TOWNS

Their take-home pay varied, and it remains hard to generalize. A turn-of-the-century study done by the Colorado Bureau of Labor Statistics found the following:

Carpenters $2.75–$4.00 per day
Blacksmiths $2.25–$4.00 per day
Laborers $1.50–$2.50 per day
Smeltermen $1.50–$3.50 per day
Miners $2.50–$4.00 per day
Bartenders $12.00–$30.00 per week
Drugstore clerks $12.00–$22.50 per week
Grocery clerks $8.00–$17.50 per week
Milliners $7.50–$15.00 per week
Waiters $4.00–$17.50 per week (plus meals)
Telephone girls $35.00–$50.00 per month
Farmhands $15.00–$25.00 per month (plus meals)
Cowboys $25.00–$35.00 per month (plus meals)
Housemaids $15.00–$25.00 per month (plus room and board)

These figures can serve only as rough indicators. Durangoans thought their wages were higher than wages "back East," but specific statistics for Durango and Sandwich are lacking. Wages aside, there is also the question of the cost of living.

A nickel went a long way in those days. For a nickel, you could buy a beer, a cup of coffee, a streetcar ride, a phone call, a dozen roses (on sale), or a ride on the midway at the fair. "A nickel's worth" had meaning in Sandwich and Durango. Prices advertised in the newspapers provide a means of comparison, but we cannot be sure of brand quality. For example, in 1894–96 a one-pound can of baking powder sold for thirty-three cents in Sandwich and fifty cents in Durango. For a dollar, a shopper could buy twelve cans of tomatoes in Sandwich and seven cans in Durango. Crackers were six and a half cents a pound in Sandwich and ten cents a pound in Durango. Eggs sold for twenty cents a dozen in both towns, and coffee in Durango cost twenty cents per pound, a nickel less than in Sandwich. There can be little doubt that Durango's cost of living was higher. After the smelter strike broke out in 1899, this comment appeared in the June 17 issue of the

Engineering and Mining Journal: "Durango employees should receive such differential as they are entitled to, owing to Durango being a more costly place to live in than Pueblo or Denver."

The answer, of course, was always to live within one's income. The *Sandwich Free Press* (Feb. 5, 1890) admonished that one should as "far as possible pay as you go." Buy only what "is actually necessary" because a "bird in the hand is worth two in the bush." Typically, a grocer advanced credit for a month's worth of groceries, and other stores carried accounts, too. For major acquisitions, however, it was believed advisable to have a large percentage of the purchase money in hand. This appeared to be true even for a home purchase. A "nice" house could be bought for around one thousand to two thousand dollars in either community, although some of the wealthier individuals prided themselves on more expensive dwellings. The purchase of a home represented a major step in the 1890s, a decade in which most Americans rented.[11]

Strolling down Main on an 1890s Saturday night would have been a fascinating experience for us. While there may have been social and occupational strata in the two communities, the towns were characterized by democratic, open societies. Despite setbacks, Sandwich and Durango moved ahead throughout the decade and would not take a back seat to any neighbor. The glow of arc lights, fashionably dressed people of overwhelmingly northern European stock, comfortable front porches dotted with rattan chairs and a swing, and electrically lighted businesses with well-stocked shelves bespoke middle-class America—a group of people confident in themselves and in the future of their town. In the words of a popular 1890s song, "On A Saturday Night":

> There's a time when we all feel gay, on a Saturday night;
> That's the time when we draw our pay, on a Saturday night.
> We go home and dress in our best suit of clothes,
> But just where to go to, well, nobody knows.

NOTES

1. Sarah J. Pearce, *A Guide to Colorado Architecture* (Denver: Colorado Historical Society, 1983), 18–21. Richard V. Francaviglia, "Victorian Bonanzas," *Journal of the West* (Jan. 1994), 54–56, 58–59. Virginia McAlester and Lee McAlester, *A Field Guide to American Houses* (New York: Alfred A. Knopf, 1990), 210–15. Sanborn maps: Sandwich 1892, 1897; Durango, 1890, 1896. The names of the business leaders are found in the newspapers and other records of the two communities.
2. Sanborn maps, 1892, 1897. Richard McCloud, *Durango As It Is* (Durango: Durango Board of Trade, 1892), 64, 71. *Durango Directory for the Year 1892* (Trinidad, Colo.: Bensel Directory Co., 1892). *Sandwich Free Press*, Feb. 5, Feb. 19, 1890; July 9, Sept. 3, 1891; April 20, 1893; May 6, 1897; May 12, 1898; April 20, May 4, May 11, 1899. *Sandwich Argus*, Oct. 11, 1890; Nov. 21, 1891; Aug. 5, 1893; May 8, July 10, July 24, 1897; Dec. 31, 1898. *Colorado State Business Directory* (Denver: Gazetteer Publishing Co., 1897), 126, 131–32, 138, 141.
3. *Free Press*, June 10, 1892; April 20, 1893; April 22, 1897. *Argus*, June 26, July 3, July 10, Aug. 14, 1897; April 23, 1898. Sanborn maps, 1892, 1897.
4. Annual Reports of the San Juan Smelting and Mining Company (1891–94). *Durango Directory for the Year 1892*, 12–13. William Bell Papers, Colorado Historical Society: John Porter to Henry Amy, Feb. 15 and Nov. 11, 1892; Porter to William Bell, Feb. 21, 1893. McCloud, *Durango*, 11, 14–15. *Durango Great Southwest*, Nov. 15, 1892. *Durango Herald*, April 11, 1890; April 20, 1894; April 11, 1895. *Durango Solid Muldoon*, Jan. 1, 1893. *Engineering and Mining Journal*, March 23, April 27, Nov. 23, 1895. Durango Land and Coal Company reports (1890–1900). James E. Fell Jr. *Ores to Metals* (Lincoln: University of Nebraska Press, 1979), 209–11, 251–55, 279–82.
5. *Herald*, *Durango Democrat*, and *Engineering and Mining Journal*, May–Aug. 1899.
6. Fifth, Sixth, Seventh, Eighth, and Ninth Reports of the Inspector of Coal Mines (Denver: Smith-Brooks, 1893–1901); each report was published separately. *Herald*, Jan. 1, 1890; Nov. 13, Nov. 27, 1891; Nov. 11, 1893; June 17, 1897; Jan. 8, 1898; June 7, June 14, Aug. 18, 1899. *Durango Directory for*

the Year 1892, 11. *Democrat,* Dec. 19, 1897. *First Report of the Porter Coal Company* (Denver: C. J. Kelly, 1892), 1–12. Durango Land and Coal Company reports (1890–1900).
7. *Free Press,* Nov. 27, 1890; May 21, June 11, Sept. 3, 1891; Sept. 9, 1897; Sept. 29, 1898. *Durango Directory for the Year 1892,* 12–15. John G. Canfield, *Mines and Mining Men of Colorado* (Denver: Carson, Hurst & Harper, 1893), 75–78. *Argus,* July 19, 1890; Dec. 15, 1894. *Solid Muldoon,* Jan. 1, 1893. *Great Southwest,* April 11, Dec. 25, 1893. *Herald,* Dec. 17, 1897.
8. Ila Smith and Stanley Smith, interviews by author, Aug. 30–31, 1989. *Herald,* Sept. 28, 1898. *Durango Weekly Tribune,* May 25, 1891. *Argus,* March 3, 1894; Jan. 11, Oct. 24, 1896; Dec. 17, 1898. *Free Press,* July 2, 1896; July 21, July 28, Aug. 18, 1898; Feb. 23, April 27, 1899. Canfield, *Mines and Mining Men,* 78–80.
9. Schlereth, Thomas J., *Victorian America* (New York: HarperCollins, 1991), 115–16, 188–91. McCloud, *Durango,* 49. *Herald,* Jan. 1, 1890; March 20, 1894. *Argus,* Dec. 30, 1893; Jan. 6, March 3, April 7, 1894; Jan. 15, March 5, April 9, 1898. *Free Press,* Aug. 14, 1890; April 13, Dec. 14, 1893; Aug. 30, 1894; Aug. 1, 1895; May 19, 1898; March 9, April 13, 1899.
10. *Durango Weekly Tribune,* May 18, 1891. McCloud, *Durango,* 52. Western Colorado Power Company records, Center of Southwest Studies at Fort Lewis College, Box 20. *Great Southwest,* Aug. 1, Oct. 20, 1892; Jan. 2, 1893. Durango Land and Coal Company annual reports (1897–1900). *Free Press,* Sept. 6, Sept. 27, 1894; Jan. 24, 1895. *Argus,* March 6, 1897. *Durango Record,* Jan. 17, 1881. *Herald,* July 26, 1889; July 29, 1892.
11. *Western Colorado* (Grand Junction, Colo.: *Grand Junction News,* 1893), 52. Schlereth, *Victorian America,* 33, 77, 79–85. McCloud, *Durango,* 86–87. *8th Biennial Report of the Colorado Bureau of Labor Statistics* (Denver: Smith-Brooks, 1892), 91–93, 275, 380. Prices compared were found in issues of the *Free Press, Argus,* and *Herald* dated 1894 through 1896. *Engineering and Mining Journal,* June 17, 1899. *Free Press,* Feb. 5, 1890.

Photographic Essay

THE TOWNS: THE LIGHT AND THE SHADOW

Sandwich and Durango of the 1890s have been preserved in photographs, moments frozen in time.

> Frank Gonner will find time to photograph you before the holidays. Drop around and arrange for a date. Secure the shadow ere the substance fades.
> *Durango Democrat*, Dec. 21, 1899

> Hendrick's Gallery: makers of all up-to-date photos, also headquarters for all the leading makes of cameras.
> *Sandwich Free Press*, Dec. 14, 1899

Historians owe photographers an unpayable debt of gratitude for what they have accomplished in preserving the "shadow" of their times. Fortunately, the American generation with which this book deals, starting with the Civil War, became the first to be widely photographed and, with a commendable sense of history, they saved their photos.

The following photographic essay looks at Sandwich and Durango and some of the events that took place in the two towns. It views the life and times of the nineties through the eyes of photographers like Frank Gonner, Charlie Orr, Frank Carpenter, and Jacob A. Boston. Come for a fleeting moment and glimpse a world long gone but hauntingly familiar.

A TALE OF TWO TOWNS

Durango about 1890, looking down from Smelter Mountain. The Graden flour mill and Rio Grande Southern bridge sit in the foreground, with the D&RG depot on the right. (Courtesy La Plata County Historical Society)

Durango in the mid-1890s, looking southwest from Reservoir Hill, showing the result of the building boom before the 1893 crash. Trees planted on the Boulevard (Third Avenue) can be seen on the right, Central School stands in the center foreground, and the smelter is in full, smoky operation. (Courtesy Roderick A. Ironside, La Plata County Historical Society)

PHOTOGRAPHIC ESSAY: THE TOWNS

Sandwich, looking across the railroad tracks toward Railroad Street and the heart of the town's business district. The Main Street tower was a town fixture for generations. Its keeper lowered the gates as trains approached. (Courtesy Roger Peterson)

Goodman's general store and Kleinsmid's hardware store were popular businesses on the corner of Main and Railroad Streets, which together formed the hub of Sandwich's business district. (Courtesy Roger Peterson)

A TALE OF TWO TOWNS

The heart of Durango's business world, Ninth and Main, with the streetcar clanging past the First National Bank. It cost a nickel to ride the trolley. On this summer day, the sides of the car have been removed. (Courtesy La Plata County Historical Society)

Durango, in the one thousand block of Main Avenue. This area was part of the district that was rebuilt after the 1889 fire. Only a few Durangoans can be seen loafing around here on a slow day. The architectural styles of Durango and Sandwich were very similar. (Courtesy La Plata County Historical Society)

PHOTOGRAPHIC ESSAY: THE TOWNS

The Sandwich Manufacturing Company, a major contributor to Sandwich's economic well-being in the 1890s. The *Sandwich Free Press* proudly noted in 1897 that few manufacturing concerns in the country "equal this one and none are better." (Courtesy Roger Peterson)

Durango's Omaha & Grant Smelter just before the 1899 strike. Both the strike and the acquisition of this plant by the gigantic American Smelting and Refining Company heralded a changing world. (Courtesy Center of Southwest Studies)

A TALE OF TWO TOWNS

The fire that caused this damage on Sandwich's Main Street in 1893 led to the construction of the Marcy Block, the town's finest business block, on the site. Both Sandwich and Durango suffered a major fire, and each town rebounded finer than before. (Courtesy Gary Moss)

Durango's fire wagon heads out of the new station. City Hall was on the second floor of the fire station. Children loved watching the horses take their daily run but dreaded the ringing of the nightly curfew bell. (Courtesy La Plata County Historical Society)

PHOTOGRAPHIC ESSAY: THE TOWNS

The Sandwich Opera House stands prominently in the background in 1896, as local farmers come to town, bringing wagons full of hogs. The linkage of town and country can be no more clearly shown. (Courtesy Gary Moss)

Both Durango and Sandwich owed their existence to railroads, but this freight train wreck displays the dangers of being on the "main line." The wreck occurred in the center of Sandwich, between Main and Eddy Streets. (Courtesy Roger Peterson)

A TALE OF TWO TOWNS

The Interior of the Sandwich Bank, owned by Miles Castle. Both Sandwich and Durango were very fortunate to have sound, conservative banks to help them weather the economic storms of the 1890s. (Courtesy Gary Moss)

A six-team freight outfit with boxes of apples from neighboring Farmington, New Mexico, stops in the eight hundred block of Durango's Main Avenue. Local farmers, too, raised apples that they shipped to markets throughout Colorado. (Courtesy George Hassan)

PHOTOGRAPHIC ESSAY: THE TOWNS

Mary and Joseph Dyas ran the renowned Sandwich House hotel on Center Street, a half block from Main. A community had to have a fine hotel to greet visitors. Durango had the Strater. (Courtesy Roger Peterson)

Durango's Boulevard (Third Avenue), a street lined with homes and churches. Trees are being watered on the parkway. Muddy and dusty streets bedeviled housewives throughout both Durango and Sandwich. (Courtesy La Plata County Historical Society)

Sandwich's renowned Union Band played at a variety of local functions and celebrations. Director Henry Wilder stands in the back row, third from the left. (Courtesy Sandwich Township Library)

All three of Durango's new streetcars were needed to carry these well-dressed fans to the baseball game at Athletic Park north of town. The park included a bicycle track and dance pavilion. (Courtesy George Hassan)

5

THE BOYS GOT WHAT THEY WANTED

The old party is on the downward track,
Good-bye, my party, good-bye.
—Populist Party campaign song (1890s)

Talking to a group of Harvard and Yale undergraduates, the hero of the Rough Riders, Theodore Roosevelt, observed, "The most practical kind of politics is the politics of decency." Mark Twain, who criticized corrupt politicians repeatedly, told a newspaper reporter upon the death of a New York City Tammany leader, "I refused to attend his funeral. But I wrote a very nice letter explaining that I approved of it."[1]

Between Roosevelt's observation and Tammany's machinations roamed U.S. politics. As conducted in Durango and Sandwich, politics were fought at the local, state, and national levels in a style more nearly approaching Roosevelt's than the Tammany leaders'. While every campaign generated partisanship, and partisan newspapers saw only immaculate candidates in their own party and corruption in the opposition, politics still provided a combination of seriousness and entertainment for the two communities in the 1890s. On the local level, personalities and issues intertwined, and although sometimes elections could become heated, it seemed that once the campaign ended, things always returned to a more normal pace. While some people never forgot, the general electorate did not seem to hold grudges. Neither town generated much of an impact on the state level, and hardly any nationally, but that did not stop the voters from becoming interested and immersed in larger issues and state and national candidates.

Some elections created little interest. School board races generally appear to have fallen into that category. But they were not alone. The *Sandwich Argus* (July 20, 1895) went so far as to recommend that an election for a town justice not be held, because it was too costly (two hundred dollars) and because nothing existed for the other five justices "to do now to preserve the peace." The electorate had the opportunity to vote often enough, city elections being held every year in each town. The elections could be "quiet affairs" and often passed "hardly noticed." Yet liquor stirred the pot and aroused emotions that ran deep in Sandwich.

There, the one ongoing issue was the Wets versus the Drys, or as they expressed it, the "license" folks versus the "no-license" folks. The issue was saloons and whether they should be allowed in town. Unfortunately, because there were no identifiable working-class sections or ethnic neighborhoods, it is impossible to discover whether the vote reflected class or ethnic divisions.

Throughout the 1890s, the two groups squared off, with the license faction carrying off most of the honors through the first three-quarters of the decade. The dispute started with the "ministers and ladies of the WCTU" winning control of the town council in the 1891 election (*Sandwich Free Press*, April 23, 1891). "After the 1st of May the saloon will have to seek more congenial quarters," said the *Free Press*. All four of the town's saloons closed. Down but not out, the license folks bounced back in a "very quiet affair" in 1892, sweeping all three Sandwich wards (*Argus*, April 23, 1892).

The quarrel could become emotional. When the license supporters organized in 1893 to keep the saloons open, the *Free Press* blasted them. On March 30, the newspaper claimed that the license people stood "for drunkenness, broken homes, and all their surroundings," and their opponents stood for "temperance, sobriety, industry, and their surroundings." The editor saw no difficult choice for the voter. The lines were sharply drawn, and "it [was] purely and simply a question of principle."

In the end, the license slate carried the field. The two sides battled on a year later when the two local parties, the Citizens Party (no-license) and the People's Party (license), squared off again (*Argus*, April 14, 1894). The license group held its ground, although the no-license people almost pulled off a victory in the Third Ward. In the years that followed, the Republican Party emerged again in place of the Citizens Party. Democrats never fielded a ticket by name in this heavily Republican town. On April 13, 1895, the *Argus* breathed a sigh of relief, when the "old question" of license or no license disappeared from the contest. Just how or why the issue vanished, the newspaper did not say. Another quiet election followed the next year, with another license victory.

THE BOYS GOT WHAT THEY WANTED

The 1897 campaign focused on whether the incumbent mayor, A. Gates White, had enforced a law that prohibited liquor and the opening of saloons within a mile of each polling place on election day. According to a *Free Press* report of April 15, 1897, the mayor personally saw "that the boys got what they wanted" on town meeting day. What they wanted was beer or some other alcoholic drink. Unfortunately, Sandwich voters had not come out to the caucuses, abdicating their responsibilities, or so the paper charged, and White was reelected. The *Free Press* felt that most Sandwichites opposed "this man and his methods and [were] in favor of the enforcement of wholesome legal restrictions on gambling and the illegal selling of intoxicants," but because of their disinterest "he [was] as good a man as they deserve[d]." The *Argus* did not become so agitated, and reported on April 17 that the election was a "quiet affair." To make matters worse, from the point of view of the *Free Press*, both parties had nominated White.

Finally, after years of arguing, planning, and working, the no-license group won in 1898. It came as something of a surprise, "but none were more surprised—happily—than those who had been laboring so earnestly for the no-license cause." On April 30, the *Argus* recorded that after May 1, "Sandwich [was] a dry city." The turn-around vote, however, did not resolve the issue or quiet people's feelings about it.

In 1899, Sandwich's People's Party determinedly aimed to "wrestle the scepter" from the no-license people. The campaign lines had "been drawn tight," but the struggle, according to the *Free Press* (April 20), was marked "with no unpleasant words or deeds," and both sides were "sanguine right up to closing." Each group used house-to-house canvasses and, according to newspaper reports, several "very brilliant speeches were given." When the votes were counted, it proved nearly a clean sweep for the no-license group, and White lost the mayor's race. Crowed the *Free Press*, "In years to come we can look back upon Tuesday, April 18, 1899, as the date of one of the most exciting struggles in city politics. It has been many a year since a large vote was polled, if ever." Two victories in a row showed that Sandwich attitudes were changing. Would national prohibition be far in the future?[2]

Durango did not have a passionate, ongoing issue to arouse the electorate. The election of 1893 was typical. The Republican, Democratic, and People's parties all placed tickets in the field. The electioneering that did occur was done in "quiet ways by friends of the various candidates." The only innovation was the Australian ballot system, but the "majority of voters seemed familiar with its workings." The *Durango Herald*'s coverage on April 5 simply said the election "passed off very quietly and the vote was light." "With one or two exceptions," the saloons remained tightly closed, making it "impossible to obtain" anything in the line of a drink.

The 1894 election proved different; for the first time, women voted. To discuss issues and candidates, women held a special meeting at the courthouse before election day, and, according to the *Herald* (April 1), "no gentlemen" were admitted. The *Herald* called for an improved "moral tone" in the city, but such issues never became a major factor. "Ladies" were advised to vote early in the day to avoid the rush. They did so and voted in "surprising" numbers at the polling places. On a "beautiful, warm and clear day," the *Herald* reported on April 4, candidates and carriages called at all residences "from which women registered." The men and women split their votes, the Populist Party and Democrats winning most races, but even the Republicans, damned because of their anti–Free Silver stand, won a share.

By 1898, the Populist and Republican Parties fielded a combined ticket against the popular Democrats. Not a "drop of bad blood was engendered" during the campaign, and the Democrats swept the field. The Herald, which had supported the Populist-Republican, or "fusion" ticket, forthrightly stated on April 6 that there was "no use disguising the fact that the Republicans and Populists did not fuse worth a cent." Rather than finding fault, the newspaper simply stated, "Voters have a right to do as they please and vote as they please."[3]

Local newspapers thrived on partisanship, and both Sandwich papers outrightly supported or leaned toward Republican candidates. The *Sandwich Free Press* never wavered from the Republican banner; the *Sandwich Argus* was for years a lukewarm supporter of the GOP, but in 1896 became nominally independent and supported Democrat William Jennings Bryan. Durango's newspapers represented a varied political lot. The *Herald* was Republican with a Free Silver twist, Dave Day's *Solid Muldoon* and *Democrat* were ardently Democratic, and the rest became supporters of the Populists until after the 1896 election. Even the *Herald* had definite Populist overtones that year.

Until the 1890s, the two towns and counties held a long Republican heritage. Sandwich and De Kalb County had voted for GOP presidential candidates since the days of Abraham Lincoln; younger Durango had voted for Republicans James Blaine and Benjamin Harrison in the 1880s. Durangoans, however, voted for Democrats in state races. All this changed in the West when the Free Silver issue emerged, followed by the formation of the People's, or Populist, Party.

Free Silver! Never did an issue unify Coloradans and other Western mining people like this one. It was triggered primarily by a fall in the price of silver, from $1.20 per ounce at the start of the Leadville bonanza in 1877 to ninety-eight cents per ounce a decade later. By 1898, it had sunk to an average of sixty cents per ounce (for a brief time, it went as low as forty-nine cents), and that was the price for smelted and refined silver, not the ore coming from the mine, which received an even lower price. For the number one silver mining state in the United States, and for a town whose chief industry depended on the neighboring San Juan silver mines, those prices represented a terrible blow.

Without emotion and from hindsight, it is easy enough to pinpoint the causes. As mentioned earlier, an increase in the production of silver from U.S. mines intersected a sharp decline in the use of the metal worldwide. The decline in use resulted mainly from countries stopping or reducing their production of silver coins. Industrial uses of silver had not yet become widespread, and the manufacture of jewelry and silver plate had not greatly increased. The resulting metal surplus and price collapse created extremely hard times for Colorado silver mining, the rock pillar of the state's economy.

It all started, the Silverites claimed, when the U.S. government stopped coining the silver dollar in 1873. The Silverites referred to that emotionally charged event as the "crime of '73." It had happened because the government's mint price for silver was lower than the world market price, which meant that silver coins were worth more than their face value. Not surprisingly, they disappeared from circulation. At first there was little concern, but when the world price went lower than the once government-guaranteed $1.25 per ounce, miners came selling only to find out that there were no buyers.

Then, the end of the silver dollar became a "crime." Predictably, Western miners wanted government help. They had two things in mind: first, a guaranteed price of $1.25 and, second, U.S. government purchase of silver. What they got was the Bland-Allison Act of 1878, which was passed over President Rutherford Hayes's veto. The Treasury would have to buy not less than $2 million nor more than $4 million worth of silver bullion each month at the prevailing price, and that bullion was to be coined into silver dollars. The law did not provide the elixir for which the Westerners thirsted, but it did call for the coinage of silver dollars. Then, in 1890, because of some political logrolling, Congress passed the Sherman Silver Purchase Act. The measure required the Treasury to buy 4.5 million ounces of silver per month. Westerners cheered, and the price of silver temporarily shot above a dollar per ounce, only to dismally slide back down again.

What the Westerners did not gain and desperately desired was what neither bill provided—a guaranteed silver price. What the Westerners wanted back again was the old government gold-silver price ratio of 16:1, originally set under Andrew Jackson's administration. With gold pegged at $20.00 per ounce, silver would then be worth $1.25. Nor did they appreciate the notion that for all practical purposes the United States had emerged on the gold standard, not the bimetal gold-and-silver standard they coveted.

To make matters worse, secretaries of the treasury in the 1880s invariably purchased as little silver as the Bland-Allison Act allowed. Western silver interests, plus those preferring inflation, were appalled. The free and unlimited coinage of silver—and a return to the bimetal standard—emerged as the demand of the day. Conservatives reacted with horror to this demand, and swiftly the battle lines were drawn between the Silverites and the Goldbugs.

Into the growing unrest came yet another volatile issue—the rights of the common man. The two major parties generally differed very little on the questions of the day. Neither appeared to sense the significance of the money problem, of the critical nature of the labor-capital relationship, or of the vast transformation that was coming over the country. The Republican Party existed to oppose the Democratic Party, and the Democrats existed to oppose the Republicans. Real issues cut across both parties, but even when recognized (a rare occurrence), they seemed to be evaded or ignored. As a result, in the 1870s and 1880s, an array of third parties tried to provide alternatives.

The public may have yawned at the tariff question, but the issue seemingly turned politicians on. At least, it helped to distinguish the two parties. The Republicans supported, and the Democrats opposed, protective tariffs. Otherwise, the two parties seemed to be guided by conservative big-business and Wall Street interests that were too little concerned about ordinary Americans and their worries. Farmers and Western miners, at least, thought that to be true, and the perception infuriated them. As a result, they marched out of the political mainstream and organized their own parties.

First came the Farmers' Alliances, which had only limited impact in Sandwich and hardly any in Durango. Then, the Populist Party (also known as the People's Party) burst on the scene, with its first national meeting in Omaha in July 1892. It was a wildly enthusiastic gathering; a cause was born. As Mary Lease, who later spoke in Sandwich, cried, "Wall Street owns the country. It is no longer a government of the people, by the people, and for the people, but a government of Wall Street, by Wall Street, and for Wall Street."

The Populists nominated a presidential candidate that year, former congressman and Civil War veteran James Weaver, and adopted a platform. Such basically conservative groups as farmers, miners, and small-town folk became radical in defense of their conservatism. The Populists called for, among other things, a graduated income tax, the Australian ballot, initiative and referendum, and, most excitingly from Durango's viewpoint, the free and unlimited coinage of silver and a guaranteed gold-silver price ratio of 16:1.

Durango fell into line with the Populists instantly. In the presidential election of 1892, La Plata County gave James Weaver 1,062 votes, Republican Benjamin Harrison 545, the Prohibition candidate 16, and, unbelievably, Democrat Grover Cleveland zero. De Kalb County, on the other hand, gave 3,789 votes to the Republicans, 1,927 to the Democrats, 489 to the prohibitionists, and only 36 to the Populists. Somonauk Township, in which Sandwich cast more votes than any other town, tallied no votes for Weaver. The startling contrast between Sandwich and Durango was understandable. The Sandwich Democrats, having done better than usual, held a victory celebration in the park for Grover Cleveland. "Fireworks, Chinese lanterns, several bonfires, cannon booming and a band playing" told everyone who did not hear the main speech that the party was alive and well (*Sandwich Argus*, Nov. 19, 1892).

Despite the overwhelming Populist victory in Durango, the *Great Southwest* had stood staunchly behind the Republicans. It tried the impossible, to support Free Silver and at the same time to support the party that doggedly fought the idea and championed the gold standard. The paper got into a nasty shouting match with the *Solid Muldoon* and the *Herald,* the sort of thing that Sandwich never witnessed. The voters did not pay heed to the *Great Southwest*'s admonition that "a vote for Weaver is a shot at a shadow" (Sept. 23). In a way, the paper was right when it said, "Scratch a Weaver man and you will uncover a Democrat" (Aug. 16). On the other side, the *Herald* (July 13) said, "Give us Weaver and a silver bill to sign, and Durango will double its population inside of twelve months."

The horrified *Sandwich Free Press* blasted the gains made by the Populists in the West. The Populists won over nine percent of the total U.S. vote, and Weaver carried Kansas, Nevada, Colorado, and Idaho. According to the *Free Press* (Nov. 17), "The candidates were selected and the elections were carried by the worst elements in society. We do not believe the People's party or Prohibition party—as presently organized—will accomplish much needed reforms." The Republican Party, the writer went on to say, needed to throw overboard the "Jonahs who so successfully steered it up Salt Creek" and to return to their early history.[4]

The Republicans would not do that, and the newspaper had sadly misjudged the times—revolt whirled in the Western and Midwestern air. Yes, right in Sandwich roared one of Illinois's leading Free Silver advocates, the *Sandwich Argus*. There is nothing in Miles Castle's life that would suggest that this banker, businessman, newspaperman, and loyal Republican in his late sixties would support a cause that almost all his neighbors and certainly his party and banking friends considered heresy. In truth, it seems that he would have done just the opposite. However, Miles proved a man of contrasts, favoring government control of railroads (*Argus,* Dec. 30, 1893) and supporting trusts, because they "have attained success by cheapening the products to the citizen, and therefore benefitting the majority" (*Argus,* May 8, 1897).

This Sandwich pioneer followed his own reasoning, this time as he did on the issue of woman suffrage. His lawyer son John came from the same background, and he joined his father to coedit the paper. The *Argus* raised eyebrows throughout the state, especially in business and banking circles, for its strong advocacy of Free Silver. The Castles apparently believed a little inflation, which Free Silver would produce, would benefit local farmers and merchants.

Castle's editorials would have fit nicely into those written in Ouray, Leadville, Boulder, and scores of Colorado towns. The reader could not have told the difference. A sampling of his editorials furnishes an idea of the emotionalism and the optimistic, if sometimes rickety, logic of the "cause."

> What we want is that bi-metallism that gives us silver to use as money just as we have gold, and worth just as much for daily use. (Sept. 16, 1893)

> What the people demand is the use of both silver and gold, or bi-metallism as advocated by the republican platform. We believe it should be free coinage of both gold and silver of American production. It is a folly to be afraid of "too much money." (Oct. 21, 1893)

> It is time the bankers retire from dictating the financial policy of the nation in the interest of the gold ring, and let the common people have a chance at it, for we have too many bankers in our financial policy now working for themselves. (Oct. 6, 1894)

> This silver question is to be one of the leading issues of the next campaign [1896] and the silverites are going to win the strong sympathy of the country. (Dec. 15, 1894)

> It is wonderful what an amount of venom the gold papers manifest, but as they are popularly supposed to be paid for their opinions on this gold and silver question just as they are on other questions, the sum of ardor they manifest is the index for the sum of cash they charge for "disinterested" opinions (May 30, 1896)

If these were not enough, Castle gave a stirring Free Silver address before the Banker's Association meeting on November 16, 1892. He definitely knew what they thought. "My views are possibly at variance with those of a majority of my hearers," he said. Nevertheless, he went on to defend that "orphanized and ostracized factor in finance,—coined silver." His main points had been repeated by two decades of Western silver spokespeople. They included the point that silver was a recognized money, the money of the masses, and a valuable product. It was "honest to the debtor class" and provided the most natural means of expanding "our currency." Considering what happened within a year, Castle's forecast in the *Argus* on November 26 that "gold alone does not furnish sufficient coin basis to sustain confidence in times of depression" proved all too accurate.

Like Castle, the Durango papers never gave up. For example, the *Weekly Tribune* (June 1, 1891) said, "Senator [Horace] Tabor is always sound on the silver question, and is worth more to Colorado than all the goldbug, gold spectacled politicians and statesmen in the state." Durango's *Great Southwest* (Oct. 19, 1893) proclaimed, "The fight will be kept up until silver is properly recognized."

When the panic of 1893 descended on the country, President Grover Cleveland, big business, and the Republican Party blamed the Sherman Silver Purchase Act and its provision for the redemption of silver certificates in gold. They conveniently overlooked the pressing national and international causes. As emotional as the Silverites, the Goldbugs locked in on the Silver Act as *the* cause. In Durango, editor Dave Day could not believe the act would be repealed without "a free coinage law substituted for it" (*Solid Muldoon,* July 21, 1893). Dave was wrong. So was Sandwich's Miles Castle, who on August 12 called repeal "a national suicide."

After an impassioned Senate fight, Congress repealed the act and down went the price of silver. On November 8, Castle warned the Republicans not to boast, for the time was coming "when Republicans [would] desire that record forgotten." That set the stage for one of the nation's greatest presidential campaigns, that of 1896.[5]

The issue stood squarely before the electorate. It climaxed with Republican nominee William McKinley and gold against Democrat William Jennings Bryan and silver. Or as the rhetoric of the day called it—rich versus poor, East versus West, debtor versus creditor, common man versus banker and big business, Americans versus international bankers, and, with reason, old America versus new America. The Populists suddenly became a party without a platform when the Democrats boldly stole their program nearly lock, stock, and barrel. For the first time in the decade, Sandwich witnessed a heated newspaper war. The *Free Press* had never been particularly political but was always loyal to the Republicans. It remained so. Castle, when asked if the *Argus* would still be a Republican paper, replied, "It will be just what it has always been; independent with strong Republican leanings" (July 18, 1896). That did not fool anyone.

> OUR PLATFORM This nation's money should be gold, silver and legal tender government circulating notes. Gold and silver should have the same mint privileges . . .
>
> We confess to a profound admiration of Wm. J. Bryan. A boy so poor that he had to borrow the coat of a room mate to graduate in, but a few years later stood at the head of the bar of his state, a place won by merit, commands admiration and respect. (July 18, 1896)

Castle's sentiments did not mislead the *Free Press*. The Democratic Party, it declared on July 16, played on a weather forecast of "cyclonic, with occasional cloud bursts, interspersed with dry, hot winds, threatening serious injury for agricultural interests of the country." On July 23 it went on to say, "The whole free coinage superstition is a delusion." The paper interjected many humorous barbs, including one on August 27 about what happened to the ancient Egyptians when they based their currency on a ratio of "sixteen onions to one cat." Meanwhile, the paper forecast a record Republican victory.

Castle fought back against all adversaries: "So long as we believe most fully that the prosperity of the farmers and wage earners and manufacturers of this nation depend on the re-monetization of silver we cannot do otherwise" (*Argus,* Aug. 1, 1896). For once, Durango's papers united with both eyes on silver and, as the *Durango Herald* proclaimed on August 13, "look[ed] neither left or right." Harkening back to the fabled Civil War years, the paper predicted, "Bryan's march to the White House will be like Sherman's march to the sea—an occasional squall, but triumphant as a whole."[6]

Both parties organized, sponsored speakers, held rallies, paraded, praised their leaders, damned the other side, predicted doom and gloom if they lost, and generally had a great time. "Tons" of literature, including *Coin's Financial School,* sought to educate the voters. Bands, banners, buttons, bonfires on crisp evenings, torchlight parades, McKinley clubs, Bryan clubs—

all inundated the voters. Eighteen ninety-six quickly swirled into a "dirty" campaign with truth falling an early victim to emotion. Cheered the *Durango Herald* (May 28, 1896), "Free silver is sweeping the country."

The *Sandwich Argus* advised on October 31, "Keep cool, vote as you believe best all things considered, and be as happy as possible." The result in Durango and La Plata County raced beyond the fondest hopes of the Silverites. Almost incredibly, Bryan received 2,796 votes and McKinley only 88. Despite Castle's finest efforts in Sandwich, the results there and in De Kalb County were predictable: McKinley won 5,598 votes and Bryan 1,868. Even in Somonauk Township, Bryan had lost by more than three to one. Said unbowed editor Castle on November 7, "We all had our opinions, pro and con, and someone must be wrong, experience will tell who." Coloradans had believed in the silver cause. Mining engineer James Hague, who was visiting Colorado, wrote his wife on November 9, "In Colorado Bryan is regarded as a Moses, a divinely appointed leader of the people, or, at least, a Lincoln, raised up to save and redeem his people." Coloradans not only believed, they also voted. Over eighty-five percent of the state's voters supported the "silver-tongued orator."

The results in Sandwich and Durango mirrored those in the rest of the country. Bryan's appeal and the Democratic platform evoked a wild response in Durango; in Sandwich and rural Illinois, the candidate and platform seemed too wild. The alleged benefits of inflation did not have much appeal, and Sandwich voters listened to Republican warnings that Free Silver would impoverish the urban market and bankrupt railroads. Both were essential to the prosperity of Sandwichites. Throughout areas east of the Mississippi River, where most Americans lived, factory workers and urban dwellers found little appeal in Bryan's rhetoric. And there remained that generation-long loyalty to the GOP. The Republican cause benefited, too, from a rise in the price of wheat near election day, a rise that seemingly hinted of better times to come.[7]

In the years that followed, Castle continued to support Free Silver, though he devoted fewer newspaper articles to the cause. Durango newspapers never lost the faith. David Day, for example, predicted in the *Democrat* (April 19, 1899) that Bryan's latest speech "is trouble for the gold bugs." The American people generally forsook Free Silver and moved on to other matters, including the Spanish-American War and its aftermath. Some issues raised during the campaign—for example, the initiative, the direct election of senators, the overwhelming power of big business, the income tax—did not die. Although the Populist Party died, its platform lived on, as did the idea of "power to the people." For Sandwich, Durango, and the country as a whole, this had been a watershed election. There would be no turning back to yesterday's seemingly simpler world.

The 1896 election marked a turning point in the struggle between rural-agricultural and urban-industrial America. Urban-industrial America won, and the future rested in its hands. Both Durango and Sandwich symbolized urban America; they represented a tiny part of that wave of the future. In a most recognizable sense, however, they depended on rural America and remained part of it as well. They did not truly understand slums, sweatshops, ethnic neighborhoods, traffic and crime concerns, immigrant problems, or big-city political machines. Urban as they were, they also stayed integrated into the earlier world of the miner and farmer. This dichotomy would not be easy to resolve, and the resolution would not occur until generations later. The echoes of a vanished America did not quickly disappear; nor did the heartaches of the urban-industrial birth.

NOTES

1. Suzy Platt (ed.), *Respectfully Quoted* (Washington: Library of Congress, 1989), 266. Alex Ayres (ed.), *The Wit & Wisdom of Mark Twain* (New York: Harper & Row, 1987), 179–80.
2. *Sandwich Argus,* April 5, 1890; April 9, April 23, 1892; April 26, 1893; April 14, April 21, 1894; April 13, April 20, 1895; April 26, 1896; April 17, April 24, 1897; April 2, April 23, April 30, 1898. *Sandwich Free Press,* April 16, 1890; April 23, April 30, 1891; March 30, April 6, April 13, 1893; April 9, 1896; April 1, April 15, 1897; April 6, April 20, 1899.
3. *Durango Herald,* March 30, April 1, April 5, 1893; March 31, April 1, April 3, April 4, April 5, 1894; April 2, April 3, April 5, 1898. Unfortunately, no issues of other Durango papers that covered the 1893–94 elections have survived.
4. *Durango Great Southwest,* Aug. 16, Sept. 13, Sept. 22, Sept. 23, Oct. 1, 1892. *Herald,* July 8, July 9, July 12, 1892. *Free Press,* June 4, Aug. 7, Nov. 13, 1890; March 28, Oct. 13, Oct. 27, Nov. 10, Nov. 17, 1892; May 18, 1893. *Argus,* Oct. 11, Nov. 5, Nov. 19, 1892. John Moses, *Illinois Historical and Statistical* (Chicago: Fergus Printing Co., 1895), 1208–10.
5. Robert W. Larson, *Populism in the Mountain West* (Albuquerque: University of New Mexico Press, 1986), 25–40. *Argus,* Jan. 16, Nov. 26, Dec. 31, 1892; July 1, Sept. 16, Sept. 23, Oct. 21, Nov. 8, 1893; May 26, Oct. 6, Dec. 15, 1894; July 13, Nov. 16, 1895; May 30, 1896. *Durango Weekly Tribune,* June 1, 1891. *Great Southwest,* Oct. 19, 1893. *Herald,* July 9, July 12, July 14, 1892; July 1, 1893. *Durango Solid Muldoon,* July 21, 1893.
6. *Free Press,* July–Nov. 1896. *Argus,* July–Nov. 1896. *Herald,* July–Nov. 1896. Paul Glad, *McKinley, Bryan, and the People* (Philadelphia: J. B. Lippincott Company, 1964), 70–82, 113–27. James Edward Wright, *The Politics of Populism* (New Haven: Yale University Press, 1974), 205–13.
7. Richard J. Jensen, *Illinois* (New York: W. W. Norton & Co., 1978), 83–88. *Argus,* Aug.–Nov. 1896. *Free Press,* Aug.–Nov. 1896. *Herald,* Aug.–Nov. 1896. Richard F. Snow, "William Hope Harvey," *American Heritage* (Dec. 1981), 34–35. James Hague to Mary Hague, Nov. 9, 1896, in the James D. Hague Collection, Henry E. Huntington Library, San Marino, California.

6
TWO-FOR-A-QUARTER STATESMEN

She may have seen better days,
When she was in her prime.
—"She May Have Seen Better Days" (1894)

Seldom praised, more often damned, and generally assumed to be muddling along, the city governments of Durango and Sandwich provided better service and more dedication than many of their too often apathetic constituents deserved. If they raised taxes, became ensnared in a controversy, or failed to provide some needed assistance, the mayor, council, and city officials heard an earful of complaints and concerns.

Occasionally, something did go wrong. After weeks of filibustering and bickering, the Durango City Council exploded in late August and September 1891. Although some of the causes have been lost to history, the records show that the mayor resigned, in part because "important business called him east" (Durango City Council Minutes, Aug. 21, 1891). The council suspended the police magistrate, amid charges that he "wanted to enjoy" a prostitute "known as Mattie Cook," and had been seen on the streets in "a drunken condition with said prostitute scandalizing the official position" he held. There was not much left for him to scandalize, after the whole story came out about how he had forced Cook's husband to leave town, did not collect fines from her, and allowed her to live outside the red-light district.

A wholesale housecleaning followed. The council suspended the marshal, charging that he had "failed and neglected" to perform his duties, and the city attorney and city clerk followed him out of office. The clerk was accused of incompetence, "employing numerous persons for his own private gain," failing to collect fees, and transferring funds without authorization. The street commissioner resigned, and the council was busily engaged in looking into everyone's books and accounts. Durangoans on the streets asked,

"What's wrong with city government?" It was generally believed, the *Durango Examiner* reported on August 24, 1891, that Durango was "under some sort of gang rule."

There seemed more to this than a Colorado resurrection of New York's infamous Tweed machine. A group of voters filed a protest to the council against this "monstrous outrage," the removal of officials without the "slightest cause," which was due, they claimed, to the action of a "high handed" majority of city council members. The motion supporting the protest lost a vote in the council and, on council's order, was "expunged." Even small-town America could have its tempest.[1]

Peace soon returned, but, in 1896, Durangoans organized a Taxpayers' Federation. Their avowed purpose was to "scrutinize receipts and disbursements of public monies" and work with public officials to make every effort to "increase receipts, reduce expenditures and lessen taxation." "Nonpolitical in character," the federation organized committees and looked into city and county operations. Although it may have accomplished some good initially, it may be doubted that the federation had much staying power, particularly after the council voted unanimously on February 16, 1897, to "table indefinitely" the federation's recommendation to reduce city salaries. Reformers could not spend all of their time looking into city and county government; they had businesses to conduct and jobs to perform.

Sandwich had its share of tempests, too, but none quite like Durango's August 1891 debacle, the one described above, which the press referred to as that of the "Kilkenny cats." A May 2, 1898, ruckus in Sandwich, fairly typical, resulted in a debate over the resignation of the chairman of the finance committee. The debate took so much time that the mayor's annual address could not be given. (An account in the *Sandwich Free Press* on May 19 does not say whether that was a blessing!) Voters seemed to complain every year of council slowness, though the council could respond rapidly, as it did when reacting to the "air-gun" menace in 1899 (*Sandwich Argus*, Dec. 2, 1899). City authorities took quick action to stop the nuisance after a "BB shot" struck a little girl in the face. They ordered the marshal to take charge of boys caught shooting air guns.

Occasionally, someone fired off a barb. The *Durango Tribune* (May 28, 1891), for example, said, "Durango has reached that period of its life when there is no question of permanency to justify two-for-a-quarter statesmen in delaying public improvements." *Sandwich Free Press* editor William Deacon complained on June 15, 1893, that "Sandwich and the township of Somonauk, by their official representatives, and lawsuits, are rapidly making widely extended reputations as the two famous jack asses from the south end of the county."

Sandwich Mayor A. Gates White, who already had been lambasted for his shenanigans by the no-license crowd, came under sharp fire in 1897 for permitting saloons and gambling dens to operate openly, thereby condoning "sabbath desecrations" (*Free Press,* Sept. 8, 1897). Four years earlier, Durango's city council had encountered the wrath of local newspapers for allowing "unsafe meat to be sold." The council responded with an investigation that finally resulted in a requirement that meat not be sold in Durango, unless it had been inspected and a fee paid for the inspection. In 1895, Sandwich citizens organized a Civic Federation that sounded very much like Durango's Taxpayers' Federation. The group wanted "honest and economic" expenditure of public funds in town and township (*Argus,* March 2, 1895). After the Civic Federation hinted darkly about the "forces of evil," nothing more was heard from it.[2]

Those "forces of evil" probably referred to the same things that got Mayor White in trouble—"demon rum" and its accompanying problems. As our discussion of the city elections showed, the Wets and Drys skirmished repeatedly. City government tried to satisfy both camps but satisfied neither. Following the victory of the no-license faction in 1891, the city council passed a Dram Shop Ordinance in May, prohibiting the sale of "spirituous, vinous, mix, fermented or intoxicating liquor of any kind within the city of Sandwich." The four-to-three vote by which it passed reflected the heated nature of the issue. The ordinance seemed concise and clear enough, yet within a month the council had to pass an amendment to make it unlawful to give away "spirituous . . . liquor" (*Free Press,* May 14, 1891).

Nothing worked. Any action upset one side or the other. A Citizens' League, which was organized to prevent the illegal sale of intoxicating liquors, started a subscription drive to raise money to enforce the ordinance. On the other side, Samuel Dickson advised the council that it should spend its money carefully, because it would no longer have the three thousand dollars in city taxes that it once gathered from liquor licenses. "If the temperance and radical fanatics," he argued, had any interest in Sandwich, they would not throw away three thousand dollars to "save three or four or not more than half a dozen poor miserable things" (*Free Press*, May 14, 1891). Sounding much like William Jennings Bryan in 1896, Dickson predicted grass would grow "at the temperance men's doors" before five years passed. "We will wait and see."

Grass really never had a chance to grow. The 1893 election reversed the prohibition decision. The consequence was a licensing ordinance, but no wide-open town resulted. Saloons could not be open on Sundays and had to close each night at 10:00 p.m. The *Free Press* (May 11, 1893) noted, "We will watch the enforcement of this ordinance with interest." Enforcement never seemed to please either side; it proved either too loose or too harsh. However, when the saloon keepers, in September 1895, requested that their closing time be extended to 11:00 p.m., the council denied it.

The victory of the no-license group in 1898 did not end the battle. A petition to the council, in December 1898, complained that liquor sales and gambling openly went on in defiance of the law. Two months later, it was still a problem, and the council instructed the marshal to investigate the sale of "intoxicating liquors" in drug stores. Foreshadowing what would happen nationally, Sandwich found that it proved costly, contentious, and time-consuming to try to regulate peoples' morals or drinking habits. The town did not stop with liquor and gambling but also passed ordinances against cigarettes "containing drugs or opiates" and that evil of evils, billiards.[3]

Citizens not only were appalled by officials' conduct, rigidity, or lack of law enforcement, they also did not hesitate to sue their town. A rash of lawsuits kept city attorneys busy and city expenses high. The causes appeared sometimes serious, sometimes humorous. A building that "obstructed light and air" to a neighboring lot caused one suit. A water-main accident, false imprisonment, poorly built sidewalks, a fall into a hole on Main Street, and a horse frightened by a streetcar produced others. The cities sued as well, to collect payments for curb and gutter work, to condemn property, and to prevent saloons from opening on Sundays.

Lawsuits, complaints, and citizens' anger—it all must have made some people hesitant to run for city council or mayor. But every year candidates toed the mark. They were generally conservative, business-oriented people. For example, in 1892 Durango's city council included a real estate agent, a livery stable owner, a blacksmith, a contractor, and the smelter superintendent. In 1898, Sandwich's council had a newspaper owner, a hardware merchant, a machinist, and the owner of a monument works. As the *Durango Examiner* observed on August 17, 1891, the owners of property did not feel like having municipal affairs handled "recklessly or boyishly." The "strictest economy should be observed" was a warning that all councils took to heart, as did Sandwich Mayor White in his address to the new council, in which he promised an economical administration that would adhere strictly to business (*Argus*, May 8, 1897).

Typically, council meetings hardly stirred public interest—minutes were read, bills were paid, reports were heard, appointments were made, and petitions were presented. Occasionally the mayor addressed the council with a special report or gave farewell remarks, as Durango's Thomas Graden did in April 1891, thanking "council and citizens" for all the "courtesies of the past year" and expressing satisfaction at Durango's "prosperous condition" (Durango City Council Minutes, April 20, 1891).

Petitions came in all forms and expressed many types of concerns. For instance, Sandwich barbers wanted an ordinance to require that all shops be closed on Sunday (they achieved it). Petitioners in both towns desired curfews for children, and Durangoans urged that the license of the Phenix Theater, a site of drinking and lewdness, be revoked.

Government, as Sandwich's Mayor White pointed out in 1897, "must not forget that we have the best interests of the whole people to look after, the minority as well as the majority, and we as their representatives must work for that purpose" (*Argus*, May 8). To help reach this objective, the Sandwich and Durango City Councils organized a multitude of committees, which dealt with such matters as finance, health, streets, building, parks, and printing, to mention just a few.[4]

The city governments generally seem to have governed on behalf of all; the voters, despite petitions and complaints, seem usually to have been complacent. City appropriations went up steadily in the 1890s in both towns, despite government economizing during the depths of the 1893 crash and depression. Sandwich's appropriations grew from $9,000 in 1890 to $15,000 in 1899. Fortunately, income also went up. Durango spent more, jumping from $24,000 in 1890 to $33,000 in 1899. The major difference between the two towns' budgets arose from salaries. In 1899, for example, the total budget for city workers in Durango was $8,500 a year, while city workers in Sandwich earned a total of $4,300. For workers in the waterworks and the electric lights department, Durango set aside $11,000 a year, while Sandwich workers received $5,650. Durango's city marshal's salary alone, at $1,020 a year, was $400 more than the entire amount budgeted for Sandwich's marshal and special police force.

For these expenditures, Sandwichites and Durangoans received police and fire protection, water, electricity, and street maintenance. The marshal and his police force, besides enforcing all the ordinances, were expected to carry out other duties, including maintaining the jail. Dogs and drunks, those perennial problems, needed to be corralled. In Durango, women of "ill-fame" had to be kept in their section of town. The marshal enforced quarantine in cases of infectious diseases, posting appropriate notices. He also tried to capture fast riders and drivers and saw to it that children did not wander about after curfew. In Durango, the curfew went from 9:00 p.m. to 5:00 a.m. for children who were without a parent or guardian or were "not . . . able to give a good account of themselves, himself or herself."

Durangoans also received another benefit, city parks. Parks had been planned in the original plat, and finally, in the 1890s, the city council started beatifying the three parks and the parkway in the center of the Boulevard and employed a man to take care of them. All did not turn out as planned, however. Trees were planted and fences were "placed in condition to prevent the ingress of cattle and horses." After some vandalism, including "several trees broken" by children playing, youngsters were "forbidden to enter parks," unless accompanied by parents or guardians. Boys were also prohibited from "playing games" in parks, because the "practice was a detriment thereof"! According to the council, children and parks did not seem to go together. Trees continually had to be replaced because of "winter kill," and finally, in September 1899, a councilman exploded, "It is a useless expenditure to go on trying to care for City Parks." Fortunately his attitude did not prevail.

Fire! No more dreaded cry could be uttered. Everyone expected the city to provide protection. Volunteer fire companies, prominent fixtures in both communities, with their horses, carts, and wagons, stood ready not only to fight fires but also to take part in parades and races. Starting in February 1894, Durango had a paid fire department of two firefighters and a chief, plus volunteers. Sandwich paid its chief, who coordinated volunteers. That winter, Durango also opened a new fire station and purchased a "thing of beauty," a black-and-bronze hose wagon (*Durango Herald,* Jan. 21, 1894). The press could not contain itself. The city, said the *Herald* (Feb. 18, 1894), "boasts of one of the most practical, efficient and best equipped fire departments in the West."

Sandwich warned its citizens of fires by means of blasts from the Sandwich Manufacturing Company's whistle. The number of blasts indicated the district in which the fire blazed. Durango provided a fire alarm system that worked fine, except for occasional false alarms. Apparently, some children or adults enjoyed seeing the horses and wagons racing through the streets!

Durango found an unexpected problem with its fire department horses. The city had three, rotating one to a pasture every month while the other two stood on duty. The issue was the cost of feed. In January 1897, the council had a long discussion about whether $2.50 or $3.00 was an appropriate amount to pay.

Fortunately, neither town suffered a major fire in the 1890s, like Durango's 1889 disaster. The worst one occurred in Sandwich in February 1893, when, with a "strong wind blowing," a fire destroyed a barber shop, restaurant, and cigar shop and damaged the Sedgwick Bank building (*Argus,* Feb. 18, 1893). Within a year, the Marcy Block building stood on the site. Small fires, however, kept the "laddies" busy and the citizens uneasy. A fire in Dr. Charles Winne's drug store in June 1894, for instance, brought the Sandwich firemen in their "usual prompt" manner (*Free Press,* June 7, 1894). Using a "vast amount of water," they quickly put the fire out, only to have the insurance adjuster complain that more damage had been caused by the water than by the fire!

Fires always created interest. "High leaping tongues of flame; dark smoke rising heavenward in dense clouds; a mighty roar like that emitted from a furnace blast" is a description found in the *Durango Herald* (June 21, 1893). Local reporters seemed to enjoy using such hyperbole to magnify the importance of their news stories. In the above instance, the *Herald* was trying to capture the scene as the Phenix Theater burned on a June evening in 1893. Readers probably showed more interest in the rest of the coverage: "Here and there by back door routes hurried citizens who had been suddenly aroused from positions more or less compromising. They were pale looking and anxious until they reached the crowds and could mingle with them without fear of being asked unpleasant questions." Any curiosity would have to be resolved by rumor because the reporter did not give the names of the men who had been visiting the "denizens with blanched faces," who rushed from their houses around the theater.[5]

In Sandwich, to help increase the water supply and to provide enough water for fire control, the town built a new waterworks. The drilling of a deep well and the installation of an engine and pump completed the project in 1894. That same year, the town further modernized by building an "electric light plant." This happened after a "majority of the citizens and taxpayers signed a petition" in favor of the project, which Sandwich borrowed seven thousand dollars to finance. The council busied itself establishing rates and was pleased, by May, that the electric lights were "giving good satisfaction." The arc lights on the street corners soon brightened the community and increased nighttime activities. The chairman of the electric light committee acted with alacrity, when fourteen "lady residents of Church street" petitioned for a light on the corner of Church and Dayton (*Free Press*, April 2, 1896). He "immediately instructed a force of men to hang and have burning before another setting of the sun an arc lamp on that corner." The council also saved money by heating City Hall with the otherwise wasted steam from the electric plant and waterworks.

Yet all was not completely smooth sailing. As in Durango, the bugs in the system had to be worked out. The *Sandwich Argus* (Jan. 11, 1896) laconically observed, the electric lights "are variable again. They flicker and go out without asking our consent." Such problems proved to be easily resolved.

Sandwich folks could be pleased with their council. It had answered their petitions and needs and modernized their town. The lights made it safer to go out at night and more comfortable inside their homes and places of business. The availability of more water for firefighting and for private use improved the quality of life. These accomplishments illustrated local government at its best. The voters of Sandwich should also have been pleased when the council found an economical way to have the town's streets numbered. According to the *Argus* (Dec. 23, 1893), a directory company wanted to publish a Sandwich volume, so it offered to place "one style of numbers" for the "remarkable low price" of five cents per building! The directory would be of small benefit, the council noted, unless numbering was done, but "numbering is not compulsory." Durango did not get around to seriously considering numbering its houses until 1899 and finally passed an ordinance on the matter in January 1900.

The councils of both towns passed a wide variety of ordinances. Those dealing with health and morality issues received much attention. Contagious diseases, filth, and privies received particular notice. The public did not mind government intruding upon private rights for the sake of securing such public benefits. The presence of minors in saloons, billiard halls, gambling houses, or houses of ill-fame was forbidden. Sandwich's curfew law defined a minor as any person under the age of sixteen. Misdemeanors and nuisances were carefully defined according to Victorian standards. They included, for example, profane, obscene, or offensive language; inhumanely or cruelly beating an animal; appearing in public in "lewd dress"; and discharging a "cannon or gun." Other measures, such as the prohibition against allowing hogs or cattle to run at large, aimed at improving the city's image and its health. A whole group of regulations were fire ordinances relating to stoves, chimneys, pipes, ashes, and the burning of combustible material in streets or lots. The public did not object to the government regulating their homes and businesses for the sake of these matters, either.

Both towns passed ordinances regulating a common source of problems, dogs. Owners had to buy licenses (seventy-five cents in Sandwich, two dollars in Durango) to allow their dogs to run at large, and, despite having licenses, they had to keep bitches in heat at home. Fines (five to fifty dollars) were to be levied against those who did not buy the dog tag or allowed a "barking, howling, whining" dog to disturb "the quiet." One fear that prompted canine regulation was rabies; so did the fear of dogs attacking people and other animals. Sandwich went so far as not to allow certain breeds—bull dogs, Newfoundlands, dalmatians, St. Bernards, and mastiffs—to run at large without muzzles. The marshal had the right to kill dogs violating these rules, which must have led to some confrontations and sad scenes.[6]

Citizen concerns prompted both councils to pass bicycle ordinances, while the biking fad soared to its zenith. Apparently, enthusiastic bikers rode on sidewalks and rode without lights at night. These became "no no's," as did fast riding, which must have been hard to define. For bicycle riders in Durango, that turned out to be greater than eight miles per hour on any public street. Sandwich Mayor White further called upon riders to be careful not to frighten teams and always to be courteous and to respect the "rights of others" (*Argus,* May 8, 1897).

Government functions cost money, and neither community displayed much interest in raising taxes. As a result, both used business licenses. The less "acceptable" the business, the higher the fee (Durango's liquor license cost three hundred dollars for each six-month period). Business licenses and water and light fees ranked as the top three revenue raisers, accounting for seventy-five percent of the towns' total income. Fines contributed a small share, especially in Durango, which sanctimoniously passed ordinances prohibiting gambling and prostitution, then allowed both to flourish and collected the fines every month. In Sandwich, rental of the town's Opera House helped a little, as did collection of a road and bridge tax.[7]

A breakdown of the revenue collected for Durango in June 1894 found the police magistrate gathering $271 in fines, thanks to thirty-eight arrests by the marshal. The city clerk issued $716 in business licenses, and the superintendent of the waterworks did the best of all by issuing $1,226 in water licenses.

Each town was part of a county and as such had to maintain economic, political, and social ties with an outlying area. Durango held an advantage, because as the county seat, it gained a variety of benefits, not the least of which were government jobs and a seat at the center of power. The brand new 1892 courthouse, built at a cost of $30,000, was a Victorian gem in a town that had many architectural "jewels." The city council, after some discussion, generously donated $650 to help put the clock in the tower. The *Durango Great Southwest* (Nov. 14, 1893) advised visitors that the cupola offered "one of the finest points in the city" from which to view "Durango and its environments."

Durango also had the good fortune of being the seat of the Sixth District Court. Lawyers settled in Durango in larger numbers than one might expect. The town had fourteen attorneys in 1892 and twenty-six, five years later. During court and county-commissioner sessions, people flocked to Durango, increasing business; the crowded streets hummed with activity and gossip.

Sandwich people, meanwhile, had to travel to Sycamore to conduct court or county business. It was not a long trip, but it could entail a day or more away from home, and money left the community.

The marriage of county and city did not prove all love and kisses; occasionally, the partners scrapped. For instance, in 1899, the *Durango Herald* (Oct. 25) took offense at the way the county poor farm was being run, and particularly the manner in which "old women" were being treated there. The Women's Club was investigating the situation when the century ended.

Durango's economic hinterland also provided more benefits, being much larger than Sandwich's. The only rival town within a hundred miles in any direction was Silverton, which lay in neighboring San Juan County. Even that mining town could not free itself from Durango, into which Silverton's railroad connection to the outside world ran. As a result of Durango's position, all nearby communities—Animas City, Hermosa, Rockwood, Porter, La Plata City, Bayfield, Silverton, Parrott City—fell into its economic orbit. Within this region, gold and silver mining, tourism, lumbering, farming, ranching, and coal mining prospered. In the 1890s, the Denver & Rio Grande again sired a town, this time through the Rio Grande Southern, a railroad it controlled. This new town, the coal camp of Hesperus, opened in 1894, with the help of Durango investors and the railroad. Even oil and natural gas were rumored to be in the region, though exploration and development remained for a later day.

Sandwich had nothing like this variety in its hinterland, especially not the gold and silver found in the La Plata and San Juan Mountains. Reflecting the old saying about mining and saints, "many are called, few are chosen," the La Platas actually delivered little in the 1890s. The *Durango Morning Democrat* (Dec. 30, 1897) showed eternal optimism regarding the La Platas; all that needed to be done, it claimed, was "some practical advertising." The La Platas needed more than that. Low-grade ore deposits, lack of funding, and transportation difficulties kept them out of the mining limelight throughout the decade. The San Juans, on the other hand, emerged as one of the greatest mining regions of the West. They returned a steady profit for Durango's businessmen and investors.

Durango profited from federal government involvement in and around the town; Sandwich had little if any federal assistance. In the Durango area, Fort Lewis represented the main attraction. But the government abandoned the military post, in spite of heated local protests, in 1891. Facts did not warrant abandonment, complained the *Durango Weekly Tribune* (May 18,

1891) but they did from the military and national perspectives. Fort Lewis long ago lost any significant military purpose. No one threatened southwestern Colorado. Uncle Sam never left, however; an Indian Boarding School opened on the old post grounds. It provided profitable contracts and jobs, even if they were fewer than before. The school's band and athletic teams soon appeared in town as Ute, Navajo, and Apache boys were taught to walk "the white man's road," and their sisters were taught skills needed in the white world. By the turn of the century, there was even talk of setting aside a national forest, although many locals were not in the least enthusiastic about such an idea. What would happen to their "rights" to use that land's resources?[8]

Farming surrounded both Durango and Sandwich, and the two towns paid careful attention to this economic base, though Sandwich paid more attention by far. Sandwich burst with pride in 1897, when it shipped more hogs than any other single point on the "Q" line. Throughout the nineties, it called itself a "good stock market." Locals had mixed feelings of pride and concern, as farmland prices went up, particularly after the depression. Newspapers in both towns complained about the weather when it hurt crops and praised it when it helped bring in bountiful bushels. They also went out of their way to trumpet high yields, and, occasionally, Sandwich newspapers would feature outstanding farms. The press wanted visitors to take note. The "song of the thresher" clanked pleasantly for Sandwich merchants.

It was more than simple economics, however. A genuine concern existed for the farmer, whether that concern was political, economic, or personal. Simon Suydam, who lived about seven miles west of Sandwich, lost two daughters to illness and his barn to lightning in a three-month period in 1890. Sandwich folks grieved with him.

Despite the fact that one observer (Hall, *History*, 175) praised La Plata County's rich soil and abundant water ("In all the West there is no lovelier agricultural section than this"), they could not compare to those of De Kalb County. In La Plata County, the soil was not as rich, the growing season was much shorter, and the dry climate was not as conducive to agriculture as were those hot humid nights in Illinois, when "you could hear the corn grow." And beyond the river bottoms, water was never abundant in La Plata County, unless the farmer obtained it by expensive irrigation. Nor was the southern half of the county even open to general farming until the Utes ceded the land, making way for the May 4, 1899, land rush.[9]

The blessings of the hinterland did not come without some complaint. Sandwich newspapers perennially grumbled about the state of "our country roads" (as did the *Free Press*, Feb. 5, 1890). Durango tagged along only a step behind. Poor transportation hurt business and was not to be tolerated. Both communities also worried about being under the thumb of a single railroad and yearned for a "southern outlet." Durango's hope lay in tapping New Mexico's trade; Sandwich's in coal and farmland. Nothing happened except talk. Committees formed, and several Durangoans incorporated the Durango Southern Railway Company, which grandiosely planned to go to Mexico. It went nowhere.

Sandwich finally settled on the popular idea of an electric railway. Excitement soared in 1898 when the Geneva Lake, Sycamore & Southern Electric Railway promised to come right down Main Street and through town, connecting the town to Wisconsin and points between. "The future of our beautiful and busy city is in a measure dependent upon the road and there is no one who can afford to lay a stone in the way of the company," declared the *Argus* (April 16, 1898). Some locals felt otherwise and petitioned the council, protesting the grant of a right of way that would lower property values. However, a larger number of citizens argued that the right of way should be granted, and after a long, tiring meeting, along toward midnight, the council agreed. Months went by, then years, and 1900 came with no railroad. "Not Dead but Sleepeth," said the *Free Press* (Feb. 2, 1899). Sandwich fumed, while construction costs and politics to the north held up the arrival of the electric line.[10]

Durango maintained an advantage over Sandwich in the size and variety of natural resources of its hinterland. Only in agriculture did Sandwich surge ahead. With farming communities within five miles in any direction, potential economic rivals surrounded Sandwich. None, however, matched Sandwich in size, in the vitality of its business district, or in industrial "might." Each offered some of the same services, and all farmers produced the same crops and raised the same animals. Nevertheless, Sandwich kept on generally good relations with all of its rivals in the nineties.

Durango had no such threats. Even Silverton, in San Juan County, depended on its larger, lower neighbor, and not only because of the railroad connection. Strong commercial ties joined the two Colorado towns, and La Plata County provided the closest agricultural market for man and beast. San

Juan County had no agricultural land, a fact that did not matter because it sometimes had a thirty-day or shorter growing season, which prohibited farming or raising much for the grower's own consumption, except rhubarb and raspberries. The lack of a rival and the variety and potential of Durango's hinterland augured well for the town's future economic growth.

NOTES

1. Durango City Council Minutes, Aug. 21, Sept. 3. Sept. 4, Oct. 20, 1891. *Durango Examiner,* Aug. 24, 1891.
2. *Taxpayers' Federation of La Plata County* (Durango: *Durango Herald,* 1896), 3, 8–12, 16. Durango City Council Minutes, Feb. 16, 1897. *Sandwich Argus,* March 2, 1895; Dec. 2, 1899. *Sandwich Free Press,* June 15, 1893; Sept. 9, 1897; May 19, 1898. *Durango Weekly Tribune,* May 28, 1891. Durango City Council Minutes, Jan. 17, Feb. 7, 1893.
3. *Free Press,* Sept. 15, 1890; May 7, May 14, June 11, July 23, 1891; May 11, 1893; May 5, June 23, 1898; Feb. 22, 1899. *Argus,* Aug. 2, 1890; Oct. 13, 1894; Nov. 2, 1895; May 15, 1897; Jan. 7, 1899.
4. Durango City Council Minutes, 1890–99. *Free Press,* April 16, May 14, June 11, July 16, 1890; May 14, May 21, 1891; June 29, 1893; May 24, 1894; Feb. 23, May 12, Aug. 18, 1898. *Argus,* March 31, 1894; June 27, 1896; May 8, May 15, 1897; March 5, 1898; Jan. 7, Nov. 11, 1899. *Examiner,* Aug. 17, 1891. *Durango Directory for the Year 1892* (Trinidad, Colo.: Bensel Directory Co., 1892), 53, 63, 69, 75, 92, 97. La Plata County District Court Plaintiff and Defendant Books, 1890s.
5. Durango City Council Minutes, 1890–99. Durango City Ordinances 207, 279, and 310. Durango Fire Department Record Book, 40, 49–51. *Durango Great Southwest,* Aug. 4, 1892. Durango Fire Department Minutes, Feb. 1, 1894. Richard McCloud, *Durango As It Is* (Durango: Durango Board of Trade, 1892), 82–83. *Argus,* Aug. 23, 1890; Aug. 12, 1893; May 19, 1894; July 6, 1895; May 15, 1897; Dec. 3, 1898; July 22, 1899. *Free Press,* Jan. 15, April 16, May 7, June 11, Dec. 4, Dec. 11, 1890; May 14, June 11, 1891; May 24, June 7, 1894; May 11, 1899.
6. *Revised Ordinances of the City of Durango, Colorado* (Durango: n.p., 1901), 1–100. Durango Ordinance Book 1. *Argus,* Dec. 23, Feb. 24, May 5, May 26, 1894; Oct. 26, 1895; Dec. 17, 1898. *Free Press,* Nov. 16, 1893; May 17, Sept. 27, 1894; Jan. 3, 1895; April 2, 1896; Feb. 23, Sept. 21, 1899.
7. *Free Press,* May 26, Aug. 4, 1898. *Argus,* May 8, 1897; April 2, 1898. *Revised Ordinances of the City of Durango,* 77–78. Durango City Ordinance 299. Durango Register of Licenses, 1896.
8. Durango Report of City Officials, June 1894. *Herald,* July 2, 1892; Jan. 31,

March 20, April 5, 1894; Oct. 4, Oct. 7, 1897; Oct. 25, 1899. *Colorado State Mining Directory, 1898* (Denver: Smith-Brooks, 1898), 272–74. McCloud, *Durango*, 65–68. Durango City Council Minutes, Dec. 15, 1891. *Great Southwest,* Aug. 2, Aug. 4, 1892; Nov. 14, 1893. *Weekly Tribune,* May 18, 1891. *Durango Morning Democrat,* Dec. 15, Dec. 30, 1897.

9. *Free Press,* Jan. 15, Feb. 12, March 5, March 12, April 16, 1890; Aug. 13, Sept. 17, 1891; July 19, Aug. 30, 1894; July 11, 1895; July 16, July 23, 1896; April 8, 1897. *Argus,* March 17, May 14, Nov. 14, 1894; Nov. 21, 1896; July 24, 1897. Frank Hall, *History of the State of Colorado* (Chicago: Blakely Printing Company, 1895), 4:157, 175. *Western Colorado* (Grand Junction, Colo.: *Grand Junction News,* 1893), 61. *Durango Herald,* July 18, 1895; April 30, 1896; Oct. 5, 1897; Sept. 30, 1899.

10. See especially *Free Press,* Feb. 5, Feb. 12, April 2, Aug. 7, 1890; March 26, 1891; June 16, 1898; Feb. 2, 1899. *Argus,* July 26, 1890; July 24, July 31, 1897; Feb. 19, March 26, April 2, April 16, April 30, 1898; July 8, July 22, 1899. *Herald,* Sept. 9, 1897. McCloud, *Durango,* 99. Porter to Palmer, Oct. 29, 1892, in the William Bell Papers, Colorado Historical Society.

7

SCHOOL MARMS AND PRINTERS' DEVILS

I don't want to play in your yard,
If you won't be good to me.
— "I Don't Want to Play in Your Yard" (1894)

Numerous things influenced the lives of Sandwichites and Durangoans, but only two touched almost all of their lives—the schools and the newspapers. Lodges and clubs influenced many people, the churches perhaps more, but schools and newspapers, in one way or another, affected almost all on a weekly, if not a daily, basis.

Victorians agreed with the popular English philosopher Herbert Spencer, when he wrote, "Education has for its object the formation of character." They set about to see that their schools had just that object by stressing middle-class values and morality. Sandwich and Durango marched right in step with the times.

Their perception of the value of education steadily rose, the reputation of the schools improved, and taxpayers assumed a far greater burden than ever before to provide for education. Each of the two towns expanded its primary educational system in scope, size, and substance. Children spent an increasing amount of time in what evolved into a graded, eight-year system with a common course of study. By the 1890s, primary schooling for all youngsters constituted a matter of "right and practice." Public education emphasized order and efficiency in the classroom and regular attendance by the students, conditions and practices designed to train students for life. The system added years to both ends of schooling, in the form of kindergarten and high school, although most students did not attend either in the 1890s. Illinois and Colorado even toyed with compulsory-attendance laws, but objections quickly surfaced, particularly because of the need to have young men in the workforce. Women dominated the teaching profession, one of the few in which they achieved such success during this generation.[1]

Durango's and Sandwich's school systems looked like "two peas in the same pod" as Victorians loved to say. The only difference was that Durango had a Catholic school, St. Mary's Academy, while Sandwich offered nothing but public schools. Both towns followed the educational trends of the day, and, indeed, parents would have been hard pressed to notice much difference between the two educational systems had they transferred their children from one to the other. If Victorian America wished to have a general conformity in educational opportunity, then these two towns had reached the goal.

These were urban, graded schools, not the one-room, little red schoolhouses of the popular image. One-room rural schools existed in areas around both communities, but if the pupils in those schools wanted to go beyond eighth grade, they had to travel into town. There can be little doubt that, overall, urban scholars had better educational opportunities and easier access to their schools, but their rural contemporaries probably received more personal attention. Already, some complaints surfaced in both towns about overcrowded schools. This led to movements to build new schools. Both Sandwich and Durango voters approved of this plan, and new buildings appeared.

The buildings served as more than just educational institutions for the two communities; they became part of the physical image that visitors observed and noted about each town. An unidentified writer, whose letter was printed in the *Sandwich Free Press* on July 30, 1890, perfectly expressed awareness of that fact: "Our school buildings have long been a disgrace to the town and a matter of comment by all strangers who visit here."

By 1893, overcrowded conditions, poor schoolroom environment (including heating problems), and increasing cost of repairs on older buildings convinced the Sandwich school board that the time had arrived to plan for new buildings. The public concurred, and, in March 1894, the voters approved a proposal to build two school buildings. When the buildings were completed and opened in December 1894, at a cost of twenty-five thousand dollars, the *Sandwich Argus* (Dec. 29) displayed the headline, "Ornaments to the City of Which the People May Well Feel Proud."

The paper included drawings of these "most modern" stone-and-brick buildings. One of them, an eight-room structure, stood on the north side of town. The other, a six-room building, was on the south side. The north-side building included the high school, and the paper could hardly contain itself. These buildings would "be substantial ornaments to Sandwich on January 1, 1995, when we will have a population of 100,000 with trolley lines to our pleasant suburbs, Plano and Somonauk."

Durango built a stone-and-brick combination elementary and high school in 1892. The pleased school board announced that the "well ventilated and lighted" building would be "conducive to active brain work" (*Durango Great Southwest*, Feb. 22, 1893). An open house for the "handsome building," called Central School, in February 1893, provided an opportunity to encourage visitors to bring books or magazines to donate to the school's library. All would be welcome, however, whether they had "no book to give" or whether they "had a hundred." These three modern schools became jewels of civic pride, the apex of the local educational systems. The two in Sandwich were the only school buildings in town, but Durango had two other brick schools, Longfellow and Northside. Durango also added, in 1899, a "Mission School" in the south part of town, with one teacher, nineteen-year-old Jennie Martinez. St. Mary's Academy, the Catholic school, was the best known of Durango's educational institutions, with its excellent reputation "all over the western United States" in "music, drawing and painting" (McCloud, *Durango*, 59). A boarding school, St. Mary's was run by a staff of five Sisters of Mercy. Both communities could truly claim they were "cities of families and schools."

The two systems contained very close to the same number of students. For example, Durango had 583 students in 1892, and Sandwich had 575 in 1890. Public elementary schools were fine, but the high schools were what separated Sandwich, and especially Durango, from their less progressive neighbors. The opening of Durango's high school brought forth this comment in the *Durango Herald* (Jan. 25, 1893), which says much about the change in attitudes toward education: "The high school is to public schools the capstone and affords the opportunity to our young people of not alone securing a common school education, that higher training so necessary to success in this day and age."

During the 1890s, Americans witnessed a steady growth in the number of students going to high school. It should not be assumed, however, that more than a minority as yet took advantage of the opportunity. In 1893, fifty-seven students were enrolled in Sandwich's high school; in 1899, seventy-seven teenagers (fifty-eight girls and nineteen boys) attended Durango's. With no mandatory attendance requirements, with parents who probably had not gone beyond grade school themselves, and with jobs available for teenage boys, a high school education did not seem all that worthwhile to many adolescents.[2]

Still, to those in town who heartily supported education, the high schools placed their communities in a most dynamic position. Both schools predated the 1890s. Sandwich graduated its first class in 1884 (although, in some later years there was no graduating class), and Durango organized its high school in 1888. Graduation was the pinnacle of the school year for parents and students. Class colors and class mottoes needed to be chosen. (Sandwich's Class of 1890 chose for its motto, "Not for school but for life we learn." Durango's Class of 1892 chose the Latin "Certum pete finem" [Determined to make it to the finish].) A baccalaureate had to be planned, graduation addresses written, music arranged for (Sandwich's Mandolin Club made its first ever appearance in 1896, for example), and a speaker chosen. Then came the day itself. Sandwich seniors graduated at the Opera House. Durango, without such a suitable site, selected various buildings, including the Presbyterian church. Proud parents and friends crowded the auditorium to greet the "young ladies in cream and white silk gowns and the young gentlemen in black suits," who each "delivered an original oration," according to the *Great Southwest*'s description of a graduation on June 10, 1893. Occasionally, graduation addresses "shocked" some of the more traditional listeners. Two Sandwich sisters, Grace and Maude Coleman, took the occasion in their 1894 and 1897 speeches to proclaim and defend the "rights of women." One can almost hear the "Where is the present generation going?" comments echoing down the years.

Out the graduates marched into the world. Usually, there were more women among them than men. Sandwich superintendent William Woodbury told the 1897 graduating class, "This occasion marks an epoch in your life. This is your 'Commencement Day' not your finishing day" (*Argus*, June 26, 1897). The previous year's class had wrestled with that in their motto, "Our sails are set but where's the shore." Thus, "nine young ladies, veritable sweet girl graduates in their simple white gowns and carrying bouquets," and "three young gentlemen wearing the accustomed suits of black," set out on life (*Argus*, June 27, 1896).

SCHOOL MARMS AND PRINTERS' DEVILS

Toward the end of the decade, high school athletics, particularly football, started to gain more press attention. Occasionally, also, a high school column appeared in the newspaper, telling readers that the fourth-year literature class was studying *Silas Marner,* or that a new compound microscope had been purchased for the laboratory, or offering a tantalizing tidbit of school gossip.

Graduates of both high schools organized alumni associations. Durango's was active by 1892, and Sandwich's started four years later. The associations held social events, such as a "weird" Halloween "ghost party" in Durango in 1892, and more formal programs, like the one in Sandwich in 1897, that included a "sumptuous repast" followed by musical numbers, a talk on the history of the local schools, and "witty remarks" by Theodore Hammond, who had been principal of the high school a decade earlier. The associations afforded an opportunity to reminisce, gossip, renew old friendships, and simply have fun.[3]

Although the *Durango Herald* (Jan. 25, 1893) pridefully noted that the graduates of the local "accredited high school" were received without examination at state universities and colleges, it appears from the limited sources available that a larger number of Sandwich graduates continued on to higher education. Sandwich's papers reported the comings and goings of college students—including several who graduated from medical school—more frequently than did Durango's. Because colleges were located much closer to Sandwich than to Durango, and were more numerous in Illinois than in Colorado, such a difference should be expected. In addition, college glee clubs and other groups appeared quite often in Sandwich, usually with a Sandwich high school graduate proudly named; such events rarely occurred in Durango.

Although voters were sometimes scolded for not taking an interest in school-board elections and other educational matters, if the public perceived a school issue as warranting attention, that issue got attention. The need for new schools and the construction of new school buildings proved to be issues that received such scrutiny. Condensed school board minutes often appeared in the newspaper, so that interested parents and others could follow developments.

Isolated issues occasionally sparked heated discussion. One flash point was the topic of teachers, who always were measured against the highest expectations, even though they were not paid accordingly. We "are entitled to teachers of a high order of ability," asserted the *Sandwich Free Press* on April 15, 1897. The sentiment was echoed by many other Sandwichites and Durangoans. The paper went on to say that the town's teachers should be "men and women who are not only all right morally, but are mentally and physically qualified to inspire the young with high aims and noble aspirations." To get such individuals in 1899, Durango paid women teachers $70 a month and men teachers $103. In Sandwich two years before, men averaged $80 a month and women slightly over $48. The disparity between the two towns' systems at least partially reflected Durango's higher cost of living and wage scale, but both towns paid low salaries for what was expected of the teachers.

Even this salary scale seemed too high to some Sandwichites, who pressured the school board in 1897 to reduce salaries because of the "hard times." A committee established to study the issue reported, "We find that with the exception of the Grammar room and one or two cases in the lower grades, the teachers in surrounding cities are being paid higher salaries than teachers in the corresponding grades in our schools" (*Argus*, May 29). The committee opposed the reduction and concluded, "The present corps of teachers is, as we believe, one of the best, most faithful and industrious ever employed by this district." The board concurred, and no reduction occurred that year.

A breakdown of salaries in Sandwich in 1895 shows that Superintendent Woodbury received $1,000 a year. The rest of the educators received eight-month contracts: high school principal Harriet Ives earned $65 per month, Mary Graves of the grammar school $70, and the eight women who taught the primary and intermediate classes $45 each, with one exception, Lena Breed, who received $50. As was typical for the era, all the women who taught were unmarried. A woman in a "family way" might raise the wrong questions in the students' minds! Harriet Ives was one of several women who became principal of the high school; Alice Blanchard and Emma Bell also had served, but no women became superintendents in either Sandwich or Durango. Durango did not draw the line so tightly on marriage. Mrs. Sarah Scott Trew had been the first high school principal, and Mrs. Sarah Price served as principal of the Northside School in 1899. Among the nineteen women teachers in Durango's 1893–94 school year, five were married.

The public expected the teachers to "instruct and inspire" their young scholars, while keeping abreast of all current educational issues and trends. Teachers were also expected to attend teachers' institutes, or a normal institute, to listen to lectures on such topics as discipline, "character building in our public school," the necessity of teaching "patriotism in preparation for citizenship," and music in "our schools" (*Sandwich Free Press*, May 14, 1890). The Sandwich school board went so far, in 1897, as to "request [that] our teachers" attend some reliable normal school to study "advanced ideas" in education.[4]

Other concerns existed, however, beyond the teachers and their methods. Textbooks aroused ire. One letter writer asked why books "were exchanged" before the children learned their "full content" (*Sandwich Free Press*, Oct. 13, 1898). Other people worried that textbooks and schools "advertised" beer. This agitation came about when concerned readers noticed that a textbook, probably a geography book, commented that Milwaukee "is noted chiefly for its manufacture of beer," and Edinburgh, Scotland, "is famous for its production of beer." Even the textbook committee missed that one!

In 1893, Sandwich started its new term on Monday, January 2, which upset parents. Principal William Woodbury noted in his diary, "Attendance was poor. Many thought it ought to be a holiday and did not come. In a great many places schools did not open to-day." The children who did not come to the Sandwich schools thoroughly enjoyed the extra vacation, and Woodbury commented on January 3, that though more students came that day, "Pupils seem to have more of a desire to play than to work."

Some teachers and parents fretted about boys and cigarettes. One Sandwich teacher declared that a quarter of the boys were addicted to cigarettes, a dependence that "is uniformly injurious to mental and physical health" (*Argus*, March 13, 1897). The *Sandwich Free Press* (Dec. 7, 1893) worried about the number of boys not in school, boys who, consequently, were getting a "vicious street education." The editor blamed parents. "Home training," he felt, was lacking. Teachers, too, were troubled about their students' home life. How many parents encouraged their children "to be studious and ambitious"? "Does your child rehearse the shortcomings of the teacher oftener than information gathered in the school room?" (*Free Press*, Aug. 27, 1896) The teachers "earnestly desire," said Woodbury, who was now superintendent, the "hearty co-operation of every parent." Teach your children to "feel their first duty is to their school work," and, as a parent, visit school as much as possible.

Finally, that great issue of the day, the flag, emerged. The extreme patriotism and nationalism generated during the nineties, thanks to the GAR and other patriotic groups, caused a flag to be flown outside almost every school and inside school rooms. The *Sandwich Argus* supported the idea on September 13, 1890, and praised the Woman's Christian Temperance Union for presenting a new flag to the high school, which was "a constant reminder to the scholars proudly viewing it, of our great country and liberal government which fosters free education for the youth of the land." However, by 1899, the two Castles had second thoughts. An editorial blasted one of the "fool laws" requiring a flag to be placed in every schoolhouse (*Argus*, Nov. 4, 1899). Another "foolishly foolly" law demanded that no one use the national emblem in an advertisement or on a sign. That apparently got the Castles' goat. "But where is the harm if they do?" The Castles hoped such laws were a fad that "would soon wear out." Most of their readers probably no more agreed with them on this issue than they had on Free Silver and Bryan.[5]

Were the schools better in the 1890s than they had been years before? In 1896, Abraham T. VanScoy, who had been superintendent of Sandwich's schools in 1880–84, when the high school was established, congratulated the board on the construction of two new schools since then and on the increased "interest shown in school work." Durango was still too new to provide much of a comparison, though in equipment and buildings it had come a long way over the past decade.

Two men emerged as the outstanding educators in the two communities. Illinois-born, thirty-six-year-old William W. Woodbury became superintendent at Sandwich in 1894, after serving as principal of the grammar school. According to local legend, he had been brought to town initially to bring rowdy students into line. He did a good job of it, paddling and even throwing a few down stairs. He was, in one student's view, a real "bear" with a temper that occasionally got out of hand. Woodbury also taught, and like teachers before and since, agonized over his efforts. He wrote in his diary on January 10, 1893, "School teacher's confidence is like speculators stock, it fluctuates. Yesterday it seemed that I could not teach school. Nothing seemed to go right, a discouraging day. To-day, on the other hand, has been just the reverse. Things have passed off nicely, and a measure of confidence is restored." There can be no question that he did more than curb the rowdy students. Under his direction, the Sandwich school system became known as one of the strongest in De Kalb County. He insisted his teachers go to summer school, and did so himself. The *Argus* (April 25, 1896) showed Sandwich's appreciation for this man: "Prof. Woodbury is very popular . . . he has improved the schools, and proven a painstaking, careful and efficient Superintendent."

Thomas Baker served as superintendent of the Durango schools from 1888 to 1894, improving the system to the point where high school graduates did not need to take a special college examination. He instituted a thirty-eight-week school year and four high school grades. The school board was especially pleased that he took "great interest in the profession" and kept "abreast with educational advancement." Baker, born in Ohio in 1859, came to Durango in 1888. While busily working to improve the town's schools, he found time to complete his master's degree in 1892. When he resigned to teach at the University of Colorado, Baker received this tribute: "A gentleman who makes his aim to be courteous and at the same time have strict discipline among teachers as well as students." Baker laid the foundation on which the Durango school system would grow into the twentieth century.[6]

Baker and Woodbury each dominated his profession in his town, and so did David Day and Miles Castle, among newspaper editors and owners. There was no one else quite like Dave Day in either community. Civil War veteran, Medal of Honor winner for gallantry during the Vicksburg campaign, outspoken, fearless, egotistical, Day had been brought to Durango in 1892 from Ouray by Democrats to counter the Republican press. One of the sponsors reportedly exploded later about the eight hundred dollars it cost him. "Damn if I wouldn't give twice that amount to send him back." Day cajoled, badgered, and supported causes, at least those of which he approved, and attacked the causes and people he did not like with a biting, slashing, humorous pen. Dave represented personal journalism to the core. One of his more classic utterances came while he owned and edited Ouray's Solid Muldoon: "What is a Legislature? In Colorado it is a conglomeration of Rural and Metropolitan Asses elevated by Misguided Suffrage to positions intended by the Constitution for Brains, Honor and Manhood."

His great love was politics, and years later the story endured of how on election night, 1896, he sat on the corner of Ninth and Main with a big box of "good sized" firecrackers. Every time a report came in of a state's voting for Bryan he lit one, threw it as high in the air as he could, and yelled in a booming voice, "Bryan," which was followed by a loud bang that echoed down the block. Dave brought his Solid Muldoon from Ouray to Durango, but, in 1893, started the *Durango Democrat*. Although he spent three years during the decade as Southern Ute agent, Day dominated the Durango press. His columns sparkled with wit, news, and occasional practical jokes that still trip the unwary researcher. In the *Solid Muldoon* on December 29, 1893, for example, he wrote, "The police court is almost as quiet as a graveyard these days. The first thing we know the officers will pay some one to create a disturbance." As one person said of Day, "His paper was condemned by many, but was read by all."

Miles Castle, though far less flamboyant than Dave Day, equaled his impact. Castle, in fact, was much more of an entrepreneur and not solely a newspaper owner and editor. Born in Albany, New York, in 1826, he arrived in Sandwich thirty years later and opened a lumberyard. The year he arrived, he established the Sandwich Bank and, in 1878, founded the *Sandwich Argus*. Twice in the 1870s, Castle was elected a state senator, and he was hailed as "one of the foremost, enterprising and reliable representatives." All this sketched the portrait of a pioneering founding father who had become a mover and shaker and who "wielded wide influence."

Castle, however, deviated from the norm. His support of woman's suffrage and Free Silver showed an independent streak that Day would have admired. Looking back over forty years, Miles wrote in a May 16, 1896, editorial, "The three [the lumber business, the bank, and himself] are as healthy as is possible after forty years comradeship. [The *Sandwich Argus*] bears its years well. . . . It is a long business life showing what good habits, a clear conscience, and plenty of work will do for a young man. This may be deemed slightly egotistical, but can't we feel good once in a while especially as we appreciate and are thankful for our mercies?" Even the rival *Sandwich Free Press* praised Castle.[7]

Day and Castle, in their own ways, shaped their communities, Castle perhaps more so than Day. Dave remained an attention getter, Miles labored more behind the scenes over a longer period.

Both worked in a highly personal and evolving newspaper world. Sandwich, during the decade, had only two local papers, and they seemed to get along quite well, all considered, in the town's sedate, middle-class environment. Their competition came from two directions. Almost all the neighboring towns had papers, but a more serious challenge came from nearby large towns, particularly Chicago, whose latest edition arrived by train a little over an hour after hitting the streets. Durango's newspaper world furnished a complete contrast—there was little outside competition, but volatile town rivalries and cutthroat competition that killed off the weak and uninteresting.

> Durango merchants pay a royal price for stupidity when pensioning the Herald. The sheet is practically without circulation in the city. (*Democrat*, May 24, 1895)

> The fact is that since Mr. Day was imported from Ouray he has invariably been opposed to the public interest of this community whenever occasion offered. (*Herald*, Aug. 16, 1899)

During the 1890s, eight daily or weekly papers called Durango home; only three remained at the end of the decade. As the *Herald* observed on November 10, 1893, after the demise that year of the *Southwest*, Durango had to "improve considerably" for two daily papers to exist, when "one is all the people care for."

In Sandwich, Castle's longevity proved unusual even for that town. The *Free Press* changed owners five times, including three times within a six-month span. During that period, Sandwich had its only woman editor, Effie Marley, but, unfortunately, her husband's health mandated that they sell the paper in September 1892. The *Argus* hailed the Marleys for turning out an excellent paper. Irish immigrant William Deacon, who edited and owned the *Free Press* longer than anyone else (from 1892 to 1898), came down from Aurora with his wife Annie and two children. Following his retirement, he became what he described as a "capitalist." Somonauk-born Frank Lowman, who was characterized as "genial and public-spirited," purchased the paper from Deacon. The thirty-two-year-old Lowman, it was said, "got to know everybody," a good trait for an editor-owner in a small town. Each editor promised to be a "hustler who will get up a good paper" for the benefit of their town and its interests. Or as long-time western Colorado editor Frank Hartman wrote, "The *Tribune* will be what its utterances make it each week, refraining from apology, idle promise or retrospective fable. With malice to none and charity to all, it is my chief ambition to be just, even to my enemies" (May 18, 1891). Hartman, ably helped by his sister Lillian, had published several Durango newspapers but ran out of luck with the *Tribune*. It failed within a year.

The turbulence of Durango journalism reflected the town's Western youth; the older, more serene newspapers of Sandwich saw little need to bicker. Sandwich had reached its angle of repose with respect to its neighbors long ago. Durango still strove to dominate; therefore, its newspapers defended and praised their town and attacked, maligned, and generally thought little of Durango's neighbors, when they, in any way, threatened the "metropolis." And the Durango papers had calmed down, since the halcyon days of the early eighties.

Despite their transitory nature and turbulence, the two towns' newspapers were, like the schools and churches, looked upon as community assets. Booster Richard McCloud understood this when he wrote, "Durango is willing to be judged in the matter of enterprise and go aheadtiveness by its newspapers." The volatility of Durango's newspapers was not unusual. As a rule, newspapers came and went in new mining communities, and those that survived did not always turn out to be journalistic gold mines. In contrast, a settled agricultural town like Sandwich, offered journalists steady, if not spectacular, rewards.

In both towns, editors were always getting after tardy subscribers. Miles Castle spoke for all his fellow editors, when he requested on October 26, 1895, that delinquents pay up "so we can buy coal, potatoes, and a warm overcoat. You know we need these small amounts to make us happy so don't fail us." The papers of Sandwich and Durango consisted of four, six, or eight pages and carried local, national, and some world news. Both towns had daily and weekly editions. The Sandwich papers did a better job of reporting news from the surrounding towns, probably because the towns were nearby, and people went back and forth with great regularity. In so many ways, these papers were the heart and soul of their communities.[8]

Almost all had mastheads that boldly proclaimed what the paper stood for:

> Our Aim: To Fear God, Tell the Truth and Make Money.
> *Sandwich Free Press*

> MINING, SMELTING, MANUFACTURING, AGRICULTURE AND STOCK-GROWING.
> *Durango Herald*

> Orthodox in Religion and Independent in Politics.
> *Sandwich Argus*

With the Linotype replacing typesetting by hand and with faster presses, the newspaper business was changing in the nineties. The expansion of wire services and *boilerplate* (syndicated or copied material) started to limit the personal nature of the local papers even as they enabled the papers to provide broader news coverage. Sandwich and Durango newspapers reflected all of these changes and more. The papers that remained in 1899 had the ability, for example, to print photographs, something none could do in 1890.

The changing nature of the 1890s was no more clearly shown than in the schools and newspapers. Ten years had seen great transformations come about in each town. The nineties proved a watershed decade for more than just politics. Although the two communities could not have realized it, they both were well positioned for the twentieth century.

As the era's two wits, Mark Twain and the Irish sage Mr. Dooley (Finley Peter Dunne) observed:

> Soap and education are not as sudden as a massacre, but they are more deadly in the long run. (Twain)

> Th' newspaper does ivrything f'r us. It run th' polis foorce an' th' banks, commands th' milishy, conthrols th' ligislachure, baptizes th' young, marries th' foolsh, comforts th' afflicted, afflicts th' comfortable, buries th' dead an' roasts thim aftherward. (Dunne)[9]

NOTES

1. Alex Ayres (ed.), *The Wit & Wisdom of Mark Twain* (New York: Harper & Row, 1987), 66. Ira Katznelson and Margaret Weir, *Schooling for All* (New York: Basic Books, 1985), 59–60. Thomas J. Schlereth, *Victorian America* (New York: HarperCollins, 1991), 244–46. Richard J. Jensen, *Illinois* (New York: W. W. Norton & Co., 1978), 81. Lewis O. Saum, *The Popular Mood of America, 1860–1900* (Lincoln: University of Nebraska Press, 1990), 147–51.
2. *Sandwich Argus*, Oct. 21, Dec. 23, 1893; Jan. 13, Jan. 20, Feb. 17, March 24, Dec. 15, Dec. 29, 1894. *Sandwich Free Press*, Nov. 23, Dec. 7, 1893. *Durango Great Southwest*, Feb. 17, Feb. 22, Feb. 23, 1893. *Durango Herald*, Jan. 25, 1893. *Durango Weekly Tribune*, May 18, 1891. *Durango Uplift*, March 1899. Schlereth, *Victorian America*, 248. Richard McCloud, *Durango As It Is* (Durango: Durango Board of Trade, 1892), 58–60.
3. *Free Press*, June 4, June 25, 1890; June 10, 1892; May 21, 1894; July 2, 1896. *Great Southwest*, Oct. 25, 1892; June 10, 1893. *Argus*, June 27, July 4, 1896; June 12, June 19, June 26, 1897. *Herald*, Jan. 25, Sept. 26, 1893.
4. *Herald*, Jan. 25, 1893; Aug. 12, 1894; May 7, 1896. *Uplift*, March 1899. *Argus*, April 30, 1892; Nov. 14, 1896; March 13, May 29, July 6, 1897; Feb. 26, March 19, 1898. *Free Press*, April 23, May 14, July 16, 1890; Sept. 29, 1892; June 28, Aug. 16, 1894; April 15, April 22, April 29, 1897; April 13, April 20, 1899. Cecil M. McKinley, "A History of the Public Schools of Durango, Colorado" (master's thesis, University of New Mexico, 1944), 3, 4, 148–51.
5. *Free Press*, Feb. 5, 1890; Nov. 23, Dec. 7, 1893; Oct. 13, 1898. Stuart McConnell, *Glorious Contentment: The Grand Army of the Republic* (Chapel Hill: University of North Carolina Press, 1992). 230. *Argus*, Sept. 30, 1890; Jan. 13, Jan. 20, 1893; Aug. 22, 1896; March 13, 1897; Nov. 4, 1899.
6. Lewis M. Gross, *Past and Present of DeKalb County, Illinois* (Chicago: Pioneer Publishing Co., 1907), 1:163. *Argus*, May 19, 1894; June 29, 1895. Thomas O. Baker, *Thomas Orville Baker: An Autobiography* (n.p., about 1942), 1, 11, 34. McKinley, "Public Schools," 59–60, 127–28.
7. Helen M. Searcy, "Col. Dave Day," in *Pioneers of the San Juan Country* (Colorado Springs: Out West Printing, 1942), 1:76–81. *Durango Solid Muldoon*,

Dec. 29, 1893. Gross, *Past and Present*, 2:40–41. *Argus*, May 16, 1896. *Free Press*, Feb. 26, 1890.
8. *Durango Daily Tribune*, May 18, 1891. McCloud, *Durango*, 61. *Free Press*, Sept. 4, 1890; Sept. 29, 1892. *Argus*, May 7, June 11, 1892; Oct. 26, 1895; Feb. 19, 1898.
9. Ayres, *Wit & Wisdom*, 66. Justin Kaplan (ed.), *Familiar Quotations* (Boston: Little, Brown and Company, 1992), 603.

8

NO BETTER PLACE IN AMERICA TO LIVE

*While strolling through the park one day,
All in the merry month of May.*
—"While Strolling Through the Park One Day" (1884)

"Grow or die," that favorite axiom of nineteenth-century town boosters guided the movers and shakers of Sandwich and Durango. In the game of self-promotion, Durango came out the clear winner, although, because of the distance between the two towns, they obviously never competed against each other. Westerners had long been accustomed to promoting themselves and understood the need to "boom" their "city" against all rivals. Such promotion might be the best hope for a town's survival; Western town development often lived on promotion. In the boom-and-bust urban mining environment, it proved even more critical, because one never knew what tomorrow might bring.

Sandwich's urban world had long ago become circumscribed and settled. A certain security existed in knowing that agriculture and industry had been the foundation of the town's urban growth. Sandwich oozed confidence born of a generation of experience and a lifetime of examples. Yet there still remained room, and a need, for the town to promote itself against neighboring rivals, so that it could attract a few more residents, lure as many visitors as possible, and capture as much trade as the market would allow.

Durango raced ahead when it reenergized an idea of the early 1880s, the creation of a Board of Trade. Incorporated in April 1892, the board's membership read like a *Who's Who* of Durango leadership—Henry Strater, Alfred Camp, Ike Kruschke, Thomas Graden, and Ernest Amy, among others. As board member Richard McCloud wrote, "[The board] has for its members the live business and professional men of Durango and they do not intend to stop work until Durango has a population of 100,000" (McCloud, *Durango*, 55).

Durango and Sandwich did not plan to grow quietly. Both towns seemed enamored with the goal of a population of 100,000. McCloud might have gotten a little carried away with his idea of Durango's growth potential, but the three-point program drawn up at the board's first meeting, on April 23, 1892, championed such a goal. The three points were

1. Promote the general prosperity of all the varied interests of Colorado, especially Durango.
2. Procure, preserve and disseminate information in relation to Durango's commerce, finance, and industry.
3. Facilitate business intercourse.

After electing officers, organizing committees, and establishing dues, the Board of Trade raced into action. The board's plans were clearly indicated by the names of its committees—finance, commerce, railroad building, emigration, agriculture, mining, and the like. The board soon hit the usual snag of tardy monthly dues but plunged ahead.

The board's first achievement arrived almost instantly—McCloud's *Durango As It Is*, a promotional, booming pamphlet, if there ever was one, although it was well written and well documented. The board members worked to round up exhibits for the World's Fair in Chicago, to make Durango the transportation hub for the brief 1896 gold rush to Bluff, Utah, and to corral visitors going to Mesa Verde. They ordered maps and distributed a variety of information and publications during the decade. It worked with other, similar groups, including the Western Slope Congress, which issued its own boomer publication in 1893, before the depression ended its activities. The congress was followed by the San Juan Congress, but only the Board of Trade survived.[1]

Because of board initiative, or because of the initiative of others, Durango draped itself in a series of boomer catch phrases:

City of churches, noted for its beautiful residences, shade trees and well kept lawns. (1892)

La Plata is peerless and Durango is her pride. (1893)

> Other counties may have their towns and cities but no other has a Durango. (1893)
>
> The Denver of Southwestern Colorado. (1896)
>
> Smelter City of the Gold and Silver San Juan. (1897)
>
> There is no place like Colorado and Durango is the gem of the state. (1898)

The board proclaimed that Durango had become the home of mining men and of wealth. "When they reap the fortune that comes to all mining men who stick to it, they spend their money in Durango in such a way as to pay a handsome income" (McCloud, *Durango*, 18). While not all mining men who "stuck to it" made their fortunes, a few, including Charles Newman, did so and did settle in Durango.

Churches, homes, businesses, the "purest mountain water," a "clean, bright beautiful, and healthful" environment, broad streets, electricity, "modern fire apparatus"—Durango, in "all the essential requirements for a model city," lacked nothing (*Colorado State Business Directory*, 440). The board was not remiss in publicizing Durango's health benefits. The dry, clear air, "full of ozone," combined with sunshine nearly all the time, worked wonders for the ill and strengthened the healthy. Add to this, those miracles of nineteenth-century medicine, the hot springs at "its very doors," and Durango could hardly be surpassed as a health mecca.

Others picked up these themes, some writers virtually repeating them, and the beat went on. According to Colorado historian and author Frank Hall, Durango's "prospects for the future are in the highest degree favorable to a large and prosperous settlement." Otto Mears, San Juan builder of toll roads and railroads, claimed Durango was "the great commercial center of the southwest," soon to be Colorado's third largest city behind Denver and Pueblo. Finally, even foreigners caught the fever. The famous Baedeker guidebook, in its first U.S. edition in 1893, hailed Durango as a "progressive town of 2726 inhabitants, on the Rio de las Animas" and as "the commercial centre of S. W. Colorado."[2]

Local newspapers never missed an opportunity, either. Their lifeblood depended on continued growth. Special year-end editions commonly featured articles publicizing their town. For example, the *Morning Democrat,* on December 15, 1897, summarized Durango's attractions. Besides everything previously mentioned, the editor pointed out the schools, hospital, twelve doctors, hotels, newspapers, banks, twenty-six lawyers, telephones, and something that perhaps not everyone would have agreed should be mentioned, the brewery. Durango's cornucopia overflowed.

Sandwich exhibited nothing to compete with this onslaught. In 1890, locals organized the Sandwich Improvement Association, whose objectives sounded familiar: "Devising the ways and means for the furthering of the business interests of the city of Sandwich, the development or securing of new business enterprises, the securing of better transportation facilities." Editor Castle was suspicious. If this simply evolved into a "business men's association," that fastened projects on the city and raised expenses, he wanted none of it (*Sandwich Argus,* Aug. 16, 1890). "Gentlemen give us some industry" and add to our population, and "we will bless you." If, however, you only add "to our taxes we will swear at you—mildly." Something certainly happened, because the association disappeared.

Sandwich's best slogans appeared early in the decade, in 1891. There "is no better place in America to live," boosters proclaimed (*Sandwich Free Press,* Aug. 13, 1891). That might be a little sweeping, but they ran on the right promotional track. Two weeks later, back down to earth, they were promoting Sandwich as "the metropolis of DeKalb county" (*Free Press,* Sept. 3, 1891). Unfortunately, the idea got derailed somehow and did not become a theme the town built upon.

Beyond that, the Sandwich newspapers occasionally came up with tidbits boosting the town. On January 29, 1890, the *Free Press* said that traveling men had proclaimed Sandwich "one of the best towns in the state for its size and we guess they are about right." Other comments were that with "its well kept and graveled streets, made brilliant at night by numerous street lamps, our city will compare favorably with any place twice its size in the state"; that Sandwich is "one of the prettiest and best shaded places in the country"; and that "our live, wide-awake and progressive" businessmen are proof of local pride (*Free Press,* Aug. 13, 1891; Sept. 29, 1898). Sandwich nonetheless made only minor promotional efforts compared with Durango. Efforts focused mainly on nearby communities, such as Plano, Somonauk, Leland, and Hinckley, trying to convince their people to come and do business with, and find bargains in, the "saver of money" (*Free Press*, Sept. 29, 1898). Sandwich's leadership perhaps did not see any pressing long-term need to promote the town; more likely they felt their one triumph, the World's Fair, provided enough publicity.[3]

Tourism already had emerged as an important economic asset for Durango by the time the World's Fair called the country's attention to Mesa Verde and southwestern Colorado. By the decade's end, Durangoans were in the forefront of the struggle to make the cliff dwellings a national park. The tourism potential seemed unlimited, and Durango already challenged nearby Mancos as the gateway to Mesa Verde. Dave Day observed on May 26, 1892, that "Durango will undoubtedly be visited by several thousand strangers this year." Some would stay overnight, others for a "week or so to enjoy the salubrious climate." The local press suggested that Durangoans be polite to visitors, something that had not always been the case in earlier years.

Durango offered a variety of attractions for the tourist, including scenery, fishing, "ruins of the Aztecs," camping, hunting, and nearby hot and soda springs. Utes, Navajos, and Apaches who lived nearby traveled to town occasionally, much to the delight of visitors, although some of the tourists were scared of the Indians, having read too many dime novels or heard too many tales. Blasé locals passed the Indians, "without a look or sign of interest or curiosity" (*Durango Great Southwest*, Aug. 1, 1892). Nine miles north of town, Trimble Springs enticed visitors not only with waters "long known to possess prophylactic and therapeutic powers," but also with croquet, tennis, a race track, golf, archery, a baseball diamond, and a "1st-class resort" hotel that lacked "none of the modern conveniences" (Rohrabacher, *Great San Juan*, 32). A bicycle path ran from Durango to Trimble, and, from the D&RG tracks, a siding was built for those with private railroad cars.

People who wanted a longer adventure could take the circular "Rainbow Route," which started in Denver, went through Durango, Silverton, and Ouray, and then returned to Denver. People who took the route saw mountains and mining towns and even took an exciting stage-coach ride from Ironton down the Uncompahgre Canyon to Ouray. In this way, they could see the "old West" before it disappeared![4]

Sandwich had nothing to compare to this, but it did have one attraction that put it on the map, the Sandwich Fair. Durango had a fair, but it did not even rate as a pale imitation of Sandwich's. It did not take place annually or seem to be of much concern to the local people. The 1890s were the end of the golden age of fairs, and Sandwich thrived while Durango languished.

For Sandwich, the fair was the year's big event. Each year, the newspapers, getting in the spirit, advised readers to clean up their homes, their lawns, and the city. "Nothing gives a stranger a better opinion of a city than to see that everything is kept neat and clean" (*Free Press,* Aug. 18, 1898).

"Everybody come to the Fair," recommended the *Sandwich Free Press* on September 4, 1890, and many heeded the admonition, from small boys and girls to aged pioneers. Exhibits of cattle, hogs, flowers, paintings, plants, machinery, horses, ducks, and merchandise greeted the visitors. The midway, with its attractions, trotting races, and band concerts, entertained fairgoers, who could eat at either the dining hall or the lunch counter, which were run by the women of the Congregational and Methodist churches. "Big day at the Fair," Nellie Forsythe wrote on September 21, 1893. "Fed nearly 500 at dinner and such a rush." The next day, she noted that the fair was over and "the ladies fed something over 2,000 in all." She not only had waited on customers, but also baked for two days for the fair.

An estimated 28,000 people came to the fair during its four-day 1890 run. The whole community became involved. The Opera House offered shows throughout fair week and, more importantly for excited youngsters, schools closed part of the week.

Even in 1893, with competition from the World's Fair, the depression, and rainy days, the fair "panned out" in good form. The Sandwich Fair Association conducted the event each year and did a businesslike job, keeping the fair afloat while some in nearby towns folded. The association continued to improve upon the buildings and grounds until Sandwich had the "most commodious as well as most convenient and pleasantest fair ground in northern Illinois" (*Free Press,* May 21, 1891). The association policed the fairgrounds, as well, promptly shutting down "monte men" and watching "fakers" to be sure nothing illegal or immoral transpired on the midway. A motley crowd of "fakers" came like bears to honey, a condition that some people thought was the fair's "only unpleasant feature" (*Free Press,* Sept. 17, 1896). Eventually, Sandwich hired a Chicago detective to meet incoming trains and point out undesirables. Local police then gave them a choice of getting back on the train or going to jail!

"Sandwich is proud of her fair," crowed the *Free Press* on September 20, 1894, and the town should have been. As the years went by, special attractions highlighted a day or two of the event. In 1896, speakers for both the Republican and Democratic Parties presented their views, and Chicago's Clarence Darrow spoke on democracy. The Chicago Union nine came out to play a baseball game against a team from the town of Paw Paw on Friday. Fortunately, the players were greeted by sunshine rather than by the rain that had fallen earlier in the week. The tenth annual fair, in 1897, featured the "balloon lady," who flew in a hot-air balloon, in addition to the usual exhibits and events. Finally, in 1899, after more grounds improvements and the utilization of special days, such as children's day, and music that featured "our own superb musical organization the Union Band," the *Free Press* (Sept. 7) declared, "Barring the state fair at Springfield the Sandwich fair has long enjoyed the reputation of being the best in the state."[5]

For a brief, shining week every year in early September, Sandwich emerged as the place to be in northern Illinois. The fair provided a showcase for local agriculture and for the town and its industries and businesses. Old-timers came to visit friends, and former Sandwichites returned to renew acquaintances. In this gathering of town and country people could be seen the best of the Victorian Era. In the beautiful wooded grounds, fond memories were created. People would not forget their days at the fair.

Durango, meanwhile, gained a moment of national attention in 1899 with the "Ute Rush." After years of demands by locals that "the Utes must go," and that their land be opened to white settlement, the government finally acted, and Ute land south of town was thrown open to homesteading, starting at high noon on May 4, 1899. Not only did locals believe that whites could better use the land, they also feared "that the close proximity of the reservation to Durango has heretofore kept away capital" (McCloud, *Durango*, 99).

Sensing a profitable windfall, the Denver & Rio Grande Railroad, which ran right through the Ute Strip, vigorously promoted the opening of the land. According to The Fertile Lands of Colorado, a work published by the railroad in 1899, "It is the last chance for cheap, fertile and enviable homes." The opening, it was said, "cannot fail to attract a large and desirable class of settlers" (*Rocky Mountain News* [Denver], Feb. 17, 1899). Dave Day called support of the opening "one of the most important movements ever known in Southern Colorado." *The Sandwich Free Press* (April 20, 1899) even chimed in, the only time Durango was ever mentioned in a Sandwich paper. The well-watered and fertile land, the article said, had a most inviting climate and would be one of "the last Indian reservations thrown open." It seems, however, that nobody from Sandwich bothered to race to Durango.

Amid blasting smelter whistles and ringing bells, the rushers stampeded for the promised land. Unfortunately, all the hoopla failed to generate another Oklahoma Land Rush. People did move in and file claims, but they would find out that filing a homestead claim was much easier than making the required improvements on the land. Water, despite promises to the contrary, remained scarce as "hens teeth," and transportation in areas away from the railroad was difficult and time consuming. Durangoans made money from the rushers, and a few Durangoans filed claims, only to find out that they had to live on the land for part of the year. Most of them preferred Durango and forfeited their rights.

It had been a grand promotional episode for Durango, one unequaled during the nineties. If the result failed to match expectations, so be it; Durango's name had reached the far corners of the United States, including towns like Sandwich.[6]

Sandwich people may not have rushed to the Ute land, but they were steadily moving elsewhere. Chicago, with its higher-paying, more numerous jobs and "bright lights," attracted young women and men. The big city was "persistently absorbing the brightest and best minds," bemoaned the *Free Press* on June 7, 1894. Chicago, with thirty-five percent of Illinois's population and unequaled wealth and political power, towered over the rest of the state. Newer Durango offered more opportunities and lost fewer people to Denver, which could not be reached as easily as Chicago could from Sandwich.

Farmers from the Sandwich area migrated to Iowa, Kansas, Nebraska, and the Dakotas, some buying prairie land and others renting. A few people moved to Colorado, some of them going for a "health cure." It was easy to do, because the Burlington Railroad had reached Denver in 1882. A former Sandwich resident, Denverite Eden Hills, went so far as to defend the West against some old accusations in a letter he wrote to the *Sandwich Argus*. Published April 11, 1896, the letter said that Westerners were neither lawless, nor illiterate, nor morally bankrupt. Hills, who by now had become a Western advocate, charged that, in truth, these were problems of the East.

Cripple Creek tried to persuade Sandwich investors to buy gold stocks, but no Durango advertisement ever appeared in Sandwich. Not just Colorado beckoned; the warm climate of California attracted both Sandwich and Durango folks for winter sojourns, and some moved there. After residing twenty-three years in Sandwich, for example, Mr. and Mrs. Daniel Sweeney and eleven of their fourteen children left for the golden shores. The *Sandwich Free Press* (April 9, 1896) bid them a fond farewell and hoped they found "fine prosperity and pleasant surroundings." It did not work out, however; by 1900 the Sweeneys were back.[7]

There was nothing unusual in the departure of some of the towns' residents. Many rural Americans were migrating to nearby villages and from there to larger towns. That trend had been established decades before. Chicago's proximity to Sandwich accelerated the drift toward the large city, and cheaper Western land lured farmers in search of new opportunities.

Sandwich and Durango did promote themselves as well as they could. Durango understandably had more success, but Sandwich's fair, at least, gave that community a yearly event that captured outside press attention and attracted tourists. One of the two significant reasons Durango would forge ahead of Sandwich in the next century, however, was Durango's promotion of the variety of attractions and resources it offered. Durango's future appeared unlimited; Sandwich found little maneuverability for anything beyond its fair.

NOTES

1. Durango Board of Trade Minutes, 1892. Richard McCloud, *Durango As It Is* (Durango: Durango Board of Trade, 1892), 26, 54, 101–02. *Durango Great Southwest*, Oct. 27, Nov. 15, Nov. 17, Nov. 18, Nov. 19, 1892; Jan. 3, 1896. *Durango Herald*, March 3, March 12, 1896.
2. *Western Colorado* (Grand Junction, Colo.: *Grand Junction News*, 1893), 61, 65. *The Gold Fields of Colorado* (Denver: Denver & Rio Grande, 1896), 36–37. *Herald*, April 16, 1898. *Durango Morning Democrat*, Dec. 15, 1897. John G. Canfield, *Mines and Mining Men of Colorado* (Denver: Carson, Hurst & Harper, 1893), 77–78. McCloud, *Durango*, 9–10, 16–18, 92–93. *Colorado State Business Directory* (Denver: Gazetteer Publishing Co., 1897), 440. Frank Hall, *History of the State of Colorado* (Chicago: Blakely Printing Company, 1895), 4:179–80. Karl Baedeker (ed.), *The United States With an Excursion Into Mexico* (New York: Da Capo Press, 1973 reprint), 419.
3. *Sandwich Free Press*, Jan. 29, Aug. 14, 1890; Aug. 13, Sept. 3, 1891; Aug. 18, Sept. 29, 1898. *Sandwich Argus*, Aug. 16, 1890; March 28, May 23, 1896.
4. *A Week at the Fair* (Chicago: Rand, McNally & Co., 1893), 102–05. *Durango Solid Muldoon*, May 26, 1892. McCloud, *Durango*, 30–32, 53, 58. R. Copeland Rohrabacher, *The Great San Juan of Colorado and New Mexico* (Durango: Durango Democrat, 1901), 32. *Durango Weekly Tribune*, June 1, 1891. *Herald*, Oct. 17, 1894. *Great Southwest*, Aug. 1, 1892.
5. Allan G. Bogue, *From Prairie to Corn Belt* (Chicago: University of Chicago Press, 1963), 205–06. *Herald*, Oct. 19, 1899. Earlier fairs had been canceled after the buildings at Trimble Springs burned down. Nellie Forsythe diary, Sept. 19–22, 1893, Regional History Center, Northern Illinois University. *Free Press*, Sept. 4, Sept. 11, Sept. 15, 1890; May 21, Sept. 10, Sept. 24, Nov. 14, 1891; June 22, 1893; Sept. 6, Sept. 13, Sept. 20, 1894; Sept. 17, 1896; Sept. 16, Sept. 23, Oct. 7, 1897; Aug. 18, 1898; Sept. 7, 1899. *Argus*, Sept. 13, Sept. 20, 1890; Sept. 9, Sept. 23, 1893; Nov. 16, 1895; Sept. 12, Sept. 19, 1896.
6. Sources on the Ute question are numerous. See, for example, the following items: *Herald*, April 11, 1890; Jan. 1, 1895; May 4, 1899. *Great Southwest*, Nov.

10, 1893. McCloud, *Durango*, 99. *Durango Democrat*, Jan. 30, 1897. *Rocky Mountain News* (Denver), Feb. 17, 1899. *The Fertile Lands of Colorado* (Denver: Denver & Rio Grande, 1899), 4, 53–54. *Denver Times*, May 4, 1899. *Free Press*, April 20, 1899.

7. The *Argus* and *Free Press,* in the 1890s, both made numerous comments about people leaving. See especially *Argus,* Nov. 14, 1891; May 4, 1895. *Free Press,* June 7, 1894; April 9, 1896. John H. Keiser, *Building for the Centuries* (Urbana: University of Illinois Press, 1977), 323.

Photographic Essay

THE PEOPLE

"My name is Sherlock Holmes. It is my business to know what other people don't know," the perspicacious detective observed. His adventures gained great popularity among Sandwich and Durango readers in the 1890s. Historians do the same kind of work Mr. Holmes did. Even if we do not always solve the mystery, we work to uncover who did it, when, and why.

Facts can only take the inquirer so far. It is always revealing to see people captured in a moment of time by photographers whom they probably knew as neighbors and friends. What follows is a glance into the 1890s, at those Sandwichites and Durangoans whose story is told in this book. Maybe the reader, like Mark Twain, will come to say, "I know all those people. I have friendly, social, and criminal relations with the whole lot of them."

Study these photographs with an open mind, because they have much to reveal. Sample them as primary source material, interrogate them for what they have to say. Savor the people and their era, and ponder what you see; be your own Sherlock Holmes. Follow Mr. Holmes's advice: "Come, Watson, come! The game is afoot." Turn the page; the game—the people and their activities—follow.

A TALE OF TWO TOWNS

The boys are enjoying themselves gambling, drinking, reading, and simply talking in Durango's El Moro Saloon. Poker and faro are the card games being played. On the board to the right are listed the results of a city election. (Courtesy Center of Southwest Studies)

Sandwichite John Mitten earnestly makes a point to John Woodward on a summer's day. Possible topics of conversation include politics, the weather, and crops. (Courtesy Sandwich Township Library)

Two winter scenes. The top photo shows Sandwich's South Main Street on a snowy day, with blanketed horses awaiting their drivers. Sleighs provided the easiest means of transportation over wintry Illinois roads. In the bottom photo, busy delivery wagons crowd Durango's East Fifth Avenue. Most stores provided delivery service. (Courtesy Gary Moss; La Plata County Historical Society)

A TALE OF TWO TOWNS

Sunday at the Baptist Church in Sandwich, 1896. "The flower decorations were beautiful," wrote the *Sandwich Argus*. Rev. Joseph Dent stands behind the altar. (Courtesy Gary Moss)

Sandwich's Union Band relaxes at Oak Ridge Cemetery on Memorial Day, surrounded by some adoring young fans. Both communities celebrated this day with parades, speeches, and respectful tribute to Civil War veterans. (Courtesy Gary Moss)

PHOTOGRAPHIC ESSAY: THE PEOPLE

The Durango Wheel Club pauses during the Labor Day parade. The Strater Hotel, Durango's finest, looms in the background on the right. A cyclist dressed as Uncle Sam can be seen in the foreground, and the women are genteelly attired in long skirts and high button shoes. (Courtesy Strater Hotel)

The Sandwich Fair was ten years old in 1897, the year this picture was taken. The Floral Hall, *center*, beckons fairgoers with a variety of exhibits. The *Sandwich Free Press* complained that the midway, seen in the background, was "filled with fakirs." (Courtesy Gary Moss)

Sandwich picnickers at the Old Settlers Union Picnic enjoy the fairgrounds in 1899. They passed the time with good food, reminiscing, and speeches about times long gone. Women were seldom found in public without a hat. (Courtesy Gary Moss)

Durango's coal mines served all of southwestern Colorado. The miners worked long hours under extremely dirty and dangerous conditions. Note the lack of safety equipment and the ethnicity of the crew. (Courtesy Center of Southwest Studies)

PHOTOGRAPHIC ESSAY: THE PEOPLE

The "lunch bucket brigade" kept both communities going. Part of the workforce of the Sandwich Manufacturing Company (top photo) and of Durango's smelter (bottom photo) momentarily pose, rather somberly, before resuming the day's tasks. (Courtesy Gary Moss; La Plata County Historical Society)

Sandwich celebrates the Fourth of July, 1897, with a parade featuring decorated carriages and floats on wagons. The Marcy Block can be seen in the background. Many women and men stand shaded by their umbrellas along flag-lined Railroad Street. (Courtesy Gary Moss)

"Remember the Maine, to Hell with Spain." A float stops in front of George Goodman's store in Durango, while two nattily dressed young ladies stand at attention. (Courtesy Goodman family)

PHOTOGRAPHIC ESSAY: THE PEOPLE

Sandwich's firemen, schoolchildren, the GAR, and the Union Band marched in this 1898 Memorial Day parade. The city council, riding in carriages, just missed getting their picture taken. The parade is passing through the heart of the business district. (Courtesy Gary Moss)

School activities usually included a play sometime during the year. These rather serious Sandwich youngsters are all dressed up for the occasion in perfect imitations of adult attire. (Courtesy Gary Moss)

A TALE OF TWO TOWNS

William Woodbury, *left background,* and students at the Sandwich Grammar School in 1892. Parents saw to it that they clothed their children properly for the occasion. The building in the background was torn down and replaced in 1894 by what the *Sandwich Argus* called an "Elegant Structure." (Courtesy Gary Moss)

Warmly dressed ice-skaters stop for a portrait before returning to a flooded Sandwich park between the Burlington tracks and Railroad Street. The Opera House looms in the background. (Courtesy Gary Moss)

PHOTOGRAPHIC ESSAY: THE PEOPLE

The freight office of Sandwich's train depot was quiet on this day. Sandwich, however, was an important stop on the Burlington line. (Courtesy Gary Moss)

Some of the members of the Sandwich Camp #147 of the Modern Woodmen of America in 1893. The organization had 150 members four years later. This beneficent society accepted only "low-risk" members, barring, among others, miners, baseball players, and saloon keepers. (Courtesy Gary Moss)

A TALE OF TWO TOWNS

White dresses were the fashion for the summer meeting of the Durango Reading Club (top photo). White dresses with high collars seem to have been an 1890s favorite. On another occasion (bottom photo), the members appear quite formal for their Washington's Birthday party. The children seem less serious. (Courtesy Durango Reading Club)

PHOTOGRAPHIC ESSAY: THE PEOPLE

Families were the backbone of both communities. In the top photo, Estelle Camp, *center*, holds an elegant dinner party, while her husband, Durango banker Alfred Camp, *left*, peers at the camera. The bottom photo shows Agnes and William Smith of Sandwich—and their family—in a formal portrait in 1896. (Courtesy of the author)

Proud mother Hattie Gonner and son Henry stand in front of their Durango home. Her husband, Frank, took many of the Durango photographs found on these pages. (Courtesy La Plata County Historical Society)

One of Sandwich's prosperous young farmers, Bert Bark, is shown here with family and friends. When he threshed thirteen acres of rye in June 1896, the *Sandwich Argus* maintained it was the first time the "song of the thresher" had been heard that early. (Courtesy of the author)

PHOTOGRAPHIC ESSAY: THE PEOPLE

The rush to the Ute Strip is over for these folks, as they wait to register their homesteads on May 4, 1899. In the years ahead, both women and men found life hard on their homesteads. (Courtesy of the author)

Marriage and children constituted the ideal for Victorian women. These members of a Durango middle-class family seem well fed and contented. Plumpness was a sign of health and wealth. (Courtesy La Plata County Historical Society)

Church and school were two of the pillars of Victorian America. In 1899, the Methodist Sunday School Orchestra (top photo) added a local flavor to Sandwich's cultural life. Proud graduates of Durango High School's class of 1892 (bottom photo) had—at least to this point—lived up to their motto "Certum pete finem" (Determined to make it to the finish). (Courtesy Gary Moss; Jack Wigglesworth)

PHOTOGRAPHIC ESSAY: THE PEOPLE

Durango and Sandwich families had to create much of their own entertainment. However, dressing as formally as these Durangoans only to blow soap bubbles does seem a bit unusual. What might have been in those flasks? (Courtesy La Plata County Historical Society)

Fishermen of all ages understood the joy of Izaak Walton when he said, "I have laid aside business, and gone a-fishing." It was possible to go fishing right in Durango or at nearby lakes. The boys of Sandwich could fish very near their town. (Courtesy La Plata County Historical Society)

The Sandwich Opera House hosted a variety of functions, including the senior class play. Durango, much to its chagrin, never gained a real opera house. (Courtesy Gary Moss)

9

OLD-TIME RELIGION

In the sweet by and by.
We shall meet on that beautiful shore.
—"In the Sweet By and By" (1898)

The perennial Sunday school and gospel favorite "The Little Brown Church in the Vale" caught the religious emotion of the day, plus a longing for the earlier, "simpler" life it glorified. The 1890s generation sang it with enthusiasm:

> There's a church in the valley by
> the wildwood,
> No lovelier place in the dale;
> No spot is so dear to my childhood
> As the little brown church in the vale.

Durangoans and Sandwichites were caught in a changing world where the "Rock of Ages" seemed like something worth holding onto in both this world and the next. Only change proved constant, change that could cause worry, stress, and growing uneasiness. The answer was the church.

Victorians typically were a churchgoing people, or were at least nominally associated with some denomination. Their attitudes toward religion, however, were changing. The majority still embraced their religion seriously, but more separation had emerged between their private lives and their religious lives than their grandparents might have condoned. Temptations lurked everywhere, seductively beckoning. Evangelist Billy Sunday understood this, when he said, "The church gives the people what they need; the theater gives them what they want."

Some concerned people believed that the United States was moving from "sacred to profane." The church's role in the community was evolving, more noticeably in Durango than in Sandwich; much more was transpiring "outside the temple." At least, in part, this reflected women's changing roles in the two communities and within the workplace.

During the previous ten years, Durango's churches had witnessed a noticeable evolution of their role in the community, something that Sandwich's churches had gone through several decades earlier. The appearance of churches in Durango had provided a strong indication to doubters that the town was "civilized" and emerging as a typical American community. Durango boasted of being the town of "churches and homes," and, as Richard McCloud wrote as late as 1892, "Durango is known as the City of Churches in the state of Colorado" (McCloud, *Durango*, 56). Therefore, church activities were well covered in the local press. In the 1880s, Protestant churches had been the principal social outlet for Durango families. These churches had provided a rest from the materialistic world and served as the main organizational base from which women could exercise leadership and have an impact on the larger community. The Catholic church provided a school and hospital, and it and the other churches offered a meeting place for like-minded people.

In the nineties, Durango no longer needed to publicize its churches as much, so church notices grew more routine and were relegated to the newspapers' "back burner." Whereas the churches formerly reached out and firmly held the entire community, influencing people well beyond their individual congregations, they now looked inward. Other family social outlets emerged in Durango—more lodges and groups competed for individuals' time, and women gained the right to vote, thus making it possible for them to become much more active outside the church. In both the 1880s and 1890s, the churches had to compete with establishments that had arrived at the same time the ministers and priests did—saloons, gambling halls, and houses of prostitution. Also, Sunday was one of the busiest business days of the week and a wide-open entertainment day.

Sandwich and its churches had evolved more slowly and in a more settled, middle-class, agrarian environment. Sunday remained the Lord's day, even if observing a day of rest did not always mean going to church. By the nineties, the churches fit comfortably into a long-established community routine. Women were still the backbone of the congregations and could find more leadership and governance opportunities within church walls than outside them. Even the threat of "Darwinism and evolution" failed to shake the pews or pulpit. Indeed, this "heresy" seemed to make little outward impact on either community. That "old-time religion" endured and was good enough for most churchgoers. They continued attending the "old church," as their parents and grandparents had done before. If any of those earlier generations had returned to check on their descendants, they would have felt at home in the church, if not everywhere else in town.

This is not to imply that religion did not continue to have a major impact on Sandwich and Durango; it did. One only has to look at those popular turn-of-the-century town histories that featured biographies of the respected middle class to see how many listed their church affiliation. That might be expected, considering their inclinations and the times, but newspaper accounts of meetings in the homes of hostesses for church functions showed an activism that went beyond mere "golden gate insurance."

The church additionally provided one of the bastions of nationalism. Christianity became especially important in the United States during the excitement over "manifest destiny," which was more popularly known as the White Man's Burden. This was reflected in some local efforts, including those to raise funds for foreign missions through women's missionary societies. Most of the congregations' efforts, however, focused on local needs.[1]

"In" churches existed in both towns; it seemed important for some people to be a member of the right church. The newspapers' listing of Sunday services always included those of the mainline Protestant churches and less often those of the fringe or fundamental denominations. The same may be said with regard to coverage of meetings, sociables, and special celebrations. The churches might have traveled far from the path that Jesus took, yet each in its own way worked to improve the present and "to meet on that beautiful shore."

The nineties furnished an interesting range of religious styles: from emotional to serene services, from conservative to liberal theologies, and from "hell fire and damnation" preachers to soft-spoken pastors. Ministers in their churches and evangelists on the "sawdust trail" worked to bring their listeners "right with God." Into this world ran former baseball player William A. Sunday. Sunday was an ex–Chicago White Stocking, who still holds the major league record for most times struck out in his first game (four), and who said he struck out his first thirteen times at bat. The speedy, good-fielding, weak-hitting Sunday overcame that start to play for eight years in the majors. Now, he stood equally determined to strike out the devil, who had a head start in Sunday's new league! "I am in favor of everything the devil is against, and I am against everything the devil is in favor of—the dance, the booze, the brewery, all friends that have cards in their homes."

On July 10, 1897, after Sunday made a whirlwind visit to Sandwich, *Sandwich Argus* editor Miles Castle observed, "Mr. Sunday is unique in his presentation of gospel truths, making them forcible and convincing." During his visit, Billy Sunday spent a typically busy weekend in Sandwich, speaking Friday night at a YMCA meeting, Sunday morning at the Congregational church, Sunday afternoon at a meeting for "men only," and Sunday evening at a union service at City Hall.

Sandwich heard Billy Sunday at his fundamental, evangelistic best, when he was fighting demon rum, the devil, ministers with whom he did not agree, and other assorted evils. Sophistication was not his strong suit:

> Some sermons instead of being a bugle call for service are nothing more than showers of spiritual cocaine.
>
> The devil isn't anybody's fool. You can bank on that. Plenty of folks will tell you there isn't any devil . . . People who say that—and especially all the time-serving hypocritical ministers who say it—are liars. They are calling the Holy Bible a lie. I'll believe the Bible before I'll believe a lot of time-serving, society-fied, tea-drinking, smirking preachers.

Sunday never missed a chance to deliver a blow against the saloon, and his zest for prohibition could hardly be matched, nor could his hatred for the twin sins of dancing and card playing. "I believe that cards and dancing are doing more to damn the spiritual life of the Church than the grog-shops—though you can't accuse me of being a friend of that stinking, dirty, rotten, hell-soaked business."

More evangelists visited Sandwich than Durango; not, however, because they believed more sinners lived there. Ease of access guided their considerations. Sandwich sat astride the CB&Q main line, and many neighboring communities could be visited in one swing. In this sense, Sandwich was unlike Durango and Silverton, which sat at the end of a long train ride.

The railroad actually helped the evangelists by providing special rates, as it did to a Plano "camp meeting," charging only eighteen cents round-trip from Sandwich (*Sandwich Free Press*, Feb. 18, 1897). The "earnest and powerful" London evangelists, Rev. and Mrs. Edwin Baker and their song leader, Professor W. L. Anderson, held a revival in 1897 at the Baptist church in Sandwich. Lasting over two weeks, it consisted of regular services and special programs for men and women, including "Some things that every man and every boy over twelve should know" (*Argus*, Feb. 20, 1897). Boys "under 14" would not be admitted—there must have been a last-minute revelation that boys of thirteen would find the material too vivid! Mrs. Baker preached to the women, and Anderson's songs "encouraged many to lead a christian life." In the end, the town "bid them God-speed in their good work" and counted thirty-six conversions (*Argus*, March 6, 1897).

Sandwich also was carried away by the November 1897 appearance of the dynamic, stylishly dressed evangelist Milan B. Williams. According to the *Free Press* (Nov. 25), "Gattlin guns, powder magazines and dynamite bombs describe him better than common every-day talk." When no building proved large enough to hold the crowds, "a large force of men" built a tabernacle in twenty-two hours! A month-long revival ensued with testimonials, conversions, songs, and prayers, and the *Sandwich Free Press* asserted, "This preaching and singing is making our town better." Williams, joined by singer Charles Alexander and converted "bronco rider" Fred Deibert, swayed local religious emotions. After they left town, Grace Saxe of the Moody Bible Institute arrived and organized "home gospel meetings" (*Free Press*, Dec. 16, 1897). Williams, like Sunday, railed against saloons and urged church members to "vote as Jesus Christ directs." Within a year, saloons were gone, but backsliding among the converted failed to elicit any comment. Williams came back in March 1898 and, according to the *Argus* (March 26), gave a rousing temperance lecture that "can only be described as great." The visit of Billy Sunday, and especially that of Williams, provided a major prohibition push, resulting in the 1898 victory.

Ministers from local or nearby churches conducted other revival services. In January 1893, Southern Methodist John Major opened a revival at the Durango Presbyterian church with "a good crowd present and good music." The Sandwich Methodists carried on a several-week-long revival in December 1893, with Plano and Aurora preachers and their own minister, the hardworking and cheerful Horace K. Vernon, who preached one Sunday evening on "Your sin will find you out."[2]

The emotional surge of evangelism did not replace the organized church, nor did it have as lasting an impact. Billy Sunday drew attention, yet it was the work of the regular ministers, day in and day out, that made the difference. The mainline Protestant churches prevailed, the strongest denominations in both towns exhibiting state and national patterns.

Methodist (then known as Methodist Episcopal), Baptist, Presbyterian, and Congregational churches ranked in that order in Illinois, and all were influential in Sandwich. Durango had both Northern and Southern Methodist churches, but no Congregational church. The slavery issue had split the Methodists before the Civil War. The Episcopalians and Catholics were strong in Durango but not in Sandwich. In Durango and in Sancwich, impressive stone-and-brick edifices told all who saw them of the prominence of those denominations. Sandwich also had small Lutheran, Methodist Episcopal German, Universalist, and German Evangelical congregations. Their frame buildings often reminded visitors of New England churches.

Small churches faced difficult times. The Southern Methodists, for example, could only survive by having their minister ride a circuit. In 1892, the busy Rev. Oscar Sensabaugh preached at six stops in addition to his home Durango church. He visited each of the six stops, on what was called the Pine River Circuit, several times a month. Still, he found time to help edit the *San Juan Methodist* and perform all his pastoral duties throughout the circuit. Sensabaugh not only included church items in the paper—

> Mrs. Durnell has kindly consented to sing occasionally for us. Lovers of good music will be delighted to hear her sing, and that quite often.
>
> The social at the parsonage was a success. Notwithstanding the threatened storm, about eighty persons were present and all seemed to have a good time. The inmates of the parsonage certainly did.

—but he could also tweak the county officials if he thought they needed it:

> The ditch crossings from Animas City to Trimble Springs are horrible. The road commissioner should be stirred up a little.[3]

While mainline Protestant churches may have seized most of the attention and proved more active throughout the decade, the Catholics in Durango and the Mormons in Sandwich held their own. The middle-class, white, Protestant, Anglo-Saxon worlds of Sandwich and Durango held conflicting views of these two denominations.

The fact that the Reorganized Church of Jesus Christ of Latter Day Saints had a congregation in Sandwich, while no Mormon congregation took root in Durango, might seem surprising. Durango sat next door to Utah and strong Mormon settlements, but the nearest ward was in Mancos, with a branch at Kline in rural Red Mesa. Mormons who moved up the La Plata River founded the latter. Mormon missionaries canvassed Durango, but without enough success, apparently, to warrant further efforts.

Sandwich, on the other hand, since the 1870s, had contained an active Mormon membership and a Mormon building, thanks to land donated by Israel Rogers, a prosperous local farmer and the first bishop of the Reorganized Church. In 1859, Rogers's grain barn had been the site of the church conference. Neighboring Plano served as regional headquarters for the Reorganized Church from the mid-1860s to 1881. There the leadership published its newspaper, the *Herald,* and other "books and tracts." This prominence did not guarantee either understanding or acceptance. The Sandwich newspapers treated the Mormons with respect but generally ignored their activities.

The local press did not understand the Mormons very well and had a hard time separating the Utah Mormons from the Reorganized Church. Yet the press could be sympathetic. When the "Ladies of the LDS" gave their first community supper in 1897, they felt "somewhat at a loss as to what the harvest might be" (*Argus,* March 6, 1897). It "proved to exceed their utmost expectations," which seemed to please the reporter. The Mormons' church notices never appeared with the others, and they received only occasional comment in the newspapers' local columns. Mormons in Sandwich seemed definitely to have been on the outside looking in for most of the decade. As the *Sandwich Argus* stated on March 10, 1894, during a week of special services, it hoped "that our own will lay aside all prejudice and hear them patiently."[4]

Despite the fact that Catholics represented the second largest denomination in De Kalb County, behind the Methodists, they never settled in Sandwich in numbers large enough to organize their own church. Regardless of that, trouble surfaced. Miles Castle lashed out against apparent anti-Catholic bigotry: "We are sorry to find a church war in Sandwich, even if it be a small one" (*Argus*, April 21, 1894). He had heard that a "young lady" was refused a position in the Sandwich school system, because she was a Catholic. He saw no reason a Catholic should be excluded any more than a "Methodist or Presbyterian."

Durangoans seemingly accepted northern European Catholics without bias. Those Catholics lived north of Sixth Street and generally came from middle-class families with varied economic backgrounds. Their St. Columba Church sat across the river and thus not on the church street, the Boulevard. Catholics living at the south end of town were not so well treated. They were eastern Europeans and Hispanics with working-class backgrounds. They worked mostly in the smelter and coal mines and were not always welcomed, which reflected racial prejudice as much as it did religious bigotry. These Catholics had their own church, Sacred Heart, which stood at Durango's far southern end.

St. Columba Church in north Durango served as the center of the local Catholic complex, which included Mercy Hospital, a convent, and St. Mary's Academy, all conducted by the Sisters of Mercy. Under the guidance of popular, hard-working Father Luke Harney, the parish grew and, among other things, purchased land for a cemetery. Harney left in 1892 after ten years in Durango, but the pulse of his parish hardly missed a beat. Like their Sandwich counterparts, the Durango Catholics were adept at soliciting money. An 1895 fair raised $752, some of which probably went to pay for the new eight-room stone rectory. As in all of the other churches, women did most of the work. For the July 4 holiday celebration in 1896, for example, "the ladies of St. Columba's" served sandwiches, ice cream, lemonade, and a chicken dinner.

While Sandwich Catholics had to travel to Somonauk or elsewhere to attend Mass, they did organize their own Catholic society, which occasionally received press notice. In October 1897, Somonauk, Sandwich, and Plano societies combined their efforts to hold a seven-day bazaar, complete with entertainment, contests, concerts, and meals, at the Sandwich Opera House. It proved to be an outstanding success, netting one thousand dollars for the Somonauk parish church.[5]

The 1890s witnessed a church-building frenzy in both communities. After the 1889 fire, the Durango Methodists, Episcopalians, and Presbyterians lined up to build new churches, which they all eventually did on the Boulevard. The Baptists later joined them by purchasing corner lots on Tenth, thus making the Boulevard what the Durango Trust (later the Durango Land and Coal Company) had envisioned back in 1880 as *the* church street.

Sandwich, without such a catastrophe to spur construction, still went through a building decade. The Congregationalists built a new addition in 1890. The Baptists purchased the German Baptist church in 1898 and got the attention of sidewalk superintendents by moving it through town on wheels. The Baptists attached the structure to their own building. That same year, the Methodists bought a grand piano, enlarged and remodeled their sanctuary, and added a choir room. They marked the reopening of their church with a choir and instrumental concert, charging a fifteen-cent admission that helped pay for the piano. Methodist women, meanwhile, to raise more money, held a "very attractive" sale of "everything the housewife needs" (*Argus*, March 26, 1898). The German Evangelical church purchased a new bell, which was added to three others to arouse "all sleepy Christians to be a little more mindful of their duties on Sabbath day" (*Free Press*, March 26, 1890).

In a variety of ways, churches played an active role in the lives of these two communities. Durango's First Methodist Church sponsored a citizens' course in the fall of 1899. "One of the ablest pulpit orators" of the Methodist church, sixty-eight-year-old Bishop Henry Warren (Colorado's resident bishop), presented an "easily understood, marvelous" talk on astronomy, entitled "Forces in a Sunbeam," remarked a *Herald* reporter on October 24. The ladies of the Presbyterian gave "another of their enjoyable socials." The Baptist young people's society "will meet for a business meeting" and social tonight at the church (*Durango Herald*, June 3, 1898). The ladies of the Congregational church "will have a tea meeting, supper will be served" from 6:00 to 8:00 and will cost twenty-five cents (*Sandwich Free Press*, Feb. 19, 1890). The evening service of the Methodist church "will be out on the church lawn," as long as weather allows (*Sandwich Argus*, July 29, 1899). "People near by can bring chairs" and those from the country can "occupy buggies and carriages" parked in the street. The crowning of "the Queen of Fame" was held at the Opera House last Friday; the event was sponsored by the Presbyterian ladies who made "something over $100" (*Sandwich Free Press*, Oct. 30, 1890). Miss Gertrude Barnard, "as Cleopatra," won.

Methodists published recipe books in both communities. The Methodist choir in Sandwich, and Durango's Southern Methodist women, both sold such books to raise funds. Parsnip wine tasted "as good as champagne," according to the book produced by the Southern Methodists. The authors also included "important hints" such as, "Milk which is turned or changed may be sweetened and rendered fit for use again by stirring in a little soda."

Occasionally, the congregations could be ecumenical. There "will be no morning service at the Methodist, Baptist and Congregational churches next Sunday owing to the dedication service at the Presbyterian church" (*Sandwich Argus*, Feb. 5, 1892). Churches "will be united" for Sunday evening services during warm weather, next Sunday at the Congregational church (*Argus*, July 8, 1893). Different Sunday schools belonging to "this township were well represented" at the "interesting and profitable" institute held at the Presbyterian church (*Argus*, March 28, 1896).

Generally, however, each church went its own denominational way, without regard to fellow Christians. Sunday services, both in the morning and in the evening, plus Sunday school and a Wednesday prayer meeting, typified a week's religious activity. A young people's class or society met sometime during the week, as well. Sermons covered a variety of topics, including the eternal battle against sin. Sermons might be arranged in a series on such "popular themes" as the evils of dancing, theaters, cardplaying, gambling, horse racing, and Sunday newspapers. Or sermons might each be on a separate subject, such as these listed in the church news columns of various newspapers:

> Prevailing Prayer
> Jezebel, the Wicked Queen
> The Power of God
> The Second Coming of Jesus Christ

What is Hell?
The Divinity of Jesus
Your Sin Will Find You Out
The Ungodly Bankrupt
Fools
Temptation to Succeed by Unlawful Means
Personal Contact of Christians with Non-Church Goers
What Shall I Do to Be Saved?

The middle-class congregations probably approved of these sermons, which spoke of their values and aspirations and must have eased some of their worries and answered some of their concerns.[6]

"Ethnic" churches were those whose names included such words as German and Swedish. No African American churches existed, a situation that reflected the communities' racial makeup; neither town contained a large enough black community to support a full-time minister or maintain a church building. The Rev. Silas Wright, "a colored pastor of Grand Junction" and superintendent of African Methodist Episcopal mission work, did preach in Durango's Missionary Baptist church in 1892 (*Herald,* July 1). Occasionally, there would be a special offering in a church to support some cause, such as "the Freedmen's Aid and Southern Educational Society" (*Sandwich Free Press,* March 5, 1890). Neither town included enough Jewish males to organize a synagogue. Aurora and Chicago were near enough to travel to for Jewish holy-day celebrations; Denver was another matter.

Charity and assistance to the poor fell mainly to the churches' purview, except for the Ladies Relief Society and the GAR's activities. The Thanksgiving and Christmas seasons were special times to remember the less fortunate. Sandwich churches were particularly active. Their relief societies gathered money, clothes, and food for needy families. The man who more than any other involved himself in aiding the less fortunate was Ralph Houck, the agent for the Ladies Aid Society. Houck was active throughout the decade in urging farmers and townspeople to donate. New York–born and a bachelor, Houck found poverty-stricken families and then delivered wagonloads of provisions. He continued making deliveries throughout the winter, reaching out to help the poor whenever his services were needed. Aided by his hardworking assistant, Jerry Troeger, and others, Houck at times helped forty to fifty families at once. The amount of money raised was not large (it totaled $87.74 in 1895), but the good accomplished went well beyond any monetary amount.[7]

Houck, who was one of Sandwich's forgotten heroes, raised a garden during the summer for the benefit of the poor. He also served as agent for the American Bible Society and held an annual canvass for that organization. The *Free Press*, on July 21, 1898, praised this dedicated man for the "faithful manner" in which he carried out his work without "fee or reward." Like Houck, a legion of church members ministered individually to the less fortunate members of their community. Some worked through the Grand Army of the Republic, including Methodist ministers who were veterans of the Civil War and organized their own GAR campfires, and veterans' wives who joined the Woman's Relief Corps.

Throughout the year, Durango and Sandwich churches were involved in their communities. Hardly a holiday passed without church participation. Sunday school students marched in parades; ministers gave invocations and baccalaureate sermons and preached on special occasions; church women opened booths with food for sale. Christmas had evolved into both a secular and religious day by the 1890s. Sunday school programs and special services highlighted the season, but Santa Claus's domain circumscribed that of the church.

Easter, however, remained one holiday that was solely within the church's realm. Although Lent might not have been conscientiously observed, Easter week, which climaxed with Easter Day, was properly celebrated. On Easter Sunday, churches were decorated with flowers, special music was heard, and congregations filled "every nook and corner." The welcoming of new members, the promotion of Sunday school students, the taking of communion, and perhaps a special evening children's service filled the crowded day.

Easter and Christmas were religious highlights in the nominally Protestant world of Sandwich and Durango. Yet their churches' impact on the communities came from their congregations, a pattern as old as Christianity itself. This fact was well understood by the *San Juan Methodist* (June 14, 1892): "Consecration in the pew is just as essential to the life of a church as consecration in the pulpit."[8]

Like other American institutions, churches confronted an evolving world in the nineties. The age of an overwhelmingly Protestant country drifted to a close. Around the corner loomed a materialistic, pluralistic society. Materialism had always been a threat to the pew and pulpit; now in the 1890s, materialism was ascendant. Individually and collectively, Protestants, Mormons, and Catholics watched and waited, not unaware of the changes, not knowing what this new world would be like for them or their children. What they had was faith. It had sustained earlier generations, and now it would have to support them. In the words of a popular hymn of the era:

> Abide with me, fast falls the eventide.
> The darkness deepens: Lord, with me abide.
> When other helpers fail and comforts flee,
> Help of the helpless, O abide with me.

NOTES

1. Richard McCloud, *Durango As It Is* (Durango: Durango Board of Trade, 1892), 56. William T. Ellis, *"Billy" Sunday: The Man and His Message* (Philadelphia: John C. Winston Co., 1914), 73. Lewis O. Saum, *The Popular Mood of America, 1860–1900* (Lincoln: University of Nebraska Press, 1990), 102–03. Thomas J. Schlereth, *Victorian America* (New York: HarperCollins, 1991) 243, 261–64. There are numerous newspaper mentions of missionary society meetings.

2. *Sandwich Argus*, Dec. 30, 1893; Feb. 20, Feb. 27, March 7, Nov.–Dec. 1897; March 26, July 10, July 17, 1898. Craig Carter (ed.), *Complete Baseball Record Book* (St. Louis: The Sporting News, 1992), 42. *Durango Great Southwest*, Jan. 3, 1893. *Sandwich Free Press*, May 28, July 30, 1891; Feb. 18, Nov.–Dec. 1897. Ellis, *"Billy" Sunday*, 73, 80–85, 183.

3. *San Juan Methodist*, June 14, 1892. *Vital and Social Statistics* (Washington: Government Printing Office, 1894), 286, 288, 298–99, 303.

4. John Moses, *Illinois Historical and Statistical* (Chicago: Fergus Printing Co., 1895), 1069–73. Inez Smith Davis, *The Story of the Church* (Independence, Mo.: Herald Publishing House, 1948), 436–37, 471, 499–506, 552. *Free Press*, Sept. 29, 1892. Ray Reeder, interview by author, Jan. 26, 1994. *Durango Democrat*, July 30, 1899. *Argus*, March 10, 1894; Oct. 19, 1895; Oct. 17, 1896; May 22, June 5, June 19, Oct. 7, 1897; March 5, 1898.

5. *Argus*, Aug. 5, 1893; April 21, 1894. *Free Press*, Sept. 23, Sept. 20, Oct. 7, Oct. 28, 1897. Mrs. M. L. Cummins, "History of St. Columba's Catholic Church, 1881–1961," in *Pioneers of the San Juan Country* (Denver: Big Mountain Press, 1961), 4:108–10. *Durango Herald*, July 2, 1896.

6. *Great Southwest*, Aug. 3, Aug. 11, 1892; Jan. 3, March 25, July 2, Oct. 11, 1893; Aug. 3, Aug. 5, 1896. *Herald*, June 3, 1898; Oct. 17, Oct. 24, 1899. *Free Press*, Jan. 22, Feb. 12, Feb. 19, March 26, May 7, Oct. 30, 1890; May 18, June 29, 1893; July 9, July 23, 1896; June 23, Sept. 15, Oct. 13, 1898; Sept. 14, 1899. *Argus*, Dec. 3, 1892; July 8, 1893; March 14, April 14, April 21, May 12, 1894; March 28, 1896; Jan. 23, 1897; March 12, March 19, 1898; July 29, Dec. 17, 1899. *The High Altitude Cook Book* (Durango: First United Methodist Church, about 1980, reprint), 39–40.

7. *Herald*, July 1, 1892. *Free Press*, March 5, 1890; Nov. 16, 1893. *Argus*, Nov.

19, Nov. 26, Dec. 3, Dec. 24, 1892; Dec. 9, 1893; Jan. 13, 1894; Nov. 22, 1896; Dec. 17, 1898.
8. *Free Press,* April 22, 1897; July 21, 1898; April 6, Sept. 14, 1899. *Argus,* April 20, 1895; April 16, Dec. 31, 1898. *San Juan Methodist,* June 14, 1892.

10

THIS IS WOMAN'S OPPORTUNITY

My mother was a lady like yours, you will allow.
—"Mother Was a Lady" (1896)

Victorian women (the newspapers, typically, called them *ladies*) have been greatly romanticized in fiction and legend. They were idealized during the Victorian Era as well. "The True Lady," as one author described her, was "agreeable, modest, and dignified . . . well brought up, her address . . . polite and gentle." The "true Victorian lady" possessed these four cardinal virtues: "piety, purity, submissiveness and domesticity." Immersed in rules of etiquette and proper conduct, she was expected to know, for example, the proper way to converse, conduct calls and visits, and make introductions. "The rules of society do not permit you to claim acquaintance with other persons until you have been properly introduced."

In reality, middle- and lower-income women found their lives only slightly better than those of women of the previous generation. They retained their status as second-class citizens; the scientific, religious, and political structures of the day militated against equality for women. Large cities, such as Chicago, offered them more opportunities than small, rural towns did. Even in Chicago, however, women were only grudgingly received into the man's world of law, dentistry, ministry, and medicine.

Housework and home life dominated most women's lives and automatically limited their roles in society. Popular books of the day published guidelines to help them fulfill those roles. The woman, the home's "exemplary steward," should, according to one publication, strive to give total devotion to her husband and family and to maintain a clean and pleasant home environment. Nothing could be nobler than "the highest importance which belongs wholly to a woman's province." A carefully maintained and regulated household exemplified a woman's success. A neglected, unkempt family and a chaotic house reflected badly upon both the woman and her husband, but the woman was more obviously a "less moral and less successful" individual.

Wives and mothers constituted the "acknowledged custodians of moral standards." The home became their center for instruction; it was there that they diligently taught morality, Christianity (most often the Protestant ethic), and middle-class values. That, at least, was the idealized perception. Within the home, women wielded their greatest influence.

Into this regulated, conservative world came crashing some radical changes. Suffragists began to push for the vote. Where teaching had once been a woman's principal professional outlet, now nursing, thanks to the Civil War experience, had evolved into a feminine domain. The recent invention of the telephone opened new positions for females; their demeanor and voices seemed better suited to the job of "central." The movement of women into the office was the fastest-growing trend of the 1890s. Because the typewriter, a new invention, seemed to require the "greater nimbleness of women's fingers," women invaded the formerly masculine world of the office in increasing numbers. Women stenographers, bookkeepers, cashiers, and accountants made up more and more of the workforce, particularly in larger cities. Simultaneously, the number of women in some occupations—lodging-house keeper, dressmaker, and laundress, for instance—dwindled.

All these innovations did not come without debate. Should women be in the office? Were women physically and emotionally suited for these new jobs? Would they replace male workers? The broader issue also remained: should women work outside the home, away from the duties of a mother and wife? The 1890s gave rise to earnest debate on these questions. Answers were not always definitive, but they left no doubt that life would never again be the same.[1]

These issues intruded upon the limited worlds of Sandwich and Durango women. None proved more invasive than the question of giving women the right to vote. By 1890, only Wyoming had done so, but the movement had been slowly gaining momentum over the past generation. Even the most popular author of the era, Mark Twain, caught the fever: "Man has ruled the human race from the beginning—but he should remember that up to the middle of the present century it was a dull world, and ignorant and stupid; but it is not such a dull world now, and is growing less and less dull all the time. This is woman's opportunity—she has had none before" (Ayres, *Wit & Wisdom*, 248).

The *Sandwich Argus* waged a decade-long crusade to secure the vote for women. Miles Castle fired off one editorial after another in support of the cause. Why?

> Woman's ballot is an act of justice to her, and safety to the state—woman's recognition in government is the fountain of purity and the balance wheel of morals. (Aug. 12, 1893)

> While the enfranchisement of women may not revolutionize the world, it will undoubtedly evolutionize it. (July 27, 1897)

Sometimes Castle quoted suffragette speakers, at other times he expressed his own opinion, but the arguments were the same in Sandwich and Durango. Editor Castle would hear none of the familiar belief that "Woman's place is in the home." He cheered "the ladies" on and never failed to encourage them. Backing up his talk with action, Castle served for years as chairman of the executive committee of the Illinois State Equal Suffrage Association, which had been advocating suffrage for some time. The first Illinois Woman Suffrage convention had been held in Chicago in February 1869.

By the 1890s, women had managed to win limited suffrage. Since statehood in 1876, Colorado women were "eligible to any office which may be created by the school laws of the State," and they had the right to vote in local school elections, a right granted to Illinois women in 1891 for both local and general school elections. In 1894, Sandwich women had their first opportunity to cast a ballot. The *Sandwich Argus* encouraged them to register and cheered on April 28, when over three hundred voted in a school-board election: "Many women voted in a matter of fact way, adding order and dignity to the election, and proving conclusively that great benefit would accrue to the country if the right of suffrage, on every question coming before the American people, was accorded the gentler sex." That November, women voted for the first time in a general election. Mrs. Freelove Castle made a point of being the first woman to arrive at the Sandwich polling place: "She voted early and found it so easy that she wanted to vote often" (*Argus*, Nov. 10).

Sandwich women—or many of them, anyway—worked hard for the "cause" by organizing meetings, inviting speakers, and even sponsoring a July 4, 1894, picnic to celebrate "Foremothers Day" (*Argus*, May 27, 1894). They formed a suffrage club that gained twenty-three members and met twice a month in 1895. Alas, they attained no further political rights. Much ground still needed plowing before a majority of Illinois males would concur with the idea of universal suffrage.[2]

It has been suggested that the West was more liberal in its attitudes toward women. With regard to the suffrage issue in Colorado and Illinois, the contention certainly proved true. In an 1877 election, however, Colorado males had voted against granting women the vote. There the issue rested until the 1890s. Then, with the changed political climate and the rise of the Populist Party, women again charged ahead with the suffragist banner.

When the Colorado Equal Suffrage Association reorganized in the early 1890s, and the Colorado Populists demanded "equality for all American citizens without regard to sex," it appeared that another push for woman suffrage had begun. In April 1893, the Colorado legislature approved a measure to place the question of suffrage on the November ballot. Women and their supporters organized the nonpartisan Equal Suffrage Association, which launched a united, single-issue campaign. The campaigners were mostly local people, but a skeptical national organization, remembering the 1877 failure, did at least send an experienced and energetic organizer, Carrie Chapman Catt. A brilliant speaker and tactician, Catt united and mobilized women, as she traveled around the state. Catt, one woman gushed, was "a gift better than silver or gold." Reams of pamphlets, articles, and other material flooded the state.

Durangoans joined the movement, organized a Woman Suffrage League, and encouraged both "ladies and gentlemen" to join. Newspaperwoman and writer Lillian Hartman led the local campaign. The local league's major push for the "emancipation of women" came in October to keep the issue fresh in men's minds for the November election. The league held meetings (one grand rally featured a "cowboy band"), heard speeches, and cheered such statements as, "We should recognize the fact that women [are] better than men and should have equal rights" (*Herald*, Oct. 22, 1893). The *Herald* (Oct. 15, 1893) lauded the women for "energy worthy of emulation," when they canvassed the community.

THIS IS WOMAN'S OPPORTUNITY

Men, it was claimed, seemed eager to hear a "fair presentation" of the principles involved in "[recognizing] your wife as your equal" (*Durango Daily Southwest,* Oct. 23, 1893). Endorsed by the county Populist Party, the campaign hit full stride just before the election. Election day came, and the women turned out in force. Episcopal church women served "dinner" (the term was used for the noon meal in this era) and a supper in the evening. Alas, despite optimistic forecasts, Durango and La Plata County men voted down woman's suffrage, 791 to 397. The *Herald* (Nov. 9, 1893) thought that the movement had "undoubtedly received a final death blow in the state." It would be a "long time," the paper predicted, before advocates would have the opportunity to vote on the question again.[3]

The newspaper had to scrape egg off its face on all counts. Coloradans approved woman suffrage statewide, 35,698 to 29,461. Durango males had some tall explaining to do! Women, the *Daily Southwest* observed on November 11, 1893, were now entitled to "exercise all rights and privileges of voters."

Castle and his *Sandwich Argus* (Dec. 23, 1893) hailed the victory and the "intelligent votes" of Colorado men in the paper's suffrage column, a type of column Durango never achieved. When Lila Routt, wife of the ex-governor, and president of the Denver Equal Suffrage League, became the first woman to register to vote, Miles cheered. Durango received no mention in the Sandwich press.

What had happened in Durango? Statewide opposition was weak and disorganized, and in Durango no open opposition surfaced. Privately, however, the saloon and liquor interests opposed woman's suffrage—they feared a potential boost for the prohibition movement. The Catholic church was lukewarm toward the idea, and no doubt many men in their hearts feared women's equality and the potential loss of "family values." Some believed politics would harden and corrupt women, robbing them of their femininity. Another fear was that Denver would acquire more political power through woman's suffrage, thereby isolating the outlying areas even more. Because southwestern Coloradans had a conservative attitude toward many issues, it was not surprising that they voted the way they did. The vote said much more about stereotypes and ingrained attitudes than it did about politics or women.

Interestingly, many men did not bother to vote on the issue. The coward's way out! For instance, over fifteen hundred voted in other county races, such as those for treasurer and surveyor, while somewhat fewer than twelve hundred voted on suffrage.[4]

What did women themselves feel about gaining the vote? Unfortunately, the answer to that question will never be fully known. Obviously, those in support turned out to walk, talk, and work for the cause. But one of the first problems faced by suffragists was the need to convince other women that they needed and wanted the vote. Where the silent majority stood in Durango cannot be ascertained.

Illinois women had never become as singularly focused on suffrage as Colorado women had. The Populist Party did not gain as much strength in Illinois, nor did the depression seem to call for desperate measures there. In both states, women, by the 1890s, had become involved in a diversified host of issues, clubs, and projects. The situation proved very fortunate for the 1893 vote in Colorado, but the national movement failed to realize this, hence its reluctance to try again after the 1877 defeat. Colorado voters had become radical in defense of their normally conservative views, suffrage being only one of many issues they discussed and voted upon. The money question, the hard times, and the exciting radicalism of the day presented a rare opportunity for suffragists throughout the country.

Durango men seemed no different from their counterparts elsewhere in Colorado, and why they voted as they did, no one knows. Understandably, none publicly bothered to defend himself after the vote totals appeared. Women had won the day.

Durango women might have guessed the way the wind was blowing, after their abortive effort to rename the streets earlier in 1893. The city council had asked the members of the Ladies Improvement Society to rename the streets; they willingly accepted. Their task was to revise the "founding fathers' " singular lack of originality when they named them.

After some discussion, the women came up with a host of names, including Columbus, Cortez, Dolores, Hermosa, Espanola, and Indio. Apparently, the selections sounded too romantic for the unimaginative male council, and, at a March 21 meeting, the motion to adopt the new names was defeated. The women, who had every reason to expect support, thanked the council and retired. According to the press reports, they did not "feel especially grieved" over the outcome (*Durango Great Southwest*, March 21, 1893). The terse council minutes give no explanation for the body's decision.[5]

The prosaic council went on to rename the east-west streets First, Second, and so on, and left the avenues with their number names. This showed little enough imagination, but the council even went so far as to change the one name that had some character, the Boulevard, to Third Avenue.

The women had every reason to be upset, yet no outward protests occurred. If we include the vote on woman suffrage, twice in one year the men of Durango dealt, or tried to deal, the women of the community a setback. Such slaps in the face did not deter the women, however. The Ladies Improvement Society had more success in planting trees in the Boulevard's parkway. While the planting had been planned since the founding of the town, it only happened when the women became active.

Women in both communities did have many more outlets than their mothers and grandmothers had. Whereas the church once represented the primary place for women to exercise leadership and to become involved, they now had a variety of clubs and other organizations. Both Durango and Sandwich had their share of these organizations, and if the sheer numbers of them suggests anything, women must have joined.

The Woman's Christian Temperance Union and Woman's Relief Corps busied themselves in both towns, as did other relief organizations and reading and other clubs. Durango, for example, offered women the opportunity in 1892–93 to join the Ladies Band of Workers, the Ladies Improvement Society, a physical culture class, two chautauqua clubs, at least two Shakespeare circles, language clubs, a Christian Endeavor Society, and various church groups.

What did the Victorian woman do with her leisure time? In beautiful penmanship, Sandwich teacher Nellie Forsythe faithfully kept a diary that concisely recorded her daily life. In January 1895, for example, the entries reflect a wide range of activities. She went to church and prayer meetings, visited the sick and relatives and friends, sat through teachers meetings, enjoyed a "stereoptican lecture," discussed the poetry of James Whitcomb Riley and Benjamin Taylor after hearing a "fine lecture," visited with her beau, enjoyed a sleigh ride, played games with friends, and on one occasion "shoveled snow for a good hour before breakfast." Nellie also helped her widowed mother with taxes and tea parties.

Women used their leisure time outside the home in ways that their mothers had little considered or seldom enjoyed the opportunity of trying. Reading fiction and poetry had long been popular leisure activities for women; now women moved into a more formal educational setting. Women were improving their minds and their lives, and, by the 1890s, they were looking beyond themselves to improve society.

They were active. Sandwich's Ladies Relief and Aid Society, throughout the decade, raised food and money for the poor, particularly during the Thanksgiving and Christmas seasons. Durango's Ladies' Library Association struggled mightily to open and maintain a library. They set a goal of providing the reading public with the "best standard, current literature" of the day (*Herald*, May 7, 1896). Starting in 1892, the women gathered a library of six hundred volumes within a year and opened a free reading room. Then they made the mistake of turning the effort over to the YMCA, which dropped the ball. By 1896, the association was striving to revive interest. Finally, they found a home for the library in the high school. The *Herald* (May 7, 1896) admonished its readers, "In their efforts to do this they need the encouragement and support of everyone in the community."

The Ladies Reading Club of Durango worked on projects such as planting those trees in the Boulevard's parkway, and they strove to improve their minds. They met from November into the next spring, reading and discussing an eclectic selection of books, from *The Last Days of Pompeii*, *Looking Backward*, *Coin's Financial School*, and Shakespeare's plays to sermons on the Holy Land. Members presented papers, read articles, and planned an annual banquet. The club's membership included women from most of Durango's first families—the Camps, Scovilles, Newmans, Boyles, Jacksons, and others.

The members of the Woman's Literary and Study Club in Sandwich also worked to improve themselves in an assortment of ways. For example, their meeting on Monday, March 21, 1898, featured Ella Scofield reading selections from Edgar Allan Poe; Lottie Logan presenting a paper on Poe; Lida Bradley reading a "carefully prepared paper on Japan civilized," written by absent member Anna White; and Ellen Blee giving a "delightful paper on Italy" (*Argus*, March 28, 1898). Other meetings featured discussions or papers on history, music, art, philanthropy, and women's inventions; the ever popular humorous readings; and one paper that may have touched on Durango, "Cliff Dwellers."⁶

Durango women did more than study the cliff dwellings; they fought to preserve them. The mysterious and fascinating cliff dwellings at Mesa Verde, some fifty miles west of town, had been "discovered" in December 1888, and the public display of relics started the next year. Visitors began to arrive by 1890, and the exhibit at the Chicago World's Fair in 1893 called wide attention to the area. The Rio Grande Southern railroad promised to take visitors to the "Homes of the Cliff Dwellers." The little village of Mancos, which was nearer Mesa Verde than Durango was, evolved into the popular departing point for a routine three-day pack trip to see the sights. But Durango, too, discovered a profitable business in catering to Mesa Verde tourists.

All this interest and visitation started to damage the seven-hundred-year-old structures, a situation that was not helped in the least by the grand fun of looking for souvenirs among the ruins. The warning buzz of distressed resident rattlesnakes limited the fun somewhat. Some parties went to Mesa Verde for no other purpose then to gather relics to sell—a flourishing and profitable business in the 1890s. Intentional and unintentional vandalism soared. All this alarmed Colorado Springs resident and frequent visitor Virginia McClurg, who almost single-handedly started a movement to save Mesa Verde. This energetic, determined woman talked, wrote, and organized. A natural leader, she attracted others to her cause. Durango, the nearest large community, proved the perfect place to meet and organize trips to the area.

Durango women joined the movement. McClurg worked originally through the Colorado Federation of Women's Clubs, then organized her own Colorado Cliff Dwellings Association. Durangoans Estelle Camp, Alice Bishop, Jeanette Scoville, and Anna Boyle joined women throughout the state and nation in a drive to create a park to preserve the ruins and save the artifacts that remained.

What did the women do? They presented programs, lobbied the state legislature and the U.S. Congress, organized tours into the region to arouse interest, served as hostesses for visiting dignitaries, hired men to build trails and dig wells (lack of water being the greatest problem for tourists), and eventually dealt with the Utes on whose reservation the cliff dwellings sat. Virginia McClurg wrote about an 1899 visit in a report to the Colorado Federation of Women's Clubs: "The people of the Southwest are enthusiastic over the movement and your chairman received kindness from the Wetherill brothers [the Mancos ranchers who discovered the ruins in 1888], Mr. Kelly of the Mancos Times, Mr. Noland, the interpreter, Mrs. Bishop of the woman's club of Durango and many others" (*Rocky Mountain News* [Denver], Oct. 29, 1899). McClurg had traveled to the region to talk with Ignacio, the chief of the Ute Mountain Utes, about a lease. Besides trying to save the ruins, the women hoped to make them more accessible to the public, even to make them, as McClurg dreamed, "passable for bicycles."[7]

In the 1890s, although McClurg and her followers neither created a park nor made Mesa Verde accessible to bicycle-riding tourists, they did lay the groundwork for the eventual achievement of both goals. All this shocked some men. Women were not supposed to venture so far beyond the home and into the world traditionally controlled by men. Attitudes of the day were subtly expressed in such practices as identifying women only by their husbands' names, or more blatantly, in comments such as this statement in the *Durango Democrat* of June 1, 1899: "Difficult for some club women to understand that man is a superior being." Or the snide comment in the *Sandwich Free Press* of September 16, 1897, that the editor wished subscribers would pay what they owed him, because his wife had taken up bicycling: "The progress thus far made indicates that the struggle will be a long one and the drafts on us for arnica and court-plaster more than exhaust our ordinary income." Not to pick on the *Free Press,* but in the October 27, 1892, issue, this appeared: "Marrying a woman for her beauty is like buying a house because it is handsomely painted."

Even a compliment in the *Durango Democrat* (May 11, 1899) could turn out to be unintentionally sexist: "Durango has many bright, beautiful and brainy women, and an opportunity to display the charms of beauty, grace and intelligence of the sex, is the one essential necessary to convince proud man that he is not the 'entire push.' " That comment was found in a review of the annual banquet of Durango's Women's Club, to which men came as invited guests only.

An increasing number of women held strong reservations about considering man to be a "superior being." These women pushed ahead on many fronts. Sandwich and Durango had women doctors, and Frances

Chaney conducted Universalist services in Sandwich in 1899. Unfortunately, as the *Sandwich Free Press* noted on April 20, attendance was "not so far . . . very large." While Frances impressed people with her "spirituality and beauty of her exposition of the gospel," her efforts failed.

Stereotyping persisted. The question of women in the pulpit had to wait and was a long way from being resolved. It constituted a "muttering coming storm." Conservatives would have none of it. However, the San Juan Methodist said in 1892, "The admission of women into the general conference, is a smothering volcano, which will in our opinion, burst and carry everything before it."

In Sandwich, a major breakthrough had occurred two years earlier when Fanny Worthington of Sterling, Illinois, gave Sandwich's Memorial Day address. Editor Castle gushed with praise: "The engagement of Mrs. Fanny M. Worthington to deliver the Memorial address was an inspiration. The fame of this talented lady had preceded her and she was greeted at the Auditorium by an audience limited only by the number of seats and standing room on the floor and gallery; hundreds of people were turned away, unable to gain admittance" (*Argus*, June 5, 1897). Attitudes were evolving, women moved closer to being accepted in the men's world. The appearance of popular orator Mary Lease, of "raise less corn and more hell" fame, attracted a large crowd to the Sandwich Opera House, where she gave her famous "Christ or Caesar" lecture.[8]

There was novelty in all this, to be sure, which helped breed tolerance or grudging acceptance. Some traditions helped as well. Women teachers had been the norm for years, so it proved easier for them to gain the principalships of both communities' high schools than to move into other areas traditionally dominated by men. Nor did it hurt the women's cause that most of the participants mentioned in club news and other activities came from the middle or upper classes. Ellen Blee, Mollie Castle, Estelle Camp, and Alice Bishop were recognizable women who, along with their husbands, represented the people who might be termed the community movers and shakers, the first families of Sandwich and Durango. These women participated in activities outside the home and thus helped break stereotypes and serve as examples for others.

A sharp debate occurred, however, when women moved into athletics. An early debate opened over bicycle riding, which had become popular. Should women be allowed to participate? Would such activity harm their emotional and mental natures, turn them into "tomboys," place them in compromising situations, or make them physically unfit for child bearing? Or, argued the other side, would it afford them needed physical exercise in a genteel manner, broaden their horizons, and provide a family activity. The discussion ranged far beyond Sandwich and Durango, and in the end women rode their bicycles and even joined clubs such as the Durango Wheel Club. This horrified some of the more conservative men and women and no doubt moved some gloomy individuals to forecast that neither demeanor nor morality would survive the current generation.

To ease the strain, Victorians, as they were wont to do, established an elaborate system of guidelines for women cyclists. They were not to speak to strangers, but could accept help if their bike broke down. When men and women rode together, the latter should ride in front. Solitary riding was strictly forbidden. Many women probably ignored such guidelines, especially once the fad really caught on and raged full-fire in the nineties.

The basic issue persisted—exercise for women. It went back years. Finally, as the century drew to a close, the physical benefits for both sexes slowly came to be recognized. For women, though, strenuous and competitive sports continued to be generally discouraged. Walking was acceptable and open to women of all classes. Indian clubs also provided an inexpensive and accessible form of exercise, particularly for school-age girls. Only a few diehards did not consider croquet, "Presbyterian billiards," suitable for women. That game, which was popular in both towns, required "considerable skill," yet not too "much strength or technique." According to the diehards, women were deficient in both.

Durango women seemed a little ahead of their Sandwich counterparts. In 1891, they organized a Ladies Athletic Club for the "fairer sex" only. On June 1 of that year, the *Durango Weekly Tribune* declared, "Riding, driving, walking and occasional dancing, are all good, but the wives, mothers, sisters and daughters of Durango, should have a suitable building in which they can enjoy regularly such exercises as they most need for their physical development." The *Tribune* and the club's other advocates felt the club should receive the "united support" of the city's businesspeople in order to raise five hundred dollars to "give the ladies a good start." That failed to happen, however, proving to be an idea ahead of its time. By 1893, only a "physical culture" class remained, supplemented a year later with a Ladies Tennis Club.

The appearance or discussion of more "rugged" women's athletics swiftly raised eyebrows or editorial wrath. The arrival of the "Boston Bloomers" girls baseball team created a sensation in Sandwich in May 1896. "The Boston Girls in bloomers fair, will bat the ball high in the air," ran the advertisement. The Boston Bloomers impressed the *Sandwich Free Press* (May 4, 1898): "The girls are all good players, and their conduct while here was above reproach." The second point hinted at a real concern: the girl athletes might corrupt young males! The thought, however, of a "female football" team raised crusty Dave Day's ire. He proclaimed, in Durango's *Solid Muldoon* (Dec. 6, 1893), "They may think differently but girls can never compete with boys on the gory gridiron." There were definitely limits to how far and fast women could go![9]

Despite all the clubs, the fight for the vote, the bicycle trips, and other advances, the main role of the Victorian woman remained with the home and family. "Who makes the best wife? Not a weak, forceless, stupid, uneducated, giddy creature." Sandwich and Durango women of all social and economic classes could never ignore their obligation to their families. In the words of a popular song of a generation before, "Be it ever so humble, there's no place like home."

Most Victorian women labored at home. Only 5.6 percent worked outside the home in the 1890s. Like much of Victorian life, tradition and social values overlay housework and married life. Housework, for example, furnished an "extension of the woman's role in nurturing the family"; a clean and pleasant home "created a place for the inculcation of proper middle-class values." Motherhood allowed women to reach their "highest and most harmonious development." The woman who "neglected this ordained purpose" denied herself, the argument ran, the "opportunity for physical and moral development."

Despite such high-sounding ideas, childbirth denoted one of the most dangerous and feared events in a woman's life. An alarming number of deaths and illnesses resulted from pregnancy and childbirth, if newspaper accounts can be used as a means of measurement. Statistics of maternal deaths per number of births are unknown for these two communities and are difficult to discover for years in the 1890s. Most births took place at home and, at best, signified a time of pain amid the joy of the arrival of a new child.

Some conservative, all-American advocates worried because the birthrate for white, Anglo-Saxon families had been sinking alarmingly; it declined by more than half during the century. This threatened the "good native stock," the racial and ethnic purity of the United States. Critics blamed it on contraceptives, abortion, and "apartment living." Without question, interest existed in contraceptives, even those "new rubber things." Abortions, albeit dangerous, were inexpensive, common, and a definite concern for those advocating more children. So too was the fact that patent-medicine preventives (no guarantee they would be successful) could be easily bought, and abortifacients (ergot and cotton root) could be purchased through the mail or from the druggist.[10]

Legendary misinformation about pregnancy persisted. One popular belief was that if a woman engaged in vigorous exercise—dancing or horseback riding—after intercourse, she would avoid conception. Many physicians and popular health advisers had no idea when conception occurred. Abstinence seemed to some the only sure way to avoid pregnancy. No doubt this caused tension; a wife's sexual abstinence may have turned her husband to prostitution or a mistress.

When a woman was in a "family way," or as another quaint expression put it, had a "bun in the oven," she was urged to provide "good soil" for the baby. She should stop wearing corsets, avoid alcohol and tobacco, and, some argued, take up exercise such as walking. Other "experts" believed the woman should not appear in public, to avoid embarrassment in general or embarrassing questions by children. After all, this was an era in which children were told that a stork had brought their baby sister or brother, or that the baby had suddenly appeared on the doorstep!

It came down to the question of sex for pleasure versus sex for procreation. Sex without an intention to procreate was immoral, argued churches and individuals opposed to "sin." But many indicators, including the existence of Durango's red-light districts, suggested that sex for pleasure occurred with increasing frequency.

Sex education being virtually nonexistent, young married couples may have been sexually naive or at best ill-prepared to assume the responsibilities and trials of marriage. The *Golden Manual* (1891) provided a chapter on "sensible rules for love-making," which included such wisdom as "right love-making is more important than right selection." It advised the reader that love-making "becomes a work of philanthropy and social reform far transcending all others." That taken care of, the fifty-four-year-old author, Henry Northrop, spent much more time on "The Proposal, Acceptance, and Vow" and on eloping, which he discourages, "for notoriety is despicable."

Of course, in this era of double standards, young men could sow their "wild oats" with the girls in the red-light district—a far easier feat in Durango than in Sandwich. Parents regulated courtship to the closest degree to try to prevent any "accidents." The acceptable courting outlets included the church, the home parlor, and the front porch, provided that there were chaperons nearby. Middle-class couples followed accepted genteel tradition. Nellie Forsythe was courted by William Woodbury at church (both were ardent churchgoers), at concerts, at the reading circle, at home in the parlor, and maybe, very cautiously, in school as well, although that would have been frowned upon by many folks in the community. Finally, on January 19, 1893, William Woodbury asked for Nellie's hand in marriage. They recorded their reactions in their diaries.

> Called on Nellie this eve. Ask Mrs. F. for Nellie. She did not reply.
>
> Will spent the evening here. A little "White Ribbon Romance" that surprised more than one person.

Five days later the reply came, neither diarist showing the emotion of the evening.

> Called on Nellie this eve. She gave me her Mother's answer to my question of one week ago. She wants us to wait until a year from Dec.
>
> W. spent the evening here and J. H. came later. W. brought the song "O tell us merry birds." It is very pretty.

They would wait in accordance with her mother's wishes and continued their courtship in the accepted manner.

Teacher-administrator Will finally married Nellie in June 1895. The wedding was described in a typical Victorian sentimental account: "The bride was elegantly attired in white silk, and carried a bouquet of sweet peas, looking lovely as a bride should, while the groom was a manly man, conventionally dressed" (*Argus*, June 29, 1895). They settled in the new home that he had had built (he worried about the cost) and furnished, probably with Nellie's help, and they became one of Sandwich's "first families."

Despite Victorian traditions, new courtship opportunities abounded for town residents, as did old-timers' frowns. Bicycles gave couples the opportunity to be alone, and roller-skating and ice-skating provided a chance to touch and to hold hands in public. By the late 1890s, young unmarried couples even went on overnight hiking and biking trips together, chaperoned by young married couples. Alarmed critics felt certain that society's moral decay loomed at hand. But there was nothing new about that; critics had been condemning dances and balls for years.

There does not seem to have been much difference between the two towns in the ages of young couples getting married. The ages ranged from mid-teens to early thirties for first marriages, the early twenties being the most common. A woman, however, who reached the "shady side of thirty" had arrived at "old maid" status with, according to popular suspicion, a "difficult temperament." Such women were fit, nevertheless, to serve as chaperons. A consolation for these women was the notion that the life of the "old maid" would be more rewarding and useful than a life of marriage "without love."

This generation witnessed a steady increase in divorce. By 1889 the United States had the highest divorce rate in the world. In the more open society of Durango, the divorced wife, after an unhappy marriage, probably would find several potential husbands. The problem of abusive husbands and unhappy marriages had been easier to resolve in Colorado since the days of the 1859 Pike's Peak gold rush, in which men greatly outnumbered women, than in the more structured and conservative Midwestern society.

Maggie Griffith, for instance, divorced her salesman husband in 1897 after he left on a trip to "parts unknown" and never returned. Eliza Worth suffered through four months of marriage in 1890, then sued her husband, William, for "beating her & using obscene & opprobrious language towards her." She won. The judge also granted Larienia Townshend a divorce after she charged that her husband, William, "had rendered himself impotent" by his "immoral & criminal conduct." Men, too, sued. John Larsen and James Kelly each said his wife had "absented herself from her husband." It took John nine years to take that step against his wife, Ella. James's wife, Lulu, had left after six months of marriage, and six months later James gained his divorce.

Although Sandwich witnessed fewer divorces than Durango did, it saw its share, with both men and women filing for them. Abraham LaShonse accused his wife of cruelty and adultery, and Emeline Wright and Clarissa Ames charged their husbands with desertion. The amount of time that a wife or husband had to put up with an unhappy marriage, even in a conservative farm community, declined during the decade. Nevertheless it was easier, as it always had been, for the man to secure a divorce. Shocked by the increasing frequency of divorce, critics looked for reasons behind the trend. Some blamed drunkenness, others the liberation of women, the decline in family values, and the stress of the urban environment. They found no simple solution, and worries mounted about the future of the American family.[11]

Women's experience of living in Sandwich or Durango was not that of the idealized Victorian woman. Women in the two towns worked and worried. Even those who might be considered members of the upper class could not avoid life's trials. In Durango, Estelle Camp, a college-educated New Englander and banker Alfred Camp's wife, was as well off as anyone and helped lead her community and church. She came to the West in 1883 as a young bride and although initially shocked by Durango's physical barrenness, grew to love the town. Estelle had time available for outside activities. She joined the reading club, helped plant trees on the Boulevard, evolved into a social "arbitrator," became involved with preserving Mesa Verde, served as a member of the bank board, and emerged as a familiar name in newspaper columns. Her status as recorded in censuses went from "keeping house" in 1885 to "wife" with a live-in Irish maid in 1900. Yet of Estelle's three sons, two did not survive their first year and, as the newspaper expressed the sad tidings, "passed into cherub land" (*Durango Idea*, Dec. 19, 1885). There was an old saying that a family had four children—one to replace each parent, one for natural increase, and one for Death, which did visit the Victorian home.

In Sandwich, Agnes Smith did not have Estelle's advantages. Agnes was born in Illinois and raised on a farm. Her husband, Will, worked for the Sandwich Manufacturing Company as a machinist for half a century. Their family in the 1890s consisted of twin girls and six boys, all of whom lived to be adults. Agnes never had a maid, but her daughters were old enough to help her in the 1890s. One of the daughters, in fact, Mable, made big family news when in 1896 she won one thousand dollars in a newspaper contest. The family had worked on the project together, and Mable's name appeared on the winning entry. They used the money to remodel their home. Agnes made the newspaper only when she entertained a meeting at home or when her name appeared in a birth announcement: "Born to Mr. and Mrs. Will Smith, March 22 [1892], a nine pound boy."

Agnes and Estelle, the working-class woman and the upper-class woman, represent the spectrum of typical Durango and Sandwich women. Immigrant and ethnic women were, if not rare, certainly not very visible in the white, Anglo-Saxon world of these two communities.[12]

Both immigrant and U.S.-born women worked, and worked hard. Hand-cranked washing machines (Sears top-of-the-line cost $2.75) and "mangles" (clothes wringers) made wash day, Monday, easier than it was when women still needed to use washboards. By 1897, Sears advertised an "electric washer" for $3.50, although the company still advised women, "On the evening before wash-day place all the clothes you wish to wash in a tub, fill the same up with water (rain water preferred), so that they may be thoroughly soaked over night." After clothes were washed, they had to be hung out on the line and eventually ironed with stove-heated irons. Time passed busily on wash day. One had to keep the house clean, and cleaning with mop, broom or brush and dust pan, and feather duster and cloth occupied many an hour. Carpet sweepers, which speeded the process and offered some physical relief, could be purchased from Sears for as little as $1.75. Spring housecleaning meant a major effort that lasted up to a week or more. After spring housecleaning had begun in 1899, Dave Day observed, on April 13, "Life has no pleasureness for hubby now."

Cooking over even the best coal or wood stove or "range" was hot, long work, particularly in the summer. Although some prepared foods (oatmeal, pancake mix, and cereals) and canned goods (soups, vegetables, fruits, fish, and meat) were on grocers' shelves, most cooking started from scratch.

Iceboxes allowed the storage of food, but they were expensive, running from ten to fifty dollars apiece. The least expensive one represented at least a week's pay for the working man. Typically, the housewife went shopping several times a week, and if her husband raised a garden and fruit trees that supplemented the diet in season, she might spend many hours canning. Eating habits changed during the 1890s, particularly at breakfast, which was not as heavy as it had once been in rural America. Cooking breakfast was made easier by prepared foods that allowed Mom to stay in bed a bit longer. The big meal (dinner) continued to be at noon and included meat, potatoes, baked goods, and desert. The evening supper might consist of cold foods or leftovers. Every morning a long day awaited the wife and mother.[13]

Women appeared in the newspaper generally with their husbands or in connection with some social or family activity. Newspapers might report, for example, that S. P. Ford and his wife left yesterday for Colorado Springs; that Miss M. R. Clark, one of Fort Lewis's teachers, spent the day with her sister; that Mrs. Nathan concluded the girls' sewing school with general exercises; that Miss Nellie Culver and Mr. John Latham were united in marriage; and that Miss Florence Adams "very pleasantly" entertained a large company of young people.

If they had the time and inclination, women could worry about styles, from clothing to hair. The corn-fed, buxom actress, the darling of the comic stage, Lillian Russell, provided the fashion ideal. For those not so naturally endowed, Sears provided everything from the Princess Bust Developer to patent weight-gain medicines and special corsets to shape the figure. If one was too fat—and one wonder's about the Fat Woman's Club in Sandwich—Dr. Rose's Obesity Powders promised the answer. Fashionable clothes could be sewn or purchased. They seem to have been easier to come by than the perfect figure.[14]

While the women's world in Sandwich and Durango expanded in the 1890s, it still had a long way to go before it incorporated the social, political, and economic equality that some liberal reformers advocated. In this regard, there was nothing unusual or different about the two towns in the general context of Victorian America. In Durango, women had more opportunity, more political power, and generally more acceptance within the man's world. That reflected Western attitudes and conditions, and not anything unusual about Durango. But whether they lived in Sandwich or Durango, women still faced a gender bias and maldistribution of wealth, facts of life so typical that people took them for granted. The woman's world remained centered on the home and family, yet strong hints of coming innovations could not be ignored.

Definitely, there remained much sentimentality associated with women and their roles within the home, family, and community. Nevertheless, women embodied a strong force in their communities. Alexis de Tocqueville understood this when he wrote, sixty years before, "And now that I come near the end of this book in which I have recorded so many considerable achievements of the Americans, if anyone asks me what I think the chief cause of the extraordinary prosperity and growing power of this nation, I should answer that it is due to the superiority of their women."[15]

NOTES

1. Henry Davenport Northrop, *Golden Manual* (Philadelphia: S. I. Bell, 1891), 23, 53, and all of book 1. Barbara M. Posados, "To Preserve the Home," in *Illinois: Its History & Legacy* (St. Louis: River City Publishers, 1984), 100, 108. Colleen McDannell, *The Christian Home in Victorian America* (Bloomington: Indiana University Press, 1986), 45, 85, 143–44. Harvey Green, *The Light of the Home* (New York: Pantheon Books, 1983), 29–30, 57, 59–60. Margery W. Davies, *Woman's Place is at the Typewriter* (Philadelphia: Temple University Press, 1982), 51–55, 80–81, 91. Thomas J. Schlereth, *Victorian America* (New York: HarperCollins, 1991), 67–69. *Women in Gainful Occupations, 1870–1920* (Washington: Government Printing Office, 1929), 33, 35, 41–42. John S. Haller Jr. and Robin M. Haller, *The Physician and Sexuality in Victorian America* (Urbana: University of Illinois Press, 1974), 273–74.
2. Alex Ayres (ed.), *The Wit & Wisdom of Mark Twain* (New York: Harper & Row, 1987), 248. *Sandwich Argus*, Oct. 24, 1891; April 28, Nov. 3, Nov. 10, 1894; April 20, 1895; Oct. 17, Oct. 24, 1896. The *Sandwich Free Press* was less enthusiastic but still gave women a boost; see July 30, 1891, and Sept. 27, 1894. *Proceedings of the Constitutional Convention* (Denver: Smith-Brooks, 1907), 111, 187. John H. Keiser, *Building for the Centuries* (Urbana: University of Illinois Press, 1977), 15–22. Lewis M. Gross, *Past and Present of DeKalb County, Illinois* (Chicago: Pioneer Publishing Co., 1907), 2:40. Marguerite J. Pease, *The Story of Illinois* (Chicago: University of Chicago Press, 1965), 223.
3. *Durango Herald*, Oct. 10, Oct. 11, Oct. 15, Oct. 21, Oct. 22, Oct. 23, Oct. 26, Nov. 2, Nov. 3, Nov. 9, 1893. *Durango Daily Southwest*, Oct. 23, Nov. 5, Nov. 6, Nov. 7, Nov. 8, Nov. 9, Nov. 11, 1893. *Colorado Suffrage Centennial* (Denver: Colorado Committee for Women's History, 1893), 5–13.
4. *Daily Southwest*, Nov. 8, Nov. 11, 1893. *Herald*, Nov. 9, 1893. *Argus*, Dec. 23, 1893; Jan. 6, Jan. 20, 1894. Keiser, *Building for the Centuries*, 18–19.
5. Durango City Council Minutes, Feb. 7, March 21, 1893. Durango City Council Minutes, book 2.
6. Richard McCloud, *Durango As It Is* (Durango: Durango Board of Trade, 1892). Nellie Forsythe diary, Jan. 1895, Regional History Center, Northern Illinois University. *Durango Solid Muldoon*, Jan. 1, 1893. Keiser, *Building for the Centu-*

ries, 18–19. Green, *Light of the Home,* 148–49. Ladies Reading Club Journal, 1890–91 and 1893–99, Durango Public Library. *Argus,* Nov. 28, 1891; Jan. 18, 1896; March 26, 1898. *Herald,* May 7, May 26, 1896. *Free Press,* March 9, April 20, Oct. 4, 1899. Posados, "To Preserve the Home," 109.

7. Material from the 1890s that is found in the Mesa Verde National Park Archives. *Durango Great Southwest,* Aug. 2, 1892, April 14, 1893. *The Cliff Dwellers* (n.p.: H. Jay Smith Exploring Co., 1893), 15. *Rocky Mountain News* (Denver), Oct. 29, 1899. McCloud, *Durango,* 31.

8. *Durango Democrat,* May 31, June 1, 1899. *Argus,* May 28, 1892; April 18, May 6, 1896; May 15, June 5, 1897. *Free Press,* Feb. 5, 1890; Sept. 15, 1897; April 1899. McCloud, *Durango,* 71. *San Juan Methodist,* June 14, 1892.

9. Green, *Light of the Home,* 152, 162. *Durango Weekly Tribune,* June 1, 1891. *Herald,* March 29, 1894. *Argus,* May 16, 1896. *Free Press,* May 14, May 21, 1896. *Solid Muldoon,* Dec. 6, 1893.

10. Northrop, *Golden Manual,* 153. *Women in Gainful Occupations,* 76. Green, *Light of the Home,* 29–32, 59. Schlereth, *Victorian America,* 272–73. Haller and Haller, *The Physician,* ix, xi, xii, 25, 114–15, 117–18, 273. Carroll Smith-Rosenberg, *Disorderly Conduct* (New York: Alfred A. Knopf, 1985), 183, 197, 199.

11. Green, *Light of the Home,* 12–13, 20–22, 27, 33. Schlereth, *Victorian America,* 271, 279–81. Haller and Haller, *The Physician,* 114–15, 124. Smith-Rosenberg, *Disorderly Conduct,* 199. William Woodbury diary, Jan. 19, Jan. 24, 1893, Regional History Center, Northern Illinois University. Forsythe diary, Jan. 19, Jan. 24, 1893. *Herald,* June 10, 1897. *Free Press,* July 23, 1890; Sept. 2, 1897; Sept. 28, 1899. La Plata County Court Records, 1890. *Argus,* July 8, 1899. Northrop, *Golden Manual,* 111–20.

12. Colorado Census, 1885, La Plata County. Twelfth Census, 1900, De Kalb County, Illinois, and La Plata County, Colorado. *Durango Idea,* Dec. 19, 1885. *Daily Southwest,* May 24, May 25, 1893. Helen M. Searcy, "A. P. Camp and the First National Bank," in *Pioneers of the San Juan Country* (Colorado Springs: Out West Printing, 1942), 1:144–49. *Argus,* June 20, 1896. *Free Press,* May 12, 1898.

13. *Sears, Roebuck and Co. Consumers Guide, 1897* (New York: Chelsea House, 1968 reprint), 8–18, 101–40.

14. *Herald,* May 28, May 30, May 31, June 1, 1898. *Free Press,* May 3, May 10, June 18, 1896. *Argus,* May 4, 1895; Feb. 13, 1897. *Sears Consumers Guide,* 31, 33–37, 307.
15. Alexis de Tocqueville, *Democracy in America* (New York: Harper & Row, 1966), 579.

11
JOY IN MUDVILLE

Slide, Kelly, slide!
Stay there, hold your base!
—"Slide, Kelly, Slide" (1889)

In that most popular 1890s song, "A Bicycle Built for Two," Daisy's beau confesses he "can't afford a carriage, but you'll look sweet upon the seat of a bicycle built for two." Daisy Bell hesitated to accept Michael's proposal, because he seemed to promise little more than "Ped'ling away down the road of life." Most Victorians, though, looked with great excitement on the popular new sport of bicycling. Bikes became one of the great fads of the nineties.

Sandwich and Durango pedaled right along with the rest of the United States. The safety bike replaced the "ordinary," the bicycle with the six-foot front wheel, and incorporated many improvements, including brakes that worked. Pneumatic tires, enclosed gears, and coaster brakes completed the evolution to the modern bike. How popular was the bike? In 1890, 312 firms manufactured a total of ten million of them. Included in this group by 1896 was the "Sandwich Bicycle," which was locally built and "among the best on the market" (*Sandwich Argus*, Oct. 17, 1896). Once you purchased a favorite, you could join a "wheel club" and be part of the League of American Wheelmen, which lobbied for better roads and highways.

Not only would Durangoans and Sandwichites be "in" if they took up bicycling, but this new sport also promised wondrous benefits. Pedaling along broadened one's horizons, intensified "love of home and country," and furnished exercise and good health. Those "in poor health" were advised to "regain good health through judicious use of the bicycle." For businessmen, riding would "clear [the] brain," for a beautiful woman, "it would preserve . . . beauty." For women not so blessed, riding would at least "make

[one] more attractive" by brightening the eye and putting "a flush of health on the cheek" (Ralph, *Harper's,* 250).

Opponents worried. What might this lead to? Would it promote immodesty in women and harm their reproductive systems? Women wearing the popular shorter skirts could invite advances, and how would bicycling change courting? Might young men gain too much freedom? Would the bicycle seat "beget or foster the habit of masturbation?"[1]

Overcoming such apprehensions, young and old alike purchased bikes. Sears sold them for as little as $24.95, and local merchants for as high as $175.00. Alas for Michael, Sears did not offer, at least in 1897, a bicycle built for two, though it did sell tricycles. By then, bicycling had become quite a business, with bells, child's seats, cyclometers, men's and women's suits, tourist cases, and many other items a devotee could purchase to upgrade his or her bike or person. For modesty's sake, women's bicycle suits came with skirt, leggings, and bloomers. The price was $3.75 to $6.75. Men could purchase a trouser guard and "Morton's Supporters made of best quality Canton flannel."

"Cycling seems to be a craze for both sexes just now," observed the *Durango Herald* on March 28, 1895. The Durango Wheel Club and the Sandwich Bicycle Club took to the roads; Americans never overlooked the opportunity to organize! Sandwich riders had the much better terrain, the land being flatter with no mountains to labor up. But Durangoans had better views when they reached the top. Day and night they rode. In Durango, a moonlight run to Trimble Springs gained popularity; so, too, did a moonlight ride from Sandwich to Somonauk, and the Durango excursion to the "annual picnic at Baker's Bridge." Maude Gray, Ethel Coy, and DeForest Coy rode over eight hundred miles on their Illinois and Iowa tour in July 1896. Occasionally, the clubs held individual and team races. Speed interested some. Members of the Durango Wheel Club covered the nine miles from Trimble Springs to Durango in thirty-nine minutes, in 1896, "notwithstanding a delay of several minutes" when the leading rider crashed and those following barely avoided a pileup (*Herald,* Oct. 22, 1896).[2]

The arrival of the bicycle salesman might be heralded as the harbinger of spring, warm weather, and outdoor activity, but another side of bicycling existed. Both city councils heard complaints about "wild," or inconsiderate, riders. The councils responded, as has been seen, by passing ordinances "prohibiting riding bicycles on sidewalks," or riding at "a greater speed than eight miles" per hour, and requiring an "attached lighted lamp and alarm bell" for night riding. Already, government was moving cautiously into the field of regulating what citizens could and could not do. Problems existed in the country, as well. The *Sandwich Argus* (May 9, 1896) felt compelled to warn bicyclists that they should "remember that farm horses are likely to be frightened by wheelmen" approaching or passing them on the road. Great caution "should be exercised to prevent runaways." Bikers had their own complaints, causing Durango to make it unlawful to "deposit nails, tacks" and the like where they were "liable to cause" a puncture of "riding machine tires."

Bicycles did allow men and women to exercise and have a refreshing social experience. It gave women an opportunity to display athletic ability and, perchance, close the equality gap. Sandwich and Durango bikers rode out of the city and into the country more frequently than ever before, helping, hopefully, to promote understanding between country and town. Their clubs hastened to push for "good roads," because it was no fun to pedal into a deep hole, especially those that contained mud or water. Despite fears and concerns, bicycles did far more good than they harmed morals or raised "base passions."[3]

Bicycling reflected the new interest in sports throughout the United States, being simply one of the most visible manifestations. Whether participating or watching, Americans were becoming involved.

Americans also had developed a passion for baseball. "The outlook wasn't brilliant for the Mudville nine that day"; almost everyone in Sandwich and Durango had heard or read "Casey At the Bat" by the mid-1890s. No sport displayed more popularity than baseball, the national game. Fans followed it with enthusiasm, from the National League race to the local team's games. A comparison of the two communities' baseball interests is revealing. Durango fielded one team after another; Sandwich had difficulty forming teams. The "outlook" was never good for the Sandwich nine, and they never seemed to get organized.

Sandwich did field teams in 1890, 1894, 1896, and 1897, though the papers provided little coverage. For example, in 1897, the team won four of six games and concluded the season with that age-old hope for the fans, that the "addition of a few good snappy players" would create a "very swift baseball nine next year." In other years, teams played at the fairgrounds and for special occasions, such as the Fourth of July, but they came from Waterman, Plano, Paw Paw, and other nearby towns. Considering the plight of local baseball, it did not seem surprising when the Boston Bloomers team played the Sandwich "anti-overs" on a beautiful spring day (Monday, May 18, 1896), and the local boys lost. The game took place in Schrader's Pasture near the fairgrounds and was "witnessed by a large crowd, many from neighboring towns," who paid twenty-five cents admission. Press coverage praised the Bloomer nine, saying the "girls are all good players." "The game was a 'hot' one, and lasted through six innings. Naturally the girls were the favorite from the start. The Bloomers were declared winner at the close of the sixth inning by the score of 9 to 13." The press usually credited the games with drawing good crowds. The question remains, why did Sandwich not field a team each season?

While the Bloomer Girls did not play in Durango, the sport did not lack popularity there. Popular merchant Ike Kruschke sponsored a Durango team early in the decade. Otherwise, teams with various names played—the North Durango nine, the Free Silver nine, the YMCA nine, the Smelter nine, and the traditional Durango nine. The games between nearby communities heated up natural rivalries. When Durango visited Silverton in July 1892 and lost 25–6, the local *Herald* reporter aimed some pithy comments at the Silverton nine's ethics. They "imported the best battery" in the state to "help down the Durangos" (July 19, 1892). Durango, given the same chance to secure a "professional battery," declined to stoop to such activity. The *Herald* concluded that the city's "motives do honor to our club" and said, "Silverton Club's management committed a gross breach of hospitality in bringing in professional players to play against amateurs. . . . Durango can afford to lose a game of base ball, but Durango cannot afford to win by questionable means." In taking the high road on this issue, Durango salved its wounds, but this did not mean that given another occasion they might not have imported players. That practice was not unusual in Colorado baseball, or elsewhere, nor was it unusual to bring in good players and provide them with a "light" job. Sounding like the eternally hopeful baseball fans who have existed throughout the generations, the *Durango Great Southwest* (Sept. 13, 1892) predicted that Durango would field a team "next season that will meet and vanquish the best in the state."

"Wait 'til next year," that kept the "hot stove league" warm all winter. Then came spring and a new season. Occasionally, a "great deal of kicking" occurred after a game. For instance, in July 1894, Durango muttered, when it lost the second of a three-game set to Ouray 21–19 (Durango won the other two 26–18 and 25–15). The newspaper story did not say whether the blame rested with the umpiring or elsewhere. When the Durango team swept the Mancos "ball tossers" in October 1899, the result proved "somewhat of a surprise," because the "Mancos Boys [had] wiped up the earth with the Ft. Lewis nine" (*Herald*, Oct. 18, 1899). The Indian school at Fort Lewis usually fielded a very competitive team, so the *Herald* (Oct. 20, 1899) concluded that "they [Mancos] are crackerjacks when it comes to tackling amateur nines but Durango is a different proposition." According to the newspaper, the "Mancos boys are genial good fellows" who took their "defeat cheerfully," having enjoyed their Durango visit. Perhaps they did, but one thing is certain, local Durango pride soared.[4]

Durango did not take defeat so cheerfully, when their nine lost two games at Silverton on July 4, 1897, for purses of $67.50 and $75.00: "The Durango ball club returned from Silverton Monday night rather crest fallen, having lost both games. The boys claim the umpire [in the first game] gave them decidedly the worst of it while Monday they got a square deal" (*Herald*, July 5, 1897). That was 1890s baseball in its most essential form. Town pride stood in the batter's box and awaited the outcome of every fielding play. Pride soared or sagged with the final out, and local money changed hands on the outcome. The games provided a social occasion, as well. Special trains sometimes took fans, a band, and the team to another town. During the event described above, the Silverton-to-Durango train was "held" until the second game ended, although on the gloomy ride home, the Durangoans must have felt like the Mudville fans.

> Oh, somewhere in this favored land the sun is shining bright;
> The band is playing somewhere, and somewhere hearts are light,
> And somewhere men are laughing, and somewhere children shout.

Even so, a newspaper said, "The boys report a pleasant time and that the town was filled with men from the mines."

Interestingly, for all their baseball enthusiasm, some Durangoans were appalled that games took place on Sunday. In 1892, a petition arrived at city council, "praying Sunday ball playing be stopped" (Durango City Council Minutes, June 21 and July 5). Council referred it to committee, and eventually an ordinance appeared prohibiting baseball and football on the Sabbath. Enforcement remained another matter, and another well-intended ordinance soon became a dead letter.[5]

The question persists, why did baseball take hold in Durango, but not in Sandwich? Not because farm boys did not have time to play during the busy summer months, nor because there was not enough town support. Nearby, smaller farm communities regularly fielded teams and they came to Sandwich to play to reported "large, enthusiastic" crowds. Perhaps Sandwich lacked a determined organizer, civic interest, or a sponsor. Certainly, it was not because there was a shortage of potential players or because the town lacked an adequate field.

Newspapers in both communities published major-league scores, and Sandwich's papers carried major-league and some minor-league standings. Fans and interest existed, so the reason why the Sandwich nine took the field so irregularly remains lost in history. Perhaps Sandwich fans took the train to Chicago to see the National League Colts (now the Cubs) play—or to root for Chicago's team in the short-lived Players' League in 1890—and, thus, could not be enticed to heartily support the local nine.

Sandwich certainly turned out to support the high school football program. In an era when rules remained far from strict, players of various ages suited up, and it was not only school teams that took the field. With equipment at a minimum, the flying wedge a popular play, and with the forward pass still in the future, the games featured lots of rough-and-tumble action.

Again, town pride became involved, and when Sandwich lost to Plano in October 1897, the *Sandwich Free Press* (Oct. 21) felt obligated to point out, "The Plano boys are an attractive set of well trained lads who easily carried off all the honors. Our boys can get considerable comfort from the fact that football is a coarse rough game that's fast becoming outré." Well and good, but in 1899 the team came out a winner, and then the game was not, as the French say, outré anymore.

Oh rah! Oh rah! Ori!
The Sandwich High School! Ki! Ki!
Who are we?
Can't you guess?
We're the students of the S.H.S.

That cheer, "heard all over Wallace's Field" on a brisk, cloudy October Saturday afternoon in 1899, helped Sandwich defeat Plano 5–0 (*Argus*, Nov. 4, 1899). Showing little sportsmanship, Plano withdrew after nine minutes, when Sandwich scored a touchdown. Plano did play a second game in December and showed why they had left, losing 25–0. On that "cloudy and dull" December 2, Superintendent William Woodbury cheered his school to victory. "A hard fought game. . . . This squares us up with the Plano People. Was a clean, sporty game." Sandwich's season ended with a final record of three wins, two losses, and a tie.

After Earlville's eleven played Sandwich to a tie, editor Castle bristled in the *Sandwich* Argus (Nov. 11, 1899): "When Earlville's team came upon the field our high school boys seemed to be greatly in the minority or else boys go to school a long time down there." Town self-respect surfaced again later, but whether Sandwich sneaked in some overage players was never mentioned!

Durango's first reported football game matched Company K of the Colorado National Guard against the high school on November 30, 1893. The game was interrupted by a big argument over rules that governed whether a touchdown or safety had been scored. The game ended amid the controversy. The high school was finally declared a 2–0 winner, with a flying-wedge safety. Enthusiasm for the game sparked a movement to "organize a crack football team in this city" (*Durango Solid Muldoon*, Dec. 8, 1893). The idea came to naught; the 1890s depression put a stranglehold on the local economy, and nearby towns did not field teams to provide opponents.[6]

Football caught on, to some degree, in Sandwich only late in the decade and never really gained popularity in Durango. Few, if any teams, existed for Durango to play, without requiring a long journey. Injuries happened too frequently (helmets and pads remained in the future), and, for many people, the sport appeared too rough; critics even talked of abolishing it nationally. The newspapers of Durango and Sandwich never reported scores of college games, and interest did not seem generally to take hold.

Recreational opportunities surfaced in many guises, and who could resist at least one? At various times during the decade, Sandwich had a Tennis Club, which held matches against neighboring towns. Lawn tennis was popular among both men and women. The *Sandwich Argus* reported on September 2, 1893, that the home boys "put it all over 'em" in defeating Somonauk. An Athletic Club was active in Sandwich in 1890 but seems to have been replaced by the YMCA. In 1898, local gun enthusiasts organized a Rifle Club. Durango went even further and built an Athletic Park north of town, across Junction Creek. The park opened on Memorial Day, 1894, with a rematch football game between the high school and Company K, the winner receiving seventy-five dollars and the loser twenty-five. Unfortunately, no newspaper remains to tell the outcome. The football field also served as a baseball diamond, and, around it, a bicycle track (six laps to the mile) ran past the five-hundred-seat grandstand. A "dancing pavilion" offered further entertainment, where that other "Casey would waltz with a strawberry blonde."

Fire laddies in both communities occasionally participated in firemen's tournaments. These events furnished practical workouts, excited civic pride, and aroused the ubiquitous betting urge. Sandwich seemed more active in the tournaments, which included coupling contests, ladder climbing, hook-and-ladder competition, hose races, and other team and individual contests. The nearness of numerous towns meant more tournaments for Sandwich teams.[7]

Foot racing (one hundred yards or so) remained popular in both communities. In fact, it was one of the special events that opened the Athletic Park. Almost every town had a champion runner who took on challengers for a purse, side bets, and local pride. Sandwich High School also participated in track meets. In a "spirited affair" in June 1897, it edged Plano 57–54 (*Argus*, June 26). The folks at the Old Settlers Picnic witnessed the meet, probably cheering on a few grandsons. The time of 5:31 for the mile seemed particularly outstanding, if the distance and timer's watch were accurate.

Sandwich had no equivalent of Durango's single- and double-jack drilling contests. In these timed contests, contestants employed a skill fast vanishing in the mines, hand drilling. Underground, more efficient and faster power drills had begun replacing the hammer and steel. Nonetheless, the contests continued to be popular in mining regions. The contestants came from Silverton, Ouray, Rico, and other San Juan mining communities, but not from Durango. Durango provided the crowd, the granite rock for drilling, and cheered the sweating drillers; they did not forget the pillar of their local economy. Participants were required to have resided in the San Juan country for at least sixty days, and no tramp miner "ringers" were allowed to drift in and compete. A purse was offered to first- and second-place finishers, and miners, such as brothers Otto and Henry Olsen, gained regional fame for their skills.

Even if they did not drive "steel," Durangoans played checkers, though not with the enthusiasm of Sandwich in 1899. There, teams from the three town wards competed with much coverage and pithy comment in the local press. Checkers met with general approval. Boxing did not. In fact, there was a national effort to ban it. Although boxing matches may have occurred, they took place in secret, except in January 1890, when "the athletes of Sandwich" put on three boxing matches along with other athletic exhibitions (*Free Press*, Jan. 29).

The Durango Club provided more genteel recreation. Billiards, chess, cards, and reading satisfied its members, who numbered more than one hundred. The club permitted no "intoxicating liquors or games of chance" (*Durango Directory for the Year 1892*, 109). Might Durango be taking on "airs"? This sounded suspiciously like a British club with social aspirations.[8]

Vacations of a few days, or a week or two, were becoming more common, primarily among the wealthy and upper middle classes. Workers with less free time took one-day excursions to a nearby popular spot. Newspapers in both towns chronicled some of the trips people took—to visit an old home, to tour Europe, or to winter in California or Florida. A few Sandwichites reached Colorado, and as far as we know, 1893 was the only year Durangoans vacationed in Illinois.

Outdoor camping emerged as one of the most popular vacation activities. It gave the family a chance to travel out of town and to enjoy both a break from routine and a trip back to "nature." Camping essentially imitated a rustic version of middle-class home life and was not a true adventure in "wilderness" living.

Fortunate Durangoans had more opportunities to return to nature. Surrounded by mountains, they lived in a vacation paradise, and the region's main river flowed right through town. Although the Animas was severely polluted by upstream mines and mills, ranches, farms, and the town of Silverton, which dumped its raw sewage into this convenient sewer, the river still contained fish and provided many camping spots. So did the nearby mountains and streams, including the Florida and Los Pinos Rivers. A trip could be just a family outing or a major expedition, such as the one in August 1894 to the Vallecito area for ten days of hunting and fishing. A four-horse team conveyed tents, food, and a cook for the party. Durangoans had to compete with out-of-town tourists, who had also discovered the delights of a San Juan camping vacation, only a minor inconvenience, unless someone "jumped" a favorite camping spot.

Vacationing Sandwich folks encountered no such problems. Their popular spots included Somonauk Creek, the Fox River, Glen Park, and Starved Rock. The latter two, located on the Fox and Illinois Rivers, respectively, emerged as particularly favorite vacation destinations. Starved Rock, with its Indian legends and rock formations (with such romantic Victorian names as Lover's Leap), advertised itself as one of the "best places for campers and sight seers" (*Sandwich Free Press,* June 11, 1891). For the less adventuresome, a new hotel opened at Starved Rock in 1891. Glen Park, nearer Sandwich, offered "favorite" fishing spots, "hills, dells, lofty trees, green grass," a dining hall, and "cozy cottages" perched on hillsides with a "picturesque view on every side" (*Sandwich Argus,* July 29, 1899). The camp closed at 10:00 p.m. so everyone could get a restful night's sleep.

Newspapers in both communities preached the need for a restful day's or week's vacation, and these Victorians, whenever they could, took advantage of the opportunities. By buggy, wagon, or train, they departed, hopefully to return invigorated from their outdoor experiences. How restful the trip might be for mother may be questioned; she still had to pack, prepare meals on most occasions, and maintain family order.[9]

Seasonal recreation provided a variety of opportunities for young and old. Marbles, skipping rope, and vacant-lot baseball games heralded the coming of spring. Both sexes passed many a summer afternoon playing croquet, an acceptable, genteel sport for courting and visiting. An afternoon fishing trip to a nearby favorite "hole," or a picnic in the country or backyard, provided a welcome diversion from everyday routine. Buggy rides, bicycle trips, and berry-picking expeditions offered other diversions. In the winter, skating, enjoying romantic evenings when "the moon is beaming over the lake," and sleigh rides, with the "merry jingle of bells" helped brighten the cold season. Sandwich occasionally flooded a park during the winter for skating, about which William Woodbury commented, "The youngsters have lots of fun at that sport."

Dancing seems to have been less popular than in previous decades—at least, the newspapers noted fewer dances. The advent of the new ragtime dance steps, however, was near at hand, as were other new recreational possibilities. A few brave Durangoans even tried skiing, although reaching the top of mountain slopes required a lot of work. It took courage to race down hillsides on skis that could not be turned very easily, or quickly, and did not have secure bindings for attaching the skis to one's boots or shoes.

The type of recreation that was, perhaps, the most common, kids' informal fun and games, went on morning, afternoon, and evening. Edna Goodman remembered her Durango youth of the 1890s: "Oh, we had certain chores we had to do. We played and had friends. We went to each others house and we had parties and things like that. We made our fun. We played hide and seek, pom pom pull away, statues—whirl around, let loose, and have to stay in the position ended up. We had paper dolls that we cut out and we would play dolls." She remembered the circus coming to town, and how they all rushed down to see the tent put up and the parade. "I went one time and the wind blew the circus tent down."

Louis Smith fondly recalled the arc lights at intersections in Durango: "After 6:00, the streets belonged to the kids, gosh under the arc-lights they was out there playing hide and seek or kick-the-can, or shinny." Laughingly, he spoke of Halloween, when one person's enjoyment might be another's headache: "Well, in those days everybody had those little outhouses, you know. Well, everybody's outhouses were tipped over, or their gates were stolen. If you had a buggy sitting out, it would be taken to another part of town somewheres." Even the curfew bell did not stop this type of recreation!

In Sandwich, Will and Agnes Smith and their family "went all-out for picnics on the Fourth of July," with a big picnic dinner. If they went to the Fox River, the trip included fishing. They enjoyed games such as checkers, authors, dominoes, and board games. During their courtship, Will and Nellie Woodbury played Parcheesi, crokinole, hearts, and "go bang." Popular board games had been acceptable for years, as long as they taught moral or ethical lessons. The Game of Christian Endeavor and the Sociable Snake came out of this heritage in the 1890s. However, the trend was away from these kinds of games and toward such games as Banking, A Century Run (a bicycle game), and, after the Spanish-American War, the Battle of Manila and the War in Cuba. The new games emphasized making money or winning, not virtue and the good wholesome life. In most good Christian homes, card games remained suspect. Card decks were referred to as "the Devil's picture books," unless they were the old favorites—authors, or cards featuring biblical sayings.

The ever popular family reading of newspapers, magazines, and books became even more enjoyable, when the electric light made it easier and more comfortable. Children sitting around the dining room table listening to Dad or Mom read out loud, or individually enjoying a favorite story, was as popular as legend has made it. Inexpensive books for under a dollar (some as low as eight cents per volume) allowed the family library to expand beyond the Bible of earlier generations. The "dime novel," however, did not gain any popularity with Mom or with teachers, but those adventure yarns never lost their appeal to young boys.

Family singing also was one of the Smith recreations, as it was for many Victorian families who gathered around the piano or organ in the parlor. Popular songs could be purchased as sheet music or, for those music lovers who had not mastered the hand-played piano, player-piano rolls. In truth, this era might well be called the "Golden Age of American Song." From lovely, lilting songs and church favorites to sentimental ballads and John Philip Sousa marches ("The Stars and Strips Forever," 1897), and even to the oncoming "sinful" ragtime melodies ("Maple Leaf Rag," 1899), the nineties heard them all. Americans played, sang, and listened in parlor, music hall, and "saw dust" revival tent. In a romantic sense, later generations have come to see these melodies as symbolizing the 1890s, and in a popular sense they did.[10]

These Victorian Americans had more leisure time than their parents and grandparents. Even the farm folk did, thanks to improved and new equipment that reduced work hours. They used their free time in a variety of ways that would have amazed an earlier generation. The differences between Sandwich and Durango were not that great, a matter of degree rather than of substance. The majority of these Victorians did not share the sentiments of Mark Twain when he said, "I have never taken any exercise, except sleeping and resting, and I never intend to take any." They enjoyed being active to one degree or another.

NOTES

1. John Bowman and Joel Zoss, *Diamonds in the Rough* (New York: Macmillan, 1989), 373. Julian Ralph, *Harper's Chicago and the World's Fair* (New York: Harper & Brothers, 1893), 250. Thomas J. Schlereth, *Victorian America* (New York: HarperCollins, 1991), 220–21. Harvey Green, *The Light of the Home* (New York: Pantheon, 1983), 158–60. *Sandwich Argus*, Oct. 17, 1896.

2. *Sears, Roebuck and Co. Consumers Guide,* 1897 (New York: Chelsea House, 1968 reprint), 177, 281, 611–19. *Sandwich Free Press*, March 30, May 4, 1893; July 2, 1896. *Argus*, July 9, 1892; Oct. 17, 1896. *Durango Great Southwest*, April 4, 1893. *Durango Herald*, April 22, 1894; March 28, 1895; March 20, July 30, Oct. 22, 1896; May 13, 1897. Ayres, Alex (ed.), *The Wit & Wisdom of Mark Twain* (New York: Harper & Row, 1987), 248.

3. Durango Ordinance Book 1, pages 318 and 335. *Revised Ordinances of the City of Durango, Colorado* (Durango: n.p., 1901), 77–78.

4. Martin Gardner, "Casey at the Bat," *American Heritage* (Oct. 1967), 64–67. Richard McCloud, *Durango As It Is* (Durango: Durango Board of Trade, 1892), 54–55. *Argus*, May 16, 1896; Sept. 4, 1897. *Free Press*, April 23, April 30, 1890; Aug. 30, 1894; May 14, May 21, 1896. *Durango Solid Muldoon*, July 21, 1893. *Herald*, July 19, 1892; July 4, 1894; Oct. 17, Oct. 18, Oct. 19, Oct. 20, 1899. *Great Southwest*, July 30, Sept. 13, 1892.

5. Durango City Council Minutes, book 2, July 5 and 21, 1892. *Revised Ordinances of the City of Durango*. *Herald*, July 4, July 5, 1897. Gardner, "Casey," 67.

6. *Free Press*, Oct. 21, 1897. *Argus*, Nov. 4, Nov. 11, Nov. 18, Dec. 2, Dec. 9, 1899. William Woodbury diary, Dec. 2, 1899, Regional History Center, Northern Illinois University. *Herald*, Dec. 1, 1893. *Solid Muldoon*, Dec. 1, Dec. 8, 1893.

7. *Argus*, July 15, Aug. 26, Sept. 2, 1893; Dec. 10, 1898. Green, *Light of the Home*, 153. *Free Press*, April 9, Sept. 15, 1890; Aug. 6, Aug. 13, 1891. *Herald*, May 27, 1894; July 5, 1898.

8. *Argus*, Sept. 8, 1893; June 26, 1897; Dec. 2, 1899. *Great Southwest*, Nov. 17, 1892. *Herald*, July 1, 1892; July 2, July 5, 1898. *Free Press*, Jan. 29, 1890. *Durango Directory for the Year 1892* (Trinidad, Colo.: Bensel Directory Co., 1892), 109.

9. Green, *Light of the Home*, 157–58. Schlereth, *Victorian America*, 19. *Herald*, Aug. 14, 1894. *Argus*, July 29, 1899. *Free Press*, June 11, 1891.
10. Woodbury diary, Jan. 10, 1899. *Free Press*, March 12, July 16, 1896. Schlereth, *Victorian America*, 211. *Argus*, Jan. 27, 1894; Feb. 12, 1898; Jan. 6, 1900. Edna Goodman, interviews by author, Jan. 9, Jan. 19, 1980. Louis Smith, interview by author, July 18, 1977. Stanley Smith, interview by author, Feb. 21, 1994. Peter Andrews, "Games People Played," *American Heritage* (June 1972), 66–74. Ayres, *Wit & Wisdom*, 71.

12

FRIENDSHIP, LOVE, AND TRUTH

*In the battle front we stood,
When their fiercest charge they made.*
—"Tramp! Tramp! Tramp!" (1864)

"Everyone was doing it," Victorians believed as they departed for their lodge meeting. Actually, it did seem that everybody was joining a club, temple, lodge, post, or association. Americans joined in record numbers in the nineties, continuing the trend of the previous decade. Ceremony and ritual costumes appeared to be a need of the hour.

Perhaps membership in an organization offered a form of escapism, an oasis from the world, a chance to be with one's friends, access to sickness and death benefits, the opportunity for leadership, the possibility of making business contacts or of gaining entry into the community—the reasons for joining seem to have been almost as numerous as the participants. By 1901, 568 fraternal organizations, from the sublime to the supremely ludicrous, beckoned would-be members. In this high tide of fraternizing, Sandwich and Durango folk marched right in step with their fellow Americans. Both men and women joined, the women often relegated to auxiliary status.

The Masons, Eastern Star, Odd Fellows ("Friendship, love and truth" was their motto), Ancient Order of United Workmen, Knights of Pythias, Woman's Relief Corps, and GAR organized in both towns. Sandwich had a Rebecca Lodge, Knights of the Globe, Modern Woodmen of America, and the IOMA. It even contained a small, "but active," branch of the University Association. The Redmen of the World, Knights Templar, Woodmen of the World, and several unions—the Knights of Labor, the Carpenters Union, and the Western Federation of Miners—gained Durango adherents. Neither town had a chapter of the Happy Order of Goats or of the International Order of Hoo-Hoo.[1]

The lodges initiated members, held regular meetings, sponsored suppers, paid funeral and general benefits, visited other lodges, raised money for community outreach programs, and marched in parades. Their activities resembled those of corresponding groups in other towns. One interesting difference between the two towns is the lack of any evidence of labor unions in Sandwich, which apparently had none or, if it did, had ones that were so weak they went unmentioned in local newspapers and other sources. Neither town would prove supportive of "radicalism," and unionism never took hold permanently. That struggle remained too foreign, too un-American.

Durango boasted of its National Guard company, Company K; Sandwich certainly wanted one, but never secured permission from the Illinois National Guard. Company K provided a grand social organization for the boys (it participated in dances, public drills, and football games) and went along quite famously, until called up in 1894 to help stop the labor violence in the booming, but strike-torn, Cripple Creek gold-mining district. No dances, parades, and games this time; the miners proved deadly serious, with guns and dynamite, and management hired its own trigger-happy guards. Company K's enthusiasm and membership dropped off rapidly, after it returned to Durango.[2]

That attitude horrified the patriotic, nationalistic Grand Army of the Republic. Probably the single most influential group in both Sandwich and Durango, this Union veterans organization, and its auxiliary, the Woman's Relief Corps, had a community-wide impact well beyond the size of its membership. Although it was not the only national veterans organization, the GAR had become the largest and most powerful.

The Civil War had hardly ended when the participants recognized the struggle as a turning point in American history, one that should never be forgotten or ignored. This generation of Americans knew they had been tested in fire, and they never forgot that experience throughout the rest of their lives. The Civil War influenced the postwar North in hundreds of ways, even in a town like Durango, which was born fifteen years after the Confederate surrender at Appomattox. Considering nineteenth-century Americans' predilection for joining groups, veterans would be expected to organize.

Illinois gave birth to the GAR. Governor Richard Oglesby and General John Logan were as responsible as any two individuals for establishing it and moving it forward in 1866–67. By 1868, National Commander

Logan called for all posts to arrange "fitting services and memorials" on May 30 for fallen comrades, thus helping to establish Memorial Day as a national holiday. Initially, the GAR became heavily involved in politics, supporting the Republicans with such slogans as "Vote as you shot." In "waving the bloody shirt," they branded Democrats as the party of Jeff Davis and treason. The GAR forged itself into the most powerful political lobby of the age. Every president but one, from 1868 through 1900, held GAR membership.

Following the reelection of Ulysses Grant in 1872, however, partisan politics made up only part of the GAR's program. By the 1880s, the aging veterans had become more concerned about pensions, and the organization proved wildly successful in securing them. By 1900, Civil War pensions consumed one-third of all federal tax dollars. GAR membership, meanwhile, fluctuated, and, not until the eighties, when the group became more of a fraternal organization, did it reenergize itself and its membership begin to shoot up again. In many ways the GAR then resembled the immensely popular civilian lodges.[3]

The town of Sandwich, which was well established by the time of the war, furnished men, money, and materials for the Union effort. Companies were raised within De Kalb County, and men volunteered for other units. These local veterans later formed the nucleus of Sandwich's GAR Post 510, which was surrounded by like posts in almost every nearby community. Union veterans helped start Durango, and they organized the GAR's Sedgwick Post, which was named after "the best-loved general in the army Uncle John Sedgwick," who was killed at the Battle of Spotsylvania Court House in May 1864. One major difference between the Sandwich and Durango posts was that no other post existed within fifty miles of Durango.

Oliver Wendell Holmes, Jr., aptly expressed, in a Memorial Day address in 1895, the common bond that held the veterans together: "As for us, our days of combat are over. Our swords are rust. Our guns will thunder no more . . . We have shared the incommunicable experience of war, we have felt, we still feel, the passion of life to its top." Camaraderie, an orderly and happy community, nationalism and patriotism, and nostalgia for the fast-fading era of their youth headlined the GAR's agenda. The Civil War years signified for most of its members their only contact with national history.

The minutes of the Sedgwick Post provide a fascinating glimpse of the GAR in action. The members had served in regiments from almost all

Northern states and territories—Kansas, Colorado, New York, Iowa, Massachusetts, Maine, and especially Illinois. They came from all walks of life and included lawyers, farmers, watchmakers, miners, musicians, photographers, mining engineers, and carpenters. A typical meeting, such as the one on June 25, 1898, included roll call; reports from the quarter master, adjutant, and department encampments; discussion of bills for expenses; election of a sentinel; and closure. Each post followed the same routine, with military terms being used throughout. GAR songbooks allowed the "boys" to sing the stirring tunes of their war days, including the ever popular "Battle Hymn of the Republic" and "Tramp! Tramp! Tramp!"

Because of the aging condition of the veterans, they spent much time discussing assistance to ill comrades—or turning it down, as happened to W. H. Hudson, because the relief committee "did not think him worthy of assistance." The availability of grave lots in Greenmount Cemetery caused quite a flap in 1897. Although the post earlier had promised free lots to members, it decided, following heated discussions, that only comrades in good standing after three years would receive a lot. "Good standing" meant paying your one-dollar yearly dues. The post would prorate the cost of lots—for example, a member would get a quarter of a lot free for one year's membership. Delinquent dues and absenteeism generated their share of serious discussions. For instance, the members requested that Chaplain Franklin Fessing either attend GAR meetings or resign; he promised to attend. Admitting and expelling members also took time. Applications had to be checked and discharges from other posts received. In the case of Nathaniel Kilborn, some unexplained questions required several months of examination before he "was voted in."

Nationally, the GAR stressed patriotism, and the Sedgwick Post marched right in step by establishing a committee to introduce into the public schools the practice of saluting the flag. As mentioned earlier, in the 1890s, Americans, at least native-born whites, came to venerate the flag almost as a cult icon. Flag Day and the Pledge of Allegiance resulted, and the GAR joined the rush because it stood on "the right side of the line that divided loyalty from treason."

The GAR, which accepted only Civil War veterans, grew older and weaker, as the years went by, and had peaked in 1890 with a membership of four hundred thousand. The Sedgwick Post reflected this trend, and its days of significance, beyond ceremonial functions, faded away in the nineties. During the decade, for example, it corresponded with the federal government about securing a Civil War cannon for the town and made sure veterans' graves continued to be well maintained.

The Sedgwick Post might have been more energetic as a unit at the time of the Spanish-American War, if it had not lost the lease on its meeting hall. An explanation of what happened failed to appear in the terse minutes, but, when the comrades assembled on April 20, 1898, at the usual place, they found that all their furniture had been removed. It took them several weeks to clear the matter up and locate a new meeting place in the Woodman Hall. By then, the Spanish-American War had moved toward its rapid conclusion.[4]

The Sandwich Post was more active overall, as might be surmised. Two factors helped bring this about: Durango had no direct connection to the Civil War, and the war had begun fading into memory by 1880–81. Sandwich was a completely Union town; no Johnny Reb dared darken its streets. The town, therefore, provided the perfect environment for a GAR post. The Sandwich Post did not have to worry about a meeting place; it had its own hall. The post sponsored local lectures and took active roles in celebrations throughout Illinois and, occasionally, as far away as Gettysburg, Pennsylvania. It sent, for example, thirty men to the July 1897 unveiling in Chicago of a statue of John Logan. Its members also went to reunions of various regiments, such as the Eighth Illinois Cavalry, in which some had served. The post hosted the annual reunion of the 136th Illinois Volunteers in Sandwich in October 1892, a major undertaking. Comrades traveled to GAR national encampments and GAR campfires and marched on every conceivable occasion. According to "unbiased" local press coverage, the post was a featured attraction in parades in other towns.

Memorial Day marked the most significant GAR day locally in both communities. In the months before the holiday, each post spent hours planning, organizing, selecting a speaker, and resolving the many details that went into a successful celebration. The day's format did not change in the 1890s. A parade started the celebration, with a band, various organizations, citizens in carriages, school children, and, of course, the veterans. The "exercises of the day" followed, including a patriotic oration (a length of an hour or more was not uncommon), music, and GAR exercises. The day concluded with trips to the local cemeteries for services. Businesses closed during these hours, so that all might participate. Said the *Sandwich Argus* (May 23, 1896):

> Patriotism demands that we lay aside the cares of business and worldly pleasures and pursuits, and with the remaining comrades kneel, with uncovered heads, at the grave of the patriot, and with flowers sweet and voice of eulogy pay homage to him who paid life for our preservation.

Memorial Day symbolized the heart and soul of the GAR's mission, which was to make sure that people did not forget. "The memories of the heroes shall not be forsaken while there are living comrades able to celebrate the day" (*Sandwich Free Press,* April 2, 1890).

As the 1890s closed, people were forgetting the conflict, despite the best GAR efforts. The war's guns and drums, silent now for over thirty years, did not receive the new generation's undivided attention. The *Durango Democrat* observed on May 31, 1899, that while Durango celebrated the day in a "fitting way," the veterans marched "possibly for the last time by the fighting machines that went to battle in the sixties as a growing feebleness of the remnant seems to deny all further orders to parade." The veterans disproved the forecast in the short run; eventually, though, the steps faltered, the ranks thinned, and finally "nobody remained to march at all." They had marched into history and only memories lingered. "The men who fought in the Civil War, speaking for all Americans, had said something this country could never forget."[5]

The veterans could not have accomplished what they had in Sandwich and Durango without the help of the Woman's Relief Corps, which was recognized as a GAR auxiliary in 1881. The Sedgwick Post extended "a vote of complimentary thanks . . . to the ladies of the Corps" and pledged that all "loyal women," who wanted to render aid to the veteran and his family, would receive a "hearty welcome." That hearty welcome aside, women, like sons, never would be admitted to membership. The GAR remained a veteran's world. The "angels of the home" were expected to stand and cheer, while the men marched and basked in the glory, just as they had done in 1861. The women were expected also to work in the background to keep things moving.

FRIENDSHIP, LOVE, AND TRUTH

The Woman's Relief Corps served under the local posts, presenting quarterly reports and working on such GAR projects as relief for veterans and Memorial Day planning. The members of the Sandwich Corps, Number 182, proved more active than their Durango sisters. They worked within the community and sent donations to the Soldiers Home in Quincy, Illinois, and the Soldiers Widow's Home in Washington, D.C. In July 1898, they served a supper to raise money for soldiers wounded in "the present war with Spain." Always looking for a way to honor veterans, they started raising money in 1899 to purchase, for Oak Ridge Cemetery, a "suitable" monument to "commensurate the services of the boys of 61–65."[6]

The "boys in blue" charged right into the history books, and the members of the Grand Army of the Republic were determined to be masters of their own legend. By the late 1880s, the GAR had become concerned about how schoolbooks portrayed the Civil War. These books reached and shaped young minds that had no memory of those glorious days. Through speeches, Memorial Day celebrations, personal narratives, monuments, and "campfires" that recreated their wartime camps, the veterans tried to influence popular perception of the war era. In Illinois, they were aided by the veneration of "their own" Abraham Lincoln. A community, school, or church program (sometimes all three) devoted to the Great Emancipator, and an article and picture in the newspaper, usually highlighted his birthday celebration, so no one would forget. Durango might have a mention of Lincoln in the newspaper, perhaps in a description of a school program dedicated to him, but little else.

The GAR's national organization tried to prod textbook publishers and local boards of education into presenting the conflict in a way that reflected the organization's "evangelical nationalist view." No data exists on what the Sandwich and Durango posts may have done in this regard. Both, however, kept a sharp eye on the pension campaign, which also served to push public opinion of the war in the same direction. The GAR portrayed contributing to the pension fund as the patriotic thing to do, as an opportunity to come to the aid of the manly, self-sacrificing patriots who had saved the Union.

Weakened in power and numbers, the GAR, in the 1890s, constituted a declining minority in a fast-evolving world that was far different from that of the immediate postwar years. Regardless, the organization had shaped the country, including Durango and Sandwich. Its activities had transformed the public's attitude toward charity, which was no longer tied only to poverty, and the Northern view of the war now approximated, if it did not completely match, what the veterans wanted it to be. The posts had been sounding boards for community ideas and plans, because its members discussed issues and political candidates. The members were respected and honored, and with annual Memorial Day activities to remind the public, no one could forget those who had sacrificed and gone before.[7]

The Woman's Relief Corps was not the most influential women's organization of the 1890s. That honor belonged to the Woman's Christian Temperance Union. The WCTU fought for the same goals as the GAR—a white, Anglo-Saxon, Protestant, middle-class, patriotic America—with one major exception: many a hard-drinking veteran could not stomach prohibition. Although the WCTU actively organized in both communities, it garnered far more impact and influence in Sandwich. The organization provided the backbone behind the fight to end liquor sales in Sandwich, and it could look to the nearby Chicago WCTU group, the nation's most active, for support and guidance.

The fact that the Sandwich WCTU won the fight and the town finally became dry did not bring the desired millennium. Whether the ordinance was poorly or rigidly enforced, saloons beckoned in many a nearby town. Some WCTU members favored temperance over prohibition, although the latter won out eventually. The WCTU fought against the saloon as the outward symbol of what alcoholism could cause—poverty, abuse, crime, and ruined lives. The Sandwich WCTU sponsored lectures (featuring both local and visiting speakers), meetings, sociables, lawn parties, fund-raising suppers, and prayer and church meetings.

"Drunkenness is in the same category as stealing and other sins," railed one emotional minister at a WCTU meeting (*Sandwich Free Press*, Nov. 30, 1893). The drunkard is a robber "defrauding society"; intoxication "is a sin against man's own being." The arguments and their popular appeal harkened back generations, and women and increasing numbers of men responded. Interestingly, the WCTU said nothing openly about alcoholism among women; men remained the chief offenders in the eyes of the organization. A dark veil shrouds opium and alcohol inebriety among Victorian women, problems that caused both an embarrassment to, and imperfection in, the image of the mother and the wife.

Sometimes, WCTU meetings did not measure up to expectations. The *Sandwich Free Press* (May 14, 1890) observed, "It really requires very much ingenuity and talent to make an interesting temperance meeting." But, five years later, the *Sandwich Argus* gushed about an address at one of the meetings: "It bristled with thrilling facts, and convincing arguments, all on the side of temperance and pure morals, the two going together." The WCTU supported woman's suffrage, believing that the vote would strengthen its efforts, an idea with which its opponents, the saloon keepers, concurred.

The WCTU worked through the churches and schools to disseminate its message, especially to the young. In 1897, the Sandwich women organized a Loyal Temperance Legion for "boys and girls ages 10–16," that within a year had one hundred members (*Sandwich Argus*, April 30, 1898). The youngsters' meetings included "prayers for the protection of the home against the rum traffic," and one, in April 1898, closed with "three cheers for temperance and three groans for saloons." The legion was a group with many goals. All "boys and girls not already members are invited to unite with these young crusaders who are so truly loyal to their country's flag."

Both Sandwich newspapers supported the WCTU, the *Sandwich Argus* calling it the most powerful moral influence in the nation, outside the church, and the city council allowed the group to use City Hall rent free, a policy the council also followed for the services of all religious groups.

The Durango WCTU received less local support. Their much more wide-open town challenged them. The newspapers, lukewarm to the "cause," at best, only occasionally published supporting articles. The *Durango Weekly Tribune*, on May 28, 1891, swung the most telling blow against liquor with an article on "Drunkenness and the Wife." The paper admitted, "If a drunken husband does not justify woman's aggression against whiskey, hardly anything does." Yet it also opposed (June 1, 1891) a Sunday saloon-closing law, which it described as a "doubtful measure of reform" that endangered the "business interests" and did not warrant the experiment. The proponents of the law never achieved its passage but did help put a 9:00 p.m. to 5:00 a.m. curfew in place to keep youngsters away from temptations.

The Durango WCTU continued to meet, to discuss such issues as "character building," and to work for the cause (*Durango Herald*, April 23, 1896). They found, however, the town's environment continually pushing against them. Durangoans did not appear ready for temperance, and they certainly were not ready for prohibition. Even the members of the Sandwich WCTU sometimes suffered doubt. "The temperance sentiment is not as high in Sandwich as we could wish, but it is hoped the zeal of this society will not lessen anyway with the coming year [1894]." Samuel Dickson, you may recall, did not agree at all with the WCTU goals. He objected to "radical fanatics" depriving Sandwich of its revenue from liquor licenses and causing the town to lose trade. Dickson and those who concurred with him were eventually overrun.[8]

In both communities, the Young Men's Christian Association joined the WCTU in the fight to save young men. Again Sandwich far outstripped Durango, the local environment being much more receptive. Or perhaps there simply existed more recreational and outdoor activities in Durango, which undercut the YMCA. A town needed a YMCA, boosters thought, and Sandwich did not have one, so the *Sandwich Free Press* (March 24, 1892) sounded the alarm: "We don't know of any other city [the size of Sandwich] in the state without a YMCA." In a matter of months, one was organized.

Sandwich's YMCA worked closely with the WCTU in various ways. For example, in 1893, the YMCA opened its doors to the WCTU's sewing class, which, with sixty girls, had outgrown its facilities. The YMCA, too, was interested in "building character," and that was a subject of more than one lecture sponsored by the local organization. The goals of the two groups were almost identical in many ways. The YMCA sponsored lecture courses, entertainments, and a reading room "to provide a place for young men to pass evenings" (*Argus*, Feb. 19, 1894). The YMCA opened its library to the public, until Sandwich started its own. The YMCA gymnasium was "fitted with the latest paraphernalia needed for athletic sports," including hot and cold baths and electric lights (*Argus*, Jan. 18, 1896). Occasionally, the YMCA brought in outside speakers to take the pulpit in local churches, and the organization's rooms served as a social center for the entire community.

Durango's YMCA also had its own rooms and a library. And it had the backing of the local press: "We recommend [the YMCA] as a cheerful and profitable place to spend leisure hours" (*Durango Daily Southwest*, Sept. 1, 1893). At least briefly, the Durango YMCA had a gym, with such "new apparatus" as Indian clubs, dumbbells, fencing foils, parallel bars, a vaulting horse, and a "striking bag." But by 1899 the *Herald* (Feb. 9) bemoaned the "sad and regrettable fact" that the institution "had elapsed." The reporter did not say what had happened. Perhaps the fact that it resided over the Hub Saloon did not help![9]

The GAR, WCTU, and YMCA all promoted what they believed would be a better today and a wonderful tomorrow, though the GAR based its vision of the future on its own heroic yesterdays. Yesterdays also seemed more important to the pioneers who had "tamed and settled this land." Pioneer days had not transpired that long ago in Durango.

Already a romantic nostalgia had settled over the reminiscences of the pioneers, and their memories evolved into a heroic story. The larger-than-life pioneers overcame all obstacles, human or otherwise, that hindered the onward march of progress. Sandwich pioneers could belong to two local groups. One was the Old Settlers Union Picnic Association of Sandwich. It was organized in 1893 and held its picnic in June, with music, historical addresses, and the election of officers. The other group, the Old Settlers Association, was for those who had arrived in De Kalb County before 1860, and it was more established and organized. The organization flourished under the direction of Civil War veteran Silas Dexter Wesson, who served as its president throughout the decade. Wesson, a farmer, lived in nearby Victor and often visited Sandwich. The Old Settlers Association met every September at Pritchard's Grove (southwest of Waterman), as it had since 1877, for festivities and a trip down memory lane. The members did not solely live in the past, however. They enjoyed a baseball game in 1891 and, in 1896, listened to a debate between Silverites and Goldbug speakers. With a certain urgency, they read at each meeting a list of "old settlers who had died in the last year" (*Free Press,* Sept. 14, 1899). By September 1899, the list was 271 names long—the obituaries in the newspapers chronicled a steady stream of pioneers passing across "the great divide."

With their history disappearing personally and materially—old buildings were being torn down to make way for "modern" structures—Sandwichites tried to preserve what they could. Preservation of old buildings would be something for their descendants; preserving the memory of pioneering days was another matter entirely. The *Sandwich Argus,* for example, ran a series of articles in 1890–91 on local history. Yet much had already been lost, and often what Sandwichites recorded in the 1890s provided only a romanticized glimpse of yesteryear. Such romanticization was natural, but it can also be understood from another perspective: The very nature of log cabin days and a seemingly simpler life clashed dramatically with the new days and ways of the 1890s. The contrast of Abraham Lincoln's New Salem with Chicago of the World's Fair may have been hard to reconcile in their minds. The pioneers' goal had been to "civilize and settle." The reality of the nineties may have stunned them into yearning for a "better" yesterday, when they had been young and masters of what they surveyed.

Durangoans had a shorter European American settlement history to reflect upon, and the "pioneers" still worked actively within the community. With a sense of history, however, they organized the San Juan Pioneer's Association for those individuals who had arrived before July 14, 1880, thereby leaving out those Johnny-come-latelies, who started Durango in September of that year! The association had members from throughout southwestern Colorado, and the fifty-cent annual dues appeared "well within the reach of every old timer" (*Herald*, July 9, 1896). Durango hosted the 1896 meeting, and the Denver & Rio Grande guaranteed special rates. "Come," said the *Herald*, "it will revive your youth." Despite being too "young," Durango extended a "most cordial" welcome.

Whether such meetings revived anyone's youth, they did provide a chance to renew old friendships and reminisce about the "good old days." The goals of these pioneers' associations were similar to the GAR's: the members were trying to shape their history into a story acceptable to them. Many individuals joined both a pioneer association and the GAR. Ardent GAR member Deck Wesson never forgot his days with the Eighth Illinois Cavalry. He even brought his cavalry horse, Old Charley, home and, eventually, lovingly buried the faithful animal on his farm.[10]

Reminiscence, comradeship, secret gripes, a promise for the future, ritual, public projects, causes, celebrations, good times, lecture series, meetings, insurance—Durango and Sandwich clubs and associations offered something for everybody who cared to join. And join they did in this decade of phenomenal interest in such organizations. How many joined in these two communities will never be known, but the percentage does not appear to have been less than the reported forty percent of men nationally. It might even be conservative to say that fifty percent of all Sandwichites and Durangoans joined some type of club or association. Most of the movers and shakers, who clearly influenced the course of events, joined: Sandwich lawyer John Blee was a member of the Knights of Pythias, Masons, and Odd

Fellows; Sandwich editor Miles Castle was a Mason; longtime Sandwich mayor A. Gates White joined the Masons and Knights of Pythias; Durango merchant Charles Newman was a Mason; Durango banker Alfred Camp was an Elk and a member of the San Juan Pioneer's Association; and Durango entrepreneur Thomas Graden belonged to the GAR. Not all marched to the same drum. Durango's maverick newspaperman, Dave Day, belonged to no club, organization, or lodge and was proud of it.

NOTES

1. Stuart McConnell, *Glorious Contentment: The Grand Army of the Republic* (Chapel Hill: University of North Carolina Press, 1992), 85, 87. Thomas J. Schlereth, *Victorian America* (New York: HarperCollins, 1991), 213. Richard McCloud, *Durango As It Is* (Durango: Durango Board of Trade, 1892), 54–55. *Durango Directory for the Year 1892* (Trinidad, Colo.: Bensel Directory Co., 1892), 21–22. *Sandwich Argus*, July 8, 1893; Jan. 25, 1896. *Sandwich Free Press*, April 2, 1896. Alvin J. Schmidt, *Fraternal Organizations* (Westport, Conn.: Greenwood Press, 1980).
2. *Free Press*, March 5, 1890; Aug. 30, 1894; April 22, Sept. 2, 1897; Aug. 1, Oct. 6, 1898. *Argus*, May 9, 1896; July 31, 1897; Feb. 26, 1898. *Durango Herald*, Jan. 7, 1893; June 5, June 6, June 7, 1894.
3. McConnell, *Glorious Contentment,* xi, xiv, 15, 86. Robert P. Howard, *Illinois* (Grand Rapids, Mich.: William B. Ferdmans, 1972), 327–28.
4. Sedgwick Post Records: Minutes, Jan. 1897–June 1898, and Membership Roll, both found in the Center of Southwest Studies at Fort Lewis College. McConnell, *Glorious Contentment,* 206–08, 220.
5. *Argus*, May 28, June 4, 1892; May 23, 1896; July 24, 1897; Feb. 19, 1898; Dec. 16, 1899. *Free Press*, Feb. 5, April 2, May 28, June 4, Nov. 27, Dec. 4, 1890; Aug. 6, 1891; Oct. 6, 1892; April l3, 1893; May 31, Aug. 2, 1894; June 2, 1898. Segdwick Post Records, 1898. *Herald,* May 30, May 31, 1898. *Durango Democrat,* May 30, May 31, 1899. Bruce Catton, *The Civil War* (New York: American Heritage, 1960), 606.
6. Sedgwick Post Records, 1897–98. McConnell, *Glorious Contentment,* 219. *Free Press,* June 28, 1894; Jan. 10, 1895; June 2, July 14, 1898. *Herald,* Nov. 9, 1893. *Argus,* July 29, Nov. 4, 1899.
7. *Argus,* Feb. 20, 1897. *Free Press,* Feb. 9, 1899. McConnell, *Glorious Contentment,* xi, xiii, xiv, 161, 167, 207, 224, 225, 228, 232.
8. Nell Irvin Painter, *Standing at Armageddon* (New York: W. W. Norton & Co., 1987), 62–63, 105. Schlereth, *Victorian America,* 226–28. John H. Keiser, *Building for the Centuries* (Urbana: University of Illinois Press, 1977), 17–19. John S. Haller Jr. and Robin M. Haller, *The Physician and Sexuality in Victorian America* (Urbana: University of Illinois Press, 1974), 274. *Free Press,* Jan. 15,

Feb. 19, May 14, 1890; March 30, April 13, May 11, Nov. 30, 1893; Sept. 10, 1896; May 19, June 23, 1898. *Argus,* Nov. 28, Dec. 26, 1891; Sept. 18, 1893; March 17, 1894; June 29, July 13, 1895; July 17, 1897; March 19, April 30, 1898. *Durango Weekly Tribune,* May 28, June 1, 1891. *Revised Ordinances of the City of Durango, Colorado* (Durango: n.p., 1901), 79–80. *Herald,* April 23, 1896.

9. *Argus,* Feb. 10, 1893; Feb. 10, 1894; Jan. 18, Oct. 17, 1896; May 22, June 19, 1897; April 9, 1898. *Free Press,* June 1, Nov. 2, 1893; Sept. 20, 1894; Jan. 10, 1895. *Durango Daily Southwest,* Sept. 1, 1893. *Herald,* Oct. 17, 1893; March 28, 1895; Feb. 3, 1899.

10. *Free Press,* Sept. 4, Sept. 11, 1890; Sept. 10, 1891; Aug. 27, 1896; June 23, 1898; Sept. 14, 1899. *Argus,* Aug. 30, 1890; Nov. 1, 1891; June 20, 1893; June 12, June 19, 1897. *Herald,* May 7, July 9, 1896.

13

THE GOOD OLD DAYS

> *Darling, I am growing old,*
> *Silver threads among the gold.*
> —"Silver Threads Among the Gold" (1873)

Popular imagination has come to depict the 1890s as a time of a simpler, happier, and less stressful life, full of warm days, friendships, and small-town America, a veritable golden age and the long sought Good Old Days. Seldom has a decade been more misrepresented, although undeniably, it might appear to be all these things, if the impression is based only on a quick glimpse of a few faded photographs or old newspapers.

The decade did not resemble an Age of Innocence, as much as some might yearn for it to have been. As has been seen, tension, complex issues, change, and concerns touched the very meaning, the very fabric of life in the 1890s. The everyday life of the decade cannot be painted in black and white; it overflowed with shades of gray and was saturated with hues of expectation and disappointment, joy and sorrow. Walking through these two towns on a summer evening in the 1890s remains an impossibility, but just for a moment, come back and glimpse, even if faintly, two rural communities that might be presumed to have been the epitome of the "Good Old Days" in the "golden age" of the United States.

Illness and death—the constant companions of adults and children—seldom departed from a household. Victorian America suffered in an unhealthy, often deadly, age, particularly for infants and children. The leading killers—consumption, diarrheal diseases, typhoid and malarial fevers, pneumonia, diphtheria, and what the Census Bureau termed, "inanition, debility, atrophy" challenged medical science and doctors, who found no easy answers or cures. Add to these woes the number of stillborn babies, thirty-four thousand in the United States in 1890, and the total picture starts to emerge.

Old-age disabilities appeared well down the list, but if a person reached middle age, his or her life expectancy increased.

Medicine had improved in the past generation, although in some ways soldiers in the Civil War received less thorough medical care than those of the Roman Empire. While great strides had been made in nursing and hospitals, there still remained those Victorians who considered the latter as a place of last resort, where one simply went to die. Durango had an excellent hospital run by the Sisters of Mercy. Sandwich had no hospital, but nearby Aurora and Chicago offered fine ones. Even so, most operations continued to be performed in the patient's home. For the surgeon, this could become a three-ring circus, with neighbors and family watching through windows and commenting.

Doctors themselves had only recently emerged from public suspicion, thanks mainly to improved medical schools and state medical licensing laws. No longer could an individual simply declare himself or herself a doctor, hang out a shingle, and treat patients. Just as important, physicians had new ideas and methods to combat illness. Louis Pasteur's theory that germs caused diseases proved one of the most far-reaching and meaningful discoveries for the ordinary individual. Another breakthrough arrived late in the nineties with the realization that aspirin could kill pain. To everyone's relief, diagnosis was revolutionized with the introduction of the stethoscope and medical thermometer, and some doctors and hospitals experimented with the X ray. The railroad and telephone brought further medical improvement, making it quicker and easier for the patient and doctor to reach each other.[1]

Pain persisted, however. It was the major problem confronting the medical profession and a difficult one to overcome. Pain-killing drugs, commonly prescribed during the Civil War (laudanum and morphine), became standard treatment in the postwar years. Tragically, not until the 1890s did general awareness of their addictive nature gain a toehold in the profession. Anesthetics, such as chloroform and nitrous oxide, eased the trauma and pain of operations; that, in turn, led to refinement in operative techniques. However, even the simplest procedure could be deadly.

Doctors simply could not cure many diseases or even relieve many symptoms. As a result, Americans often relied on home remedies or those increasingly popular patent medicines with their alluring promises of cures that the medical profession could not produce. As a result, patients often appeared at the doctor's office too late. The physician might be only the final stop on a person's medical journey. Conversely, some Americans gained more confidence in physicians, and doctors who failed to treat them successfully sometimes faced malpractice suits. The number of cases and judgments against doctors mounted in the century's last decades. The medical profession liked to blame "unscrupulous lawyers," who enticed clients with golden dreams of wealth.

Dentistry trailed still further behind in Victorian times. The toothbrush and most Americans had yet to make a lasting acquaintance, and their mouths showed it, being virtual dental disasters waiting to happen. Preventive dentistry came later, and most people ventured to the dentist only to have a tooth pulled. Slow and painful pump drills did not encourage patients to see a dentist, although the introduction of anesthetics, particularly "laughing gas" (nitrous oxide), helped relieve fears. In the nineties, dentists worked hard to convince the general public that "good appearance and good health" came from keeping the "teeth in good order."

One Sandwich dentist carried this a bit far, when he claimed that "defective teeth often produce" neuralgia, poor hearing, dyspepsia, and "even insanity" (*Sandwich Free Press,* Sept. 29, 1898). A Durango dentist, to allay patients' fears, wrote a pamphlet entitled "Dentist and Patient" (*Durango Herald,* Oct. 15, 1893). Nonetheless, dentistry still had a long way to go before a visit was considered less than a fearful experience. Both communities were fortunate to have dentists; many towns did not. The best some communities could do was simply have a visiting dentist drop by occasionally.

The residents of Sandwich and Durango had to rely on this 1890s medical world. Sandwich suffered through two epidemics, both of which raised the twin concerns of personal health and profits. The first epidemic occurred in October 1891, when diphtheria struck the town. Before the epidemic ran its course, at least six children died and Sandwich's image was threatened. "The papers have been careful not to create a panic outside while protecting the health of our citizens." As the *Sandwich Argus* (Dec. 26, 1891) explained, the autumn trade was essential to "the prosperity of our business men," and the fear of diphtheria, sown "without reason among those who usually trade" in Sandwich, "would have injured the business of our city."

Without reason? The *Sandwich Free Press*, on October 15, contained the obituaries of four children, all of whom were victims of diphtheria. In true Victorian prose, the paper bid good-bye to Estella Rogers, a "bright, intelligent girl, the light of the home and the joy of her parents"; Edwin David, a "boy of much promise"; and two others. When Sandwichites were faced with anxieties over business profits and personal health, the former won out when the health was that of people from the world outside of Sandwich.

The smallpox epidemic three years later exhibited an even more fearsome potential. The Burke family, who recently had moved to Sandwich from Milwaukee to be with their grandmother, brought the plague. Tragically, they had not been vaccinated. Two of their children died, and, in panic, their uncle, Will Middleton, fled Sandwich, carrying smallpox with him. Physicians, when they diagnosed the disease, immediately started vaccinating people in the community and isolated the family. Fear spread. Nothing Sandwich did relieved the worries of neighboring Somonauk, which on November 24, 1894, circulated handbills and cards that said, "Small-pox at Sandwich: Beware." That aroused the *Sandwich Argus*, which, on December 1, accused Somonauk merchants of trying to "fence in" Sandwich to improve their trade.

Sandwich responded with another step, quarantining those exposed, and all "disease" houses were "thoroughly fumigated and disinfected" (*Argus*, Dec. 15, 1894). Still that was not satisfactory, and on December 10 there appeared a half-page public notice signed by Ira Converse, chairman of the Board of Health; Mayor E. Graves; and S. White, a physician. The notice read, "THERE ARE NO CASES OF SMALL-POX AT THE PRESENT TIME." Finally, fears subsided, and calm returned. With a sigh of relief, the *Sandwich Argus* pointed out, in mid-December, that increasing numbers of "farmers and others from the country and neighboring towns" were appearing on Sandwich's streets.

Before the epidemic ran its course, doctors diagnosed fourteen cases, and five people died. The last act of this tragic story, one that was sadly avoidable, occurred the next March, when the vacant house of the "smallpox family" mysteriously burned.[2]

Both epidemics could have been avoided. City government and local physicians responded quickly to the danger of these highly infectious diseases, but individual carelessness or ignorance caused far more deaths than should have occurred. While the public expressed concern for the victims in both situations, the overriding fear appears to have been what the outbreaks might do to business and Sandwich's image. Fortunately, most of the ill, and the town, survived. Durango faced no epidemics to equal these two during the decade.

"La grippe," or the flu, was a more frequent visitor in both towns. Sandwich's William Woodbury, while "struggling," as he wrote, "with la grippe," noted in his diary on January 12, 1899, "Very many are sick in town. Grip and pneumonia are making havoc." The *Durango Herald* (Feb. 9, 1899) printed a treatment that would "positively cure you." It included drinking warm sage tea, taking a sulfate quinine pill and aconite pellets, and sticking "your feet in hot water with a little mustard in it."

Doctors diagnosed many cases of "hysteria" among women, a classic nineteenth-century feminine disease. Women tried everything, from bromide to opium to wearing magnetic belts, to control such symptoms as sleeplessness, depression, and anxiety. Men suffered from some of the same symptoms but did not call their condition hysteria.

Colds, measles, cuts, broken bones, heart problems, consumption, cancer, strokes, fevers—physicians treated them all, as best they could. Patients recovered, patients died, it was all part of Victorian life. When Mabel Barker recovered from a "very difficult surgical operation," done at home to straighten her foot, the *Sandwich Free Press* (May 8, 1897) hailed Dr. George Culver for his skill and professionalism.

When twenty-nine-year-old Sarah Gunderson fell victim to "quick consumption," no cure was found. She died, as did Lydia Benoit, age twenty-one, from the flu. Other victims included Lucy Smith at eighty-one and Fred Abile at thirty-nine years of age. The young died, the old died, hardly a newspaper appeared that did not carry an obituary. In sentimental Victorian prose, the papers noted the deaths. The *Sandwich Argus* (March 10, 1894) printed a classic account of how nine-year-old Lillie Cook, "realizing" death was near, "left messages of love to her teachers, relatives, playmates and passed away to the other shore." Friends and family bid farewell to the deceased in their own way at home, church, or cemetery.[3]

Not only were medical experience and home remedies—castor oil, calomel, whiskey, turpentine, teas, quinine, and mustard plaster—pitted against illness, those "elixir" patent medicines were pitched into the battle as well. They promised wonderful cures and often included alcohol and drugs as part of their ingredients. St. Germain Female Pills and Dr. Pierce's Favorite Prescription pledged a tonic to revitalize "run-down," debilitated, and overworked women. Mineral water from Mini-myan Springs promised relief from rheumatism and stomach and kidney troubles. Syphilene offered "the magic remedy to cure syphilis."

Syrup of figs cleaned the system, dispelled colds, headaches, and fevers, and cured habitual constipation. Apollo Nervie Tablets made a man "manly." And so the advertisements ran, promising much, probably curing little, and potentially doing harm. Although, with alcohol or drugs, sometimes both, in the magic elixir, the partaker probably felt temporarily better! Durango's newspapers carried more of these ads than Sandwich's. Such advertisements, if nothing else, provided the papers with a little needed revenue. The nostrum makers were the nemeses of physicians; they mimicked, distorted, derided, and undercut the authority of professional medicine.

Preventive measures for better health, individual or collective, attracted some attention. Echoing the worries of teachers and some parents, the *Sandwich Free Press* admonished its readers on June 4, 1890, that tobacco smoking, like opium smoking, "is an unnatural vice, as well as a filthy habit." What worried the writer most was that "the little folks" were imitating the older folks.

Durango had an office of the earliest franchised medical business in the United States, the Keeley Institute. Sixty of the offices existed in late 1892. So popular did the institutes become that they spawned "fraudulent establishments using similar titles." Treating patients with its "double chloride of gold" remedies, Keeley promised to cure "liquor, opium, morphine and tobacco diseases" (*Durango Great Southwest*, Oct. 26, 1892). Patients were treated in "handsomely and luxuriously furnished" rooms. If the institute's claims can be believed, the Keeley method proved a rousing success. According to the institute, there were fifty cures in Durango in the first two months. The *Durango Great Southwest* thought "the world may be thankful." Although Sandwich never secured a Keeley Institute, Miles Castle believed the Keeley program should receive "encouragement from all temperance people" (*Sandwich Argus*, Dec. 5, 1891).

Both towns became concerned about environmental issues, even if their residents preceded by several generations today's public furor over that crucial topic. For Durango, one key issue, the polluting of the Animas River, the town's principal water source, haunted residents throughout the decade. Polluters were threatened with fines, and the city marshal posted notices prohibiting swimming within five miles of the city and "committing any other nuisance in said river." One half of any fine collected was even offered to any person giving information "which leads to conviction" of a bather or anyone committing "any other nuisance." The Animas River remained highly polluted despite such efforts. Why? Upriver, Silverton dumped its raw sewage into the Animas, mines ran their dumps into it and mills their tailings, and ranchers, miners, and farmers emptied their privy vaults into this convenient sewer, not to mention the fact that the Animas was an easy place to dispose of dead animals. Durango could do little to stop such activities, and the town was fortunate to avoid any water-related epidemics. Lightner Creek, the source of water for the smelter workmen, also received attention, and polluters were told they would "be promptly arrested" (*Herald,* July 15, 1892).

The keeping of horses and cattle in town caught both city councils' notice, resulting in sharp discussion. Like the issue of water, this one involved private rights versus community rights, and solutions proved hard to come by. Even chickens caused trouble; "domestic fowl" were not supposed to run at large. Sandwich grew particularly concerned about litter—paper, trash, and other discarded materials—not necessarily because of health hazards or unsightliness, but because such litter might blow about and scare horses. "A little care exercised will obviate all danger to life and limb" (*Argus,* April 28, 1894).[4]

Some folks continued to believe that the abolition of saloons would benefit everyone tremendously. Besides the benefits mentioned earlier, closing saloons would improve the health of the "poor wretches" who frequented such establishments. As Billy Sunday shouted, "A saloon-keeper and a good mother don't pull on the same rope." For those who did not grasp that image, he more bluntly said, "Whisky is all right in its place—but its place is in hell."

The saloon, in reality, stopped not quite a "free lunch" short of hell and ruining home, wife, family, friends, and community. It furnished a male preserve away from home and was a popular leisure environment. The saloon catered in hundreds of ways to the social and political needs of men, in an atmosphere where blue-collar and white-collar individuals mingled freely. The saloon keeper might offer a free lunch consisting of a salty, spicy fare that tempted customers to buy more beer and mixed drinks. Neither town was large enough to have ethnic or neighborhood saloons; nor did customers put much stock in upscale ("bit versus two-bit") establishments, where they could drink their "demon rum" with a little more class.

Sandwich's endangered saloons were intermingled among respectable businesses. The town had no red-light district, no conglomeration of dance halls, gambling halls, and cribs and parlor houses that would have constituted a total male entertainment district. Durango had no qualms about its own red-light district, which lured customers and generally stimulated business districts. Indeed, as discussed above, by passing ordinances against such "evils" and then allowing those "evils" to flourish, the city collected monthly fines that helped raise its revenue, kept taxes lower than they would otherwise have been, and provided various kinds of entertainment. This common practice in the West permitted taxpayers to "have their cake and eat it too." Nor did Durango try to hide this aspect of its life. The 1892 city directory dropped no discreet veil: "Durango is not a 'dry town,' and those who like to look upon the wine when it is red can do so. Games of chance are also open to those who like to indulge."[5]

The red-light district survived as part of Durango's business community, which it typically did in Western towns. It provided entertainment for the masculine world of the cowboy, railroad worker, businessman, smelter, common laborer, and miner. Without it, the town would have suffered in competition with less sanctimonious neighbors.

Durango, not about to miss the opportunity to make a profit, had two districts, one by the depot and the other on the west side of the nine hundred block of Main Avenue and extending west across the railroad tracks. The atmosphere in these districts was different from that in more straitlaced Sandwich. Sporting women and men cavorted openly, though such behavior did not occur on the Boulevard or on residential streets. "Good women" stopped that "brazen" affront by "individuals bereft of all decency." The "fair but frail," the "erring sisters," those lewd women had to know their place. Nor did the public look with favor on men "living off the shame of fallen women." A tug-of-war existed in Durango between Victorian morality and profit. For the moment, the latter won out.

The red-light district did produce its own special problems for city government and law enforcement officials. The one great fear was that young girls would be seduced into a life of shame. This concern received careful press and municipal attention, and authorities tried to prevent the corruption of local girls whenever possible. The red-light district also gave rise to such problems as robbery, fights, drunkenness, "unlawful cohabitation," and accusations that games were rigged. The police responded to complaints, but the "buyer had to beware" when venturing into the district. Durango's drug problems also were concentrated there, where "fiends" could find a supply of opium, morphine, cocaine, and belladonna. Most of these drugs, however, could be purchased over the counter at a drug store.

Drug addiction was not unknown in the life of the middle class, especially among women. In most cases, opium "enslavement" probably resulted quite innocently from a doctor's prescription or from the use of patent medicines. Perhaps addiction resulted from the life the women led, because, as one Victorian doctor suggested, women in smaller towns were "deprived of all wholesome social diversion and doomed to a life of disappointment." Whether that was true in Sandwich and Durango will never be known. In those towns, as elsewhere, a dark veil dropped over the drug habit and alcoholism among women, and to a degree among men.

Victorians did not like to discuss the "scourge" of venereal disease either. Young men "sowing their wild oats" faced the possibility of an emotional and physical trauma. Despite the claims of some patent medicines, no complete cure was available. Doctors embraced mercury as the best remedy. (As the old sayings went, "Thirty seconds with Venus, a lifetime with Mercury," and "A night with Venus, a moon with Mercury.") This treatment produced some relief but also had many side effects, to the consternation of patient and physician.

Whether the red-light fines paid for the increased need for law enforcement and other civil and social problems will never be known. The press watched the district with puritan interest, chronicling the suicide of Minnie Becker (her *nom de turf*), who left behind a daughter in Iowa. May Porter, better known as Tricksey, a "demi-monde at Julia Wheeler's maison de joie," failed in a like attempt, though her failure received excellent coverage in the *Durango Herald* on July 12, 1892. A fight between Fat Alice and an adversary ended with her wounding herself, followed by some cryptic comments in the newspaper about this "disreputable negress."

Yet, should a Durango woman cross the line into a life of prostitution, a curtain of silence dropped over the "poor mortal," who gave up a "position in society to move just across the railroad tracks to take up a life of shame" (*Durango Weekly Tribune*, June 1, 1891). Occasionally, the press took a swing at the "class of hypocrites" who "blighted and blasted the names of young girls by liaison and clandestine meetings." "It is not," said the *Durango Democrat* (April 27, 1899), the "woman with evil designs" who has so damaged the "good name of the city." These men, contended Dave Day, these "paragons of purity," should be driven out of town.

Not all agreed with the practice of fining and flourishing. The *Tribune* (May 18, 1891), during its short existence, crusaded against "Durango pursuing a policy of doubtful character—compromising city government by licensing crime." The ten-dollar fine per "bride of the multitude," or game table, was split between the city and the collecting officers (police judge and city attorney). The newspaper charged that some gamblers, pimps, and prostitutes made payments, and others were "allowed to go free." The whole system afforded "opportunities for blackmail and various abuses," and the *Tribune* claim caused much talk. On June 1, 1891, the paper urged that the gambling and sporting houses be closed so that laws would be obeyed. "Do you believe it is right to hold up these poor wretches for such a rent and such an amount? Turn them loose or shut them out entirely, and give Durango a clean skirt to flirt in." Durango did neither, even though the district's activities led to continued problems.[6]

The red-light district's crime only partially reflected the typical law-enforcement problems of the day, which regularly involved drunks and dogs—there was a surplus of both in Durango, only of the latter in Sandwich. For example, Durango's Police Magistrate Court, from January to April 1890, besides dealing with the "inmate in a house of ill-repute" and gaming-table fines, handled drunkenness, concealed weapons, and unspecified disturbances. Six years later, and more specifically, defendants were being found guilty of fast riding, leaving teams unhitched, polluting the Animas River, violating the garbage and stock ordinances, fighting, disturbing the peace, and, most frequently, drunkenness. The WCTU could only say, we told you so. Dogs did not get "hauled" to court; that problem was sometimes taken care of on the spot, with a bullet.

What minor matters did local police have to face? Tramps and other undesirable people (Sandwich had a "gypsy" problem), con men, bicycle theft, rowdiness, collisions of horse-drawn wagons or buggies, runaway teams, dogs without licenses, rabies scares, speeding horses or bikes, and boys trespassing or misusing firecrackers or guns.

The treatment of "gypsies" provided a commentary on the times. Although they were considered "colorful," with their wagons and wandering lifestyle, they were also believed to be thieves of "the first water" (that is, of the highest order). Usually camping outside of Sandwich, they came into town to an unwelcome reception from concerned store owners. In most cases, the police took care of the matter by driving them out, whether they had been accused of a crime or not.

Add to these concerns the general nuisances, including such "crimes" as loud parties and stealing from flower gardens. Of a more serious nature were burglaries, firing guns within city limits, and violations of certain municipal ordinances involving fire, the sale of intoxicating liquors, animal abuse, trash, and the curfew.

Fair week, as seen earlier, gave Sandwich's law-enforcement officers a headache, because it attracted a "drifting" crowd. To the shock of the good people of Sandwich, in September 1891, two young ladies, "dressed in men's clothes," stole a horse and carriage from the fairgrounds (*Free Press*, Sept. 24, 1891). Law-enforcement officers eventually captured them, but women were not supposed to do such things! The *Argus* congratulated the community on September 19, 1896, after a calm fair. "We were proud of our little city this week, while we have had a popular fair, with its many visitors, there has been less rowdyism and vulgar shows than we usually see."

Sometimes something more serious happened. Durango's postmaster came up short eighteen hundred dollars in 1894 and blamed his downfall on gambling. Three years later, Margaret Mercer died under strange circumstances in Sandwich. The doctors speculated the frail woman, who had seven children in twelve years of marriage, died of "exhaustion," literally worn out by caring for her large family. Later, however, the coroner's jury decided that her death had been caused by arsenic, "administered by methods unknown to us" (*Free Press*, Sept. 2, 1897). As suddenly as the story appeared, it vanished, and nothing more emerged to whet public interest.

Newspapers had a way of ignoring crimes among the well-to-do or among respected people. Whether this policy applied to Margaret Mercer's case is impossible to say; suicide seemed the most likely cause. A press cover-up definitely occurred in Sandwich in 1892, when "one of [the town's] young ladies was stabbed" by a "supposed friend" (*Argus*, June 4, 1892). "Both parties are prominent in our social circles and out of respect to their parents the affair will be kept as quiet as possible." People at the time knew who the guilty party was. Undoubtedly, gossip raced about town, but history will never know the identity of the attacker.[7]

Neither town exhibited lawlessness to any degree; the law-abiding nature of both communities clearly displayed the Victorian commitment to law and order. The most life-threatening problem in either town occurred in Sandwich, where fast trains ran through unguarded railroad crossings. This danger caused local concern and a call for regulation. Durango did not face this problem, although the city council passed an ordinance limiting trains to four miles per hour (they all were departing from or stopping at the depot) and requiring that engineers "continuously" ring their engine's bell. A flagman was supposed to be stationed at every street crossing to warn the public "against danger," although it seems unlikely that that took place very often. To keep pedestrian tempers from flaring, no train was permitted to block traffic for more than ten minutes.

A warm summer evening, the smells and sounds of small-town America, fresh-cut grass, hot roasted peanuts and popcorn drifting from the corner stand, homemade pie cooling on the back porch intermingled with stable and country "scents," laughing children running around while their parents listen to a band concert—this is a picture that epitomizes a traditional view of the 1890s. Near the park, a few fortunate folks sat on their front porches enjoying the music; the porch, with its swing and wicker chairs, was a featured attraction of the Victorian home. Intruding into this idyllic scene were the annoying hum of mosquitoes and flies and the potpourri of small-town smells. Bands, porches, warm nights, fireflies (in Illinois), Victorian families enjoying an evening concert—sentimental certainly, but such things did occur. Both communities had bands (plus other musical organizations), and they gave "lively" concerts on warm summer evenings to appreciative audiences.

In Sandwich, the band members gathered on the post office corner (the corner of Eighth and Main), and in the park, to give their "open air" concerts. Typically, a galop, a waltz or polka, a march, an overture, and a special number charmed the evening. A band might also serenade an important family (who might later be approached for a contribution) play a shivaree of a young married couple, the "hot time" at a political rally, a "hit" in a parade, and appear on a variety of other occasions. Sandwich's Union Band was by far the most famous and long lived of the town's bands. Directed by maestro Henry Wilder, it played throughout the 1890s. Only in his thirties, German-born Henry also served as the city fire marshal. Sandwich patrons donated money to pay for sheet music and other needed items for the band. Durangoans, who had much less success in maintaining their brass band, turned to the city council, which donated twenty-five dollars per month for a while. When the council stopped this contribution in 1898, a group of Durangoans petitioned for reconsideration, but to no avail.

For a time, Sandwich's musical world also featured a concert orchestra and a choral society, which promised to "do good work," and both towns enjoyed concerts by church choirs, public school musical organizations, and appearances by professional musicians. On the whole, Sandwich maintained a musical edge over Durango.

Sandwich also enjoyed another decided cultural edge: it possessed an imposing Opera House, the architectural gem of the town. Durango always yearned for an opera house: "Durango is waiting for one of its Tabors to build himself an enduring monument in an opera house." Alas, wait would be all the town did; no one stepped forward. Durango might have a theater, which occasionally claimed to be an opera house, but the town did not have a prestigious "real" one. Even if an opera seldom graced the stage, a "majestic" building stroked civic pride and enhanced the community's image.

Built in 1878, Sandwich's Opera House served two functions—the lower floor was City Hall, the upper floor the auditorium. The latter was "one of the finest in this section [of Illinois]," with a seating capacity of "one thousand" claimed the *Free Press* (Dec. 11, 1890). It fulfilled a variety of roles, from providing a place for high school graduations to hosting minstrel shows, revivals, socials, lectures, dances, and a "magniscope performance" that produced views "of a most natural character," including that of a cavalry charge (*Free Press*, April 8, 1897). Along with the magniscope was presented "magnificent Edison Phonography of the highest grade." "Trial By Jury," featuring "twenty-eight young ladies [to] delight you" (*Free Press*, March 24, 1892), probably came as close to opera as anything ever presented at the Sandwich Opera House in the 1890s.

The Opera House provided Sandwich's architectural and cultural apex. Nellie Forsythe particularly cherished one memorable February 1895 evening that featured the Mozart Symphony Concert Company. "It was the finest thing I ever heard in Sandwich. The quartette of stringed instruments was indescribable, also the trumpet solo ending with 'The Star Spangled Banner.'"

The 1897 appearance of the noted orator and former Confederate general John Gordon, sponsored by the GAR and the Woman's Relief Corps, demonstrated changing attitudes and a new conciliatory spirit. The *Sandwich Free Press* (April 8, 1897) saluted the general, the "best type there is in educated southern chivalry," as "another evidence of American Heroism." Gordon's military career warranted such praise. Wounded five times at the battle of Antietam, and nursed back to health by his wife, he went on to fight throughout the war. To present the lecture course, or series, at the Opera House, the GAR had to pay eight dollars a night for rental of the building. The city council charged ten dollars for "foreign show troupes" and fifteen dollars for dances until 3:00 a.m.

The city steadily made improvements in the Opera House. A new ticket office and new seats, carpets in the aisles, and electric lights made the evenings more enjoyable for the patrons. The heart of Sandwich's cultural life, the Opera House crowned the community's grand aspirations. Durango could only dream; Sandwich had achieved.[8]

In addition to summer band concerts and those ever popular ice cream and strawberry socials, the holiday seasons evoke warmhearted images of the 1890s. The Fourth of July was a grand day for patriotic Americans in the nineties. The Fourth gave them an excuse to exhibit their patriotism and show their national pride, and they did it with vigor. For example, July 4, 1896, saw Durango putting on "holiday attire" with banners and decorations:

> sunrise firing of salutes, ringing bells
> 9:30 grand parade

11 reading, speaking & literary exercises
1:30 Horse races
3 baseball game purse $150
5 road foot race from Hermosa bridge to postoffice
5:50 foot race $25 winner
7 Indian dances
8 meeting of the pioneer's association
9 fireworks $2,000 display

The Durango Brass Band and the Fort Lewis Indian School Band played patriotic melodies. The celebration went "smoothly" and was "voted" the grandest ever held, and the parade was decidedly the "best ever." The parade featured forty-nine young ladies and gentlemen on horseback, "representing the states and territories," along with business floats and "bicyclists on gaily bedecked wheels" (*Herald,* July 9, 1896). Durango defeated Rico 12–6 to win the baseball purse. After all this, the "tired populace lost no time in seeking their beds." Other years featured single- and double-jack drilling contests, balloon ascensions, firemen's races, and tightrope walkers.

Because Durango was the largest community in the region, it put on a full-scale celebration, which increased business and provided a splendid party for everyone. Sandwich, on the other hand, in some years celebrated the Fourth there, and in others enjoyed a quiet day, with Sandwichites going to a neighboring town to join in festivities. The fairgrounds provided a wonderful place to celebrate the "glorious fourth." When Sandwich did celebrate, it did so in a grand manner, much like Durango. One such year, 1897, was marred only by the fact that the temperature reached a humid one hundred degrees. Imagine how that sapped parade participants, bicycle racers, and the baseball players: "the enervating influences of the broiling sun" left people exhausted, except for the reporter, who did not seem at a loss for words! The Union Band and Somonauk Band "discoursed sweet harmonies" throughout the day, and the celebration ended with a "colossal" fireworks display (*Argus,* July 10).

Families celebrated the Fourth of July in their own ways in both communities. Sandwich folk picnicked along Little Rock, Big Rock, and Somonauk Creeks, Devil's Gulch, and the Fox River; Durangoans picnicked in the mountains or on the banks of the Animas, Florida, and Los Pinos Rivers. The Fourth usually was a day of much noise, many festivities, and occasional injuries. Sandwich's city council prohibited the firing of "rockets, crackers or any other explosives," because of the personal and public danger they presented. "A word to the wise is sufficient," admonished the *Sandwich Argus* on June 29, 1895; still, fireworks remained easy to buy, and everybody knew that little boys, and older ones as well, would manage to get some! So dogs, horses, and people continued to be startled and frightened, and burns, cuts, and more serious injuries marred the day.[9]

With less noise but no less enthusiasm, these Victorians celebrated the Christmas holidays. For a mining town, Christmas was one of the times the mines closed and let the miners enjoy a vacation. In both towns, the stores tempted customers with shelves crammed with Christmas gifts and holiday foods, the churches planned special programs and services, adult children returned to the family home, and restaurants outdid themselves preparing scrumptious Christmas meals. Durango's Commercial Hotel enticed dinner patrons in 1894 with young turkey, ham, veal, prime rib, chowchow, puree of fowl, French peas, sweet and mashed potatoes, tomatoes, mince pie, and chocolate eclairs, all for thirty-five cents.

Merchants loved the holiday season. It provided one of their most profitable times, especially when the gloom and despair of the depression started to wear off. William Woodbury noted in December 1899, "Merchants seem to be doing a rushing business. Lots of people in town and all seem to be buying."

Christmas trees with homemade ornaments—and maybe a few store-bought glass and tin ones—hanging from the boughs and bathed in a mellow candle glow heralded the last day or so before Santa's arrival. Beautiful to look at, the trees were a fire hazard, and somewhere nearby, a bucket of sand or water awaited an emergency. Most homes more likely had stockings hung on the fireplace mantel or in some other convenient spot, awaiting Christmas morning. Not everyone could afford the luxury of a tree or wanted to risk the fire!

Dances and parties highlighted the season, and, in 1893, Durango planned a football game between Company K and the high school boys, only to have the game snowed out. Santa Claus made his appearance, for above all, this stayed a child's holiday. "Take Christmas out of the calendar and half the pleasure of children's lives is taken away from them" (*Herald*,

Dec. 25, 1896). There was also another side to the season: the "needy" could not be forgotten, or in the words spoken by Dickens's Ghost of Christmas Present to a shocked Scrooge, "This boy is Ignorance. This girl is Want. Beware of them both." In this festive season, caring people did not neglect the poor; many of them knew by heart Dickens's story and its moral. No Scrooges in Durango or Sandwich!

Newspapers could not let the day go by without an editorial to match the occasion. "Christmas, the gladdest day of the year, is at hand," wrote editor Castle in 1898, "and all the world rejoiced in the birth of the world's Redeemer" (*Sandwich Argus*, Dec. 24, 1898). However, 1894 offered few happy prospects, and the *Durango Herald* responded on a somber note:

> Another year has nearly passed and Christmas finds the people of the land in more straightened circumstances. Our people had hoped that when this gladsome day arrived prosperity would be the heritage of the nation, but they are doomed to disappointment . . . Christmas is a day when all should be merry and happy but a hungry individual can be neither. Those who are blessed with sufficient of this world's goods can and should be happy but before indulging they have a mission to perform—that of seeing that no one in their midst suffers for food or raiment to keep them warm.

In the 1890s, Santa Claus may have been leaner and the Christmas trees fewer, with fewer presents found under them or in the socks hanging on the fireplace mantel—no matter, it was still a joyous day for the family, who even in the hardest of times tried to have something for the children.[10]

The other holiday periods required less of a fuss. Thanksgiving involved church services, scrumptious home dinners, and reminders not to forget that "the best gifts of God are promised to those who remember the poor" (*Sandwich Argus*, Nov. 22, 1896). Arbor Day and Columbus Day were celebrated mostly by the schools, Washington's Birthday by the Masons and by people at dances, Lincoln's Birthday was celebrated in special ways in Illinois, and while hardly a holiday, leap years were occasionally marked by a dance or party. Labor Day, which became a national holiday in 1894, did not receive much attention in either community. Valentine's Day could be sentimental and a lover's delight or a cruel day, depending on the cards one received or failed to receive.

The holiday parties and dinners of the "first families" got the most press attention. People in both towns aspired to be "society," which was not unusual for Victorian urban America. This aspiration was reflected in the organization of social clubs, the designation of a "party of the year," efforts to attend the right church, and a desire for special personal mention in the newspapers. Fine homes dotted both communities and were the focus of the social season and the comings and goings of the "upper crust."

Durango, perhaps, worried more than Sandwich about such society things. Older, more established Sandwich knew the pecking order very well, thank you; one did not presume to be what one was not. Younger Durango still seemed a bit equivocal about its society and their emerging world. A fortunate real estate investment or a bonanza mine could still vault a lucky individual into a position to join the "Boulevard crowd" and have one's wife become a member of the Ladies Reading Club.

There existed, of course, "good" neighborhoods in which to live, if one aspired to social status. In Sandwich, that meant Main Street, north of the railroad tracks (beyond the factories), Eddy Street, and new additions opening in that area as far north as Lisbon Street. The remainder of the town consisted of middle-class neighborhoods. There was not really a "bad" neighborhood, except, perhaps, in areas clinging to the community's fringes. Durango's Boulevard was the place to reside. North Durango, across the Animas River, and Fourth and Fifth Avenues remained solidly middle class. South of Sixth Street emerged a blue-collar neighborhood for the workers at the smelter and coal mines. South and west of these areas were small Hispanic districts. Because of the predominantly middle-class white heritage of most of the residents, crossing from one neighborhood to another became a matter of choice and finances, or bad luck, if one slipped backward.

Most people probably just ignored social pretense and went about their business. Sandwich and Durango society, nevertheless, did try to imitate its counterparts in Denver and Chicago, to whatever degree possible or permissible. That was part of small-town America in the 1890s.

Regardless of social status, Victorians loved to visit. A warm evening on the front porch, or a winter's night in the parlor, could be passed very pleasantly discussing the topics of the day (was the new two-cent stamp better than the old one?) or the latest gossip ("Fat Alice" shot herself). Nellie Forsythe's diary, for example, has numerous mentions of her visits to friends and relatives, as does William Woodbury's. It was all an enjoyable part of life in the 1890s.

So was the circus.

For everyone's children, and children of all ages, the coming of the circus headlined the summer. People turned out when the circus arrived with the "strongest man on earth," "educated" sea lions, performing elephants, and a menagerie of wild beasts, all heralded by a "spectacular" street parade. Here was something out of the ordinary, something "stupendous, a mighty monarch of all tented exhibitions." It was the chance of a lifetime, or certainly of the year, to see the wonders of the world. The circus was not to be missed.

A library might be even more "stupendous" in its attractions; teachers, parents, and others thought its advantages could hardly be equaled. However, libraries cost money, and neither town seemed able to establish a public library. "Nothing is so badly needed," said the *Sandwich Free Press* (March 26, 1890), but only YMCA reading rooms, the Ladies' Library Association, and private collections filled the gap. Need and concern finally begot interest, and by late in the decade, both communities had begun moving on the road to establishing a public library.[11]

Mark Twain, one of the most popular authors found in any Victorian library, quipped, "Everybody talks about the weather but nobody does anything about it." Durangoans and Sandwichites definitely fell into that category. Ground Hog Day always garnered a comment or two, so did hot weather or cold, rainy weather or dry. The two towns experienced a variety of conditions for residents to discuss—heavy rain or snow, cyclones or strong winds, cold or hot spells, dry periods, storms, lightning, hail, ice, floods or drought, early or late frosts, too little or too much humidity—even on those grand days that everyone enjoyed. The fresh beauty of a spring morning or a crisp fall day framed in seasonal colors must have inspired even the most philistine of townspeople.

All this was wonderful but provided no guarantee of pure, fresh air. While Sandwich had nothing like Durango's smelter, with its baleful, sulfur-scented, arsenic-laced smoke, residents of both communities noticed coal and wood smoke hanging over them on wintry days and breathed the fumes. Snow turned sooty black after a few days, no longer providing a winter wonderland of white for a walk or sleigh ride. Nor should one forget the pungent aroma that drifted across the small-town Victorian world from stables, barns, horse "chips," outhouses, chewing tobacco on hot stoves, and a potpourri of sources now forgotten or cleaned up. And that was not all. Dust cursed summer rides and, unless the water wagon had recently sprinkled the streets, a summer evening on the porch. Pollen bedeviled allergy sufferers, who partly brought on their own problems by sowing the seeds of some of the guilty plants.

Durango sometimes suffered from high water in the spring, but Sandwich faced the only flood, in mid-June 1892. Nearly two hundred acres flooded, "affecting about 160 houses," closing down the Sandwich Manufacturing Company, and inundating the neighboring *Sandwich Free Press* office. Editor Frank Marley never lost his sense of humor. He accepted Miles Castle's offer to publish at the *Argus,* observing, "We are now in a condition to better appreciate a drought."

Take a stroll and someone would certainly mention the weather. After several acquaintances hailed Mark Twain with a comment on the weather, a passerby greeted him with, "Nice day, Mr. Twain." Twain rose to the occasion with a classic rejoinder, "Yes, I've heard it highly spoken of."

Indian relics fascinated residents of both towns. While Sandwich did not have a Mesa Verde nearby, interested locals collected arrowheads, axes, spear points, and other relics of the earlier sojourners in the region. These artifacts could not, however, equal the discovery of the *Stegosaurus ungulatus,* which was over one hundred feet long! Found west of Durango, its bones passed through town on their way to "Yale College and its collections" (*Great Southwest,* April 11, 1893).

Some of the high and low points of the late Victorian Era have passed before us in review. Some are almost as vivid as the memories of old-timers who recalled, for example, that in those days they would walk down to the post office on a cold winter's day to see if that special letter had arrived in the family's box. Home delivery awaited a future government decision. Watching a funeral procession on the way to the cemetery etched other remembrances as the 1890s receded into dimming yesterdays.

Season followed season, holiday followed holiday. Spring cleaning and spring fashions, "the very latest styles and fads," political campaigns and church services, late afternoon croquet on the lawn, and conducting business downtown—all these things occupied the attention of a secure middle-class America that was seemingly in control of its social, cultural, and political destiny.

Both adults and children looked eagerly toward what seemed to be a promising future. Around their feet romped the family pets, like Goody the tailless pup or the inmates of widowed Ed Bark's "cattery," where a "fugitive feline" could find a home. Of Ed, who was a livery keeper, the *Sandwich Argus* (Sept. 5, 1896) said, "When Ed reaches Cat Heaven these cats will all welcome him with purrs and praises."

These Victorians were firm in their conviction that they all would reach the promised land and receive their just rewards for having lived the good life and made their communities better places to live. All they had to do was look around their towns to receive assurance that this was true.[12]

NOTES

1. *Vital and Social Statistics* (Washington: Government Printing Office, 1894), 224. William G. Rothstein, *American Medical Schools and the Practice of Medicine* (New York: Oxford University Press, 1987), 69–70, 89, 92–93. Brian Inglis, *A History of Medicine* (Cleveland: World Publishing Co., 1965), 155–57. Paul Starr, *The Social Transformation of American Medicine* (New York: Basic Books, 1982), 69–70. Thomas J. Schlereth, *Victorian America* (New York: HarperCollins, 1991), 287–88.
2. *Sandwich Free Press*, Sept. 29, 1898. *Durango Herald*, Oct. 15, 1893. *Sandwich Argus*, Oct. 24, Oct. 31, Nov. 14, Dec. 26, 1891; Nov. 17, Nov. 24, Dec. 1, Dec. 8, Dec. 15, 1894; March 30, 1895. Bruce Haley, *The Healthy Body and Victorian Culture* (Cambridge: Harvard University Press, 1978), 3, 17.
3. John S. Haller Jr. and Robin M. Haller, *The Physician and Sexuality in Victorian America* (Urbana: University of Illinois Press, 1974), 25–26, 197, 274. *Free Press*, Jan. 22, Jan. 29, Feb. 12, 1890; May 11, 1893; May 8, Oct. 14, 1897; Oct. 27, 1898. *Argus*, June 11, 1892; Dec. 16, 1893; May 4, June 29, July 13, 1895. *Herald*, Feb. 9, 1899.
4. Haller and Haller, *The Physician*, 273–89. *Free Press*, Feb. 5, April 2, June 4, 1890; June 1, 1893; July 9, 1896. Durango City Council Minutes, July 2, July 16, 1895; Aug. 16, 1898; Aug. 18, 1898. *Durango Great Southwest*, Oct. 26, 1892; Nov. 14, Dec. 25, 1893. *Durango Solid Muldoon*, Jan. 1, 1893. *Herald*, Nov. 13, 1891; July 15, 1892; June 30, 1893. *Argus*, Dec. 5, Dec. 12, Dec. 26, 1891; April 28, May 5, 1894.
5. William T. Ellis, *"Billy" Sunday: The Man and His Message* (Philadelphia: John C. Winston Co., 1914), 75–76. Schlereth, *Victorian America*, 225–28. *Revised Ordinances of the City of Durango, Colorado* (Durango: n.p., 1901), includes all the "sin" ordinances. *Durango Directory for the Year 1892* (Trinidad, Colo.: Bensel Directory Co., 1892), 24.
6. *Herald*, July 12, July 19, 1892; March 23, April 20, 1894; July 1, 1898; March 2, April 27, 1899. Haller and Haller, *The Physician*, xi, 237–52, 265–67, 273–76, 281, 301–02. *Great Southwest*, Aug. 6, Oct. 17, 1892. *Durango Weekly Tribune*, May 18, June 1, 1891. *Durango Democrat*, April 27, 1899.

7. The sources of this list of crimes are the Sandwich and Durango newspapers for the 1890s and the Durango Police Magistrate Court Docket for Jan.–April 1890 and May–Sept. 1896. The cases mentioned are a random selection.
8. Richard Maxwell Brown, "Violence," in *The Oxford History of the American West* (New York: Oxford University Press, 1994), 393–95, 422–23. Durango City Council Minutes, Aug. 2, 1898. *Argus*, Dec. 7, 1878; April 14, May 27, 1894; April 6, Aug. 3, Nov. 2, 1895; Jan. 11, April. 4, May 23, May 30, June 27, Aug. 15, Sept. 19, 1896; July 29, 1899. Nellie Forsythe diary, Feb. 11, 1895, Regional History Center, Northern Illinois University. *Free Press*, June 4, Nov. 20, Dec. 11, 1890; Sept. 3, 1891; March 24, Oct. 20, 1892; May 31, 1894; July 11, Aug. 1, 1895; April 1, April 8, 1897; Feb. 9, 1899. *Herald*, July 12, Sept. 9, Sept. 11, 1894; Dec. 24, 1896; July 1, 1898. *Solid Muldoon*, Dec. 6, 1894. *Weekly Tribune*, May 18, 1891. *Durango Directory for the Year 1892*, 24. 1,000 seats in the opera house is doubtful; the present seating is just over 300 in the same room.
9. *Herald*, July 2, July 9, 1896. See also *Herald*, July 5, 1898. *Argus*, June 29, July 6, 1895; July 3, July 10, 1897. See also *Argus*, July 5, 1890; July 9, 1891; July 8, 1892; July 11, 1896. *Free Press*, July 9, 1891; July 11, 1895; July 3, 1897.
10. *Herald*, Dec. 27, 1893; Dec. 23, 1894; Dec. 26, 1895; Dec. 24, Dec. 25, 1896. *Democrat*, Dec. 16, 1897. *Argus*, Dec. 17, Dec. 24, Dec. 31, 1892; Dec. 10, Dec. 24, 1898. William Woodbury diary, Dec. 20, 1899, Regional History Center, Northern Illinois University.
11. *Argus*, Oct. 29, Nov. 19, Nov. 26, Dec. 3, 1892; Dec. 9, 1893; Feb. 24, 1896; Nov. 2, 1895; Nov. 22, 1896; March 5, Dec. 17, 1898. Richard McCloud, *Durango As It Is* (Durango: Durango Board of Trade, 1892), 76–78. *Free Press*, Feb. 12, Dec. 4, Dec. 11, 1890; Nov. 16, 1893; May 31, 1894; Feb. 27, 1896; May 5, May 19, June 30, 1898. *Herald*, July 24, April 21, 1894; May 22, 1896. Schlereth, *Victorian America*, 53.
12. Schlereth, *Victorian America*, xiii, 271, 278. Alex Ayres (ed.), *The Wit & Wisdom of Mark Twain* (New York: Harper & Row, 1987), 244–45. *Free Press*, July 2, July 30, 1890; July 1, 1892; May 11, May 25, 1893; July 15, Aug. 16, 1894; Feb. 9, 1899. *Herald*, May 30, 1894; Oct. 7, Oct. 9, Oct. 11, 1897. *Democrat*, Dec. 30, 1897. *Great Southwest*, April 11, 1893. *Argus*, June 4, June 18, June 25, 1892; Feb. 17, 1894; Sept. 5, 1896.

Epilogue

AFTER THE BALL

> *The years creep slowly by, Lorena,*
> *The snow is on the grass again.*
> — "Lorena" (1857)

"Clear the volume of one more year," wrote William Woodbury on December 31, 1899. With true Victorian sentiment, he continued, "May it be such that we can meet it without fear when it faces us in the Hereafter. Farewell '99." Farewell to the 1890s, as well, and the nineteenth century.

The decade of the nineties had disappeared in the twinkling of a historical eye. It seemed like only yesterday that it had opened with such high promise for Sandwich and Durango; now the new century was upon the United States with, again, seemingly high promise. The 1890s had been a decade to remember. Maybe people already remembered more than actually happened.

Durango, despite its tribulations, had grown by twenty-two percent to a population of 3,317, while Sandwich had barely held even, gaining only four people to bring the total to 2,520. Ahead lay some fascinating and difficult decades; the economies of both communities would change over the years. Durango's mining and smelting industries would decline steadily in the years before World War I, and then, for nearly a generation, agriculture would dominate. The town's economy would, for a brief while, become more like Sandwich's. Unlike some more fortunate Midwestern towns, Sandwich would eventually watch its industries close down or be absorbed by larger rivals, and agriculture would remain the town's only major economic pillar. Nor did Sandwich benefit from the coming of the automobile and extend its hinterlands at the expense of local rivals. The highway, like the railway, passed through the town, but Sandwich never became a destination point. The town's lack of growth was dismally displayed by a stagnant

EPILOGUE

population curve. Durango, on the other hand, benefited immensely from the automobile and the twentieth-century world rushing upon it.

The boys marched off to war in 1917–18, and the world continued to pour into Sandwich and Durango with the coming of the cars, radios, and movies. The twenties "roared" for neither town nor for many other agricultural communities. Both towns suffered during the Great Depression, while old-timers debated whether the nineties had been worse than the thirties.

World War II changed all that. After the war, the factors that had so helped Durango in the 1890s—scenery and location, tourism, natural resources, promotion, ample water, and the railroad—again came into play, and a forty-year boom dawned. There would be no looking back. Sandwich never experienced such a boom. Farming changed and so did urban Illinois. Sandwich moved toward becoming a bedroom community for its larger neighbors. Meanwhile, a nationwide decline in rural population marked one of the most fundamental changes in American history.

The train does not stop at Sandwich anymore, nor do trains carry Durangoans throughout the country. The narrow-gauge trip from Durango to Silverton has become a celebrated tourist attraction, one of the few that provides visitors with the sights, sounds, and smells of the 1890s. In stark contrast, the railroad company tore down Sandwich's depot, and only the lonesome whistle of a passing freight is left to remind the listener of yesterday.

All this obviously was not clearly understood on January 1, 1900. Dave Day did not even try to speculate that far ahead, when he wrote on December 31, 1899, "The year 1900 begins on Monday and ends on Monday. The rest of us will commence the year on a Monday, but there is no telling where we end." His rival, the *Durango Herald* finished the decade as it started, by promoting; it could think of "no other hundred square miles in the world where there are so many opportunities to make a living and to make money" (Dec. 30, 1899).

On January 1, 1900, Sandwich and Durango generally appeared remarkably similar to what they had been a decade before. Merchants still provided leadership in communities dominated by conservative, middle-class, Anglo-Saxon Protestants. Victorian standards and culture predominated in the home, church, business, street, and society. Customers relied on Main Street merchants for most of their shopping needs. Railroads still provided the principal means of transportation, and local industry remained the largest employer. In the hinterland, agriculture retained a firm hold in De Kalb County, though less so in La Plata County, where coal and hard-rock mining continued to capture investors' imaginations. The recent depression was receding into memory, and, again, both towns appeared prosperous and caught up in the traditional "grow or die" urban philosophy. Physically, of course, they had changed, especially Durango, which had bounced back remarkably from the disastrous 1889 fire. Each town presented a more substantial appearance than it had a decade before, thanks primarily to brick-and-stone construction of home, church, and business.

Underneath the surface, however, change bubbled and pushed upward. The reforms of Populism stirred people's imaginations like a spring wind. Sandwichites and Durangoans had had time to read about, ponder, and discuss reform ideas, some of which no longer seemed so shocking or radical. Considering the onrushing power and prestige of big business and its "co-conspirator," wealth, a strong dose of "all power to the people" did not appear so outrageous. Rather it seemed necessary to continue democracy and maintain the middle class.

Already in small ways and large ones, the upheavals wrought by the new industrial age could be seen in these two towns. The most obvious indication was the swallowing of Durango's smelter by the gigantic smelter trust, the American Smelting and Refining Company. More subtly but more pivotally, outside business and industry steadily made inroads against their local competitors. Here emerged the real impact of large-scale operations, lower prices, and advertising. It did not take a very perceptive person to grasp what the long-range implications might be for Sandwich, Durango, and similar communities.

Agriculture, too, continued to evolve. Farms grew larger, while the "small farmer" became a potentially endangered species. Fewer farms meant fewer customers and less business to support towns and businessmen; it meant a decline in tax revenues. For Sandwich and its neighbors, this trend held dangerous implications for a somber future.

Less obvious at the moment was that a great change in transportation was dawning. Already the automobile had chugged and sputtered onto the scene, more a plaything than a means of transportation. No doubt, folks in both communities had read about this new machine. Only a real visionary would have forecast, however, that it might seriously threaten railroads and

EPILOGUE

their business. Vulnerable Sandwich and Durango faced a change in lifestyle, not only because they were created by railroads, but because they relied completely on the train.

On the other hand, a person with only a small dose of intuition could have forecast that the finite reserves of southwestern Colorado's coal and minerals would eventually run out, resulting in mining's decline and forcing the smelter to close. It had happened elsewhere and would eventually happen in Durango, despite the belief that somehow it would be different here in the Animas Valley and San Juan Mountains. A person might have needed a bit more perception to see that local manufacturing would not be able to withstand outside competition, but not all the local pride in the world could have saved it.

Part of the future of these two towns had already been defined by the recent past. Just as the Denver & Rio Grande leadership had promised back in 1880, Durango emerged as the commercial, transportation, banking, and industrial hub of southwestern Colorado. Add to this what the locals had achieved—becoming the region's educational, medical, tourist, and social center—and Durango seemed in every way to be well positioned for the new century. Sandwich continued to rely on its agricultural base, and its economy was strongly supported by the town's two manufacturing plants.

Durango was much more active in promoting itself as a place to visit, to regain health, to invest, or to come to settle. Land in the area could still be homesteaded, as the opening of the Ute reservation amply displayed; the promise of Western land still beckoned. Uncle Sam was more than willing to bet the sale of 160 acres of semidesert for ten dollars, against buyers spending five years of their lives on the homestead. Most of the eager homesteaders on the Ute Strip lost the wager, unable to stand the hardships and the disappointment of dreams gone sour.

But land was not all that Durango had to offer. A multitude of investment possibilities awaited the imaginative, hard-working individual who heeded the call to "Go west young man." After all, hardly a generation had passed since the frontier days of the promised land known as La Plata County. Now the county had, in Durango, all the benefits of modern America and still extended the age-old promise of the West. Sandwich, on the other hand, with a limited hinterland, well-established agriculture, and nothing singularly captivating to attract visitors, held few inducements for the outsider. It did promote itself, but such efforts seemingly became lost in the chorus of similar appeals from other Midwestern farming communities.

Durango proved further blessed by being the county seat and having a district court. In addition, the federal government's involvement provided benefits that promised to increase in the years ahead. Sandwich had nothing like these advantages to fall back on or to build upon.

The lure of larger cities was taking a toll on Sandwich, but less so on Durango, which became its region's big city. The bright lights, more plentiful and higher paying jobs, and other urban inducements of nearby Aurora and Chicago were major reasons for Sandwich's lack of growth in the nineties. The West also proved a factor, drawing away young farm families to a region that promised cheaper land and the opportunity for a fresh start. Denver was a day and a half from Durango by train and thus did not threaten Durango like Chicago did Sandwich. Durango dominated its neighbors and, indeed, lured some of their residents with the pleasures and opportunities of the "big city."

Durango's aggressive leadership subscribed completely to the "grow or die" philosophy and resolutely planned to grow, even if it meant crushing a few neighbors. Already, Parrott City and Animas City had fallen victim. Durango's leaders intended to create a community like the ones they had left behind, though one that was additionally blessed with all the modern conveniences and attractions. In these goals, they matched their expectations and recreated Victorian America in the Animas Valley. Yet, that signified merely the beginning; they steadfastly believed the future held grand possibilities. Sandwich, with a quarter-century head start, represented on a modest, agricultural scale what Durangoans planned for their hometown. But Sandwich's boisterous youth retreated into memory well before Durango was born, and the Midwestern town reached its angle of repose by the turn of the century. Sandwich's leadership worked within limits that had been laid out for them long ago.

Neither town condoned lawlessness. The community leaders realized that it hurt business and besmirched the civic image, thereby discouraging investment, visitors, and future settlers. These were not desired results. A law-abiding atmosphere might have been expected in Sandwich, but perhaps not in Durango. Such an atmosphere does not fit the legendary image of mining towns. Violence in the West has become "an enduring aspect of

EPILOGUE

the nation's mythology." Violence, however, was typically American and came west with the pioneers. It thereby touched at one time or another both Sandwich and Durango.

Among the multiple causes of this violence, several might have been evident in these two communities—the "doctrine of no duty to retreat" and the "ethic of individual enterprise." But no gunfights sullied the reputation of either town, nor was a man considered undressed without his gun. Guns seemingly were not worn in either town, and, although people stood up for their rights, gunfights did not result. The one example of violence in an entrepreneurial struggle occurred during the smelter strike in Durango in 1899. Because of the strike, Durango emerged antiunion and stayed that way.

In their relative lack of violence, Durango and Sandwich proved more typical than Dodge City or Tombstone. Why? The frontier had gone before each was established. Only Durango had a vigilante incident. That occurred back in April 1881, during its one period of violence. Order and stability were the goals of the movers and shakers, and these elite, well-to-do individuals controlled their communities. Only one economic conflict, the Durango smelter strike, occurred among the industrialists, the small businesses, or the professions. That strike hardly ranks among the "legendary" labor-management struggles. Each town had an ethnic and cultural uniformity that united the residents—they almost all had a common Midwestern and Eastern background. As a result, violence and lawlessness were not part of the 1890s in Durango or Sandwich.

In both towns, tension and potential tragedy lurked behind what the movers and shakers set out to do, more so in Durango and the Animas Valley than in Sandwich. Sandwich's rich agricultural land, long growing season, and abundant rainfall and water sources supported a familiar lifestyle. Pioneers, since Jamestown, Virginia, in 1607, had marched west on such a firm foundation. Frederick Jackson Turner had been right on that point, but wrong on what they hoped to achieve. Turner argued that "from the time the mountains rose between the pioneer and the seaboard, a new order of Americanism arose." On the contrary, these people were trying to recreate the world they left behind, with obviously a few modifications.

In recreating the life they left behind (generally Midwestern), Durangoans tried to remake and shape their valley as they thought it should be, ignoring the limits of reality. What once had been a sagebrush valley, with scrub oaks and a few pine trees, now contained homes, farms, grass lawns, and a variety of trees and vegetation. All this took water, and, as the homesteaders and others were finding out, water was a precious and limited commodity. When would city dwellers come to the same realization? What were the best ways to use water on farms, in industry, and in cities? Were the settlers denying the environmental and climatic limits of southwestern Colorado in trying to follow a Midwestern pattern of settlement and development? What would be the long-range impact of this "progress" on the land and people? By living out the American dream and the principle of individualism, were they being stewards or exploiters of the land and resources?

What about the complex question of the expansion and development of farm, town, and mine versus the preservation of the splendid scenery? In 1900, both bestowed economic benefits on Durango, the former more so than the latter. The tension between the two might loom small then, but there was a strong possibility it would increase in Durango and the rest of southwestern Colorado in the decades ahead and emerge as *the* issue. Even in Sandwich, this question would arise, though in a slightly different form. When Sandwich eventually expanded out onto the surrounding farm fields, people debated whether it was best to use the land for homes or for fields.

The generation of 1900 did not have the answers. But these Victorians cannot be blamed for failing to resolve questions that are still with us and still have elicited no definitive, or (some might say) practical, answers. Probably very few, if any, Sandwichites or Durangoans stopped to ponder such matters on January 1, 1900. Many more, no doubt, were caught up in that pressing question of the day, did the new century start in 1900 or 1901? Most simply enjoyed the day and perhaps pondered their chances for brighter tomorrows in the twentieth century.

Doubts about the future had little place in the minds of people who had survived the panic of 1893, the harsh depression that followed, the furor of the 1896 election, the excitement of the Spanish-American War, and the array of changes that had befallen the past decade. They had gotten a glimpse of the future at the World's Fair, and most liked what they saw. For them, the new century appeared as promising as anything they could remember. Why trouble themselves about issues better left to the future? As the Victorian Era drew to a close, life seemed good, especially for these middle-class Americans.

EPILOGUE

Nonetheless, there existed a bittersweet quality about all this. The small-town America they lived and worked in, and likely loved, neared the sunset of its influence. The America they knew stood on the threshold of change, a transformation that they themselves had helped cause. Within a generation, that America would be a fading memory overrun by the automobile, World War I, the radio, the movies, the crash of 1929, and the worst depression in the nation's memory. All of these experiences would bring the world and its problems to their doorstep.

Through it all, Sandwich and Durango moved into new periods of their histories. Towns, like people, evolve during their lifetimes. Weep not for what was; these Victorians built on the past and dreamed of tomorrow.

Charles Harris undoubtedly was not expecting to draft an epitaph for the 1890s when he composed his popular song "After the Ball." When he wrote it in 1892, most of the decade still stretched out ahead of him, his contemporaries, and the United States. Sandwich editor Miles Castle groused about the song and observed (May 30, 1896), "The composer of 'After the Ball' has sued for $3,000 damages. If he is in custody don't let him off with a fine." Castle did not say what the suit was about; nor did he explain what irritated him, but maybe it was the fact that the song made Harris a millionaire.

Regardless, Harris provided a fitting epitaph for the two towns as they existed in the 1890s and for the towns' Victorian residents. The people of Sandwich and Durango had seen the best of times and the worst of times, the failure of hope and the triumph of hope, and now it all receded into history. The decade was over, the new century born, the "sweet tunes and bright lights" faded. As Harris wrote in the chorus to his popular hit,

> After the ball is over,
> After the break of morn,
> After the dancers' leaving,
> After the stars are gone:
> Many a heart is aching,
> If you could read them all;
> Many the hopes that have vanished,
> After the ball.

ESSAY ON SOURCES

Researching and writing urban history is a fascinating and rewarding, if occasionally frustrating, endeavor. For example, a project such as this one, involving small towns, presents special research problems. Short of traveling through a time warp, the scholar has to rely on the limited sources available—newspapers, a few diaries and letters, remembrances, photographs, census records, various reports, an occasional book, and a smattering of interviews—to recapture a vanished America and discover the answers to questions posed.

The most significant sources I used for Sandwich and Durango were the newspapers, which covered a large variety of topics, even if they did not always do so in an unbiased manner. The 1900 census records provided invaluable help, but, unfortunately, the 1890 records have been destroyed for both Sandwich and Durango, as they have been for most of the rest of the country. Occasional state and federal reports touch upon the two towns or their counties. Because of the towns' limited size and seeming lack of importance on the larger state scene, writers had very little to say about either community in pamphlets and books. Durango had a little better success getting into such publications, because it was a tourist community and promoted itself more actively.

Unlike the letters and diaries from the Civil War years, which were cherished family heirlooms, similar materials from the 1890s either have not survived or have not surfaced. A few reminiscences and interviews provide glimpses of the decade, and photographs prove invaluable tools for understanding small-town America of the 1890s.

For exact references, the reader is encouraged to return to the endnotes. Be not discouraged. Researching small-town America is a unique opportunity to study the roots of the United States and is indispensable for gaining insight into where we have been and how we have developed into

ESSAY ON SOURCES

what we are today, as a country and a people. If, as Tolstoy suggested, "the subject of history is the life of peoples and of humanity," then the world of the small town offers the place to commence.

INDEX

"A Bicycle Built for Two," 191, 192
Abile, Fred, 225
Adams, Augustus, 6, 49
Adams, Henry, 49
Adams, J. Phelps, 49
African Americans, 8, 13, 229; families, 22; few, 18, 161; racism, 23–24
"After the Ball," 17, 252
Agriculture, 4, 12, 72, 128; evolves, 13, 247; farmers, 22, 28; hinterland, 55–56, 100–01; Sandwich, 248, 250; Ute rush, 127–28
Alexander, Charles, 155
Altgeld, John P., 33
American Bible Society, 162
American Smelting and Refining Company, 51–52, 69, 247
Anderson, W. L., 155
Animas City, 9, 24, 45
Aragon, Lucindo and Lucia, 20
Arbor Day, 237
Architecture, 59, 68; schools, l06–07; Victorian, 43–44
Attorneys, 98
Aurora, 11, 222

Baker, Edwin, 155
Baker, Mabel, 225
Baker, Thomas, 113
Baptists, 136, 156, 160
Bark, Bert and Grace, 22, 146
Bark, Ed, 241
Barnes, Thomas, 54
Barnett, George and Jennie, 22
Barrows, Arthur and Elizabeth, 20
Baseball, 74, 215, 235; Sunday, 195; town, 193–95; women, 179, 194
Baumer, Harry, 19
Becker, Minnie, 229

Bell, Emma, 110
Benoit, Lydia, 225
Bicycles, 182, 191–92, 193; ordinances, 97–98, 193; women, 178, 191–92
Bishop, Alice, 175
Blanchard, Alice, 110
Blanco, Ramon and Pacifica, 19
Blee, John and Ellen, 21, 216
Boston Bloomers, 179, 194
Boyle, Anna, 175
Boynton, Nellie, 23
Boxing, 199
Bryan, William J., 84, 86
Burke, Frank, 31
Business: district, 43, 48; leaders, 19–21, 23; role, 10, 246–47; trusts, 39. See also Durango; individual firms; Sandwich

Camp, Alfred, 145, 217; banker, 12, 20, 48
Camp, Estelle, 20, 145; career,183,184; Mesa Verde, 175
"Casey At the Bat," 193
Castle, Freelove, 20, 169
Castle, John, 82
Castle, Miles, xiv, 6, 8, 46, 177, 217; "After the Ball," 250; banker, 47; Billy Sunday, 154; career, 9, 113–14, 116; discrimination, 157; Enterprise Company, 50; "Free Silver," 82–86; Keeley Institute, 226; Philippines, 39; Spanish-American War, 36, 38; woman's suffrage, 169–71
Catholics, 152, 156, 157; churches, 158–59; discrimination, 158
Cats, 90, 241
Catt, Carrie, 170
Central School, 66

255

INDEX

Chaney, Frances, 177
Chicago, 10, 249; migration to, 128, 129; railroads, 4, 5; rival, 11; World's Fair, xiii–xviii
Chicago, Burlington and Quincy RR, 5, 46, 50, 246; "Clean Sweep," 49; freight office, 143. *See also* railroads
Chicago Cubs, 196
Children, l62, 232, 236; circus, 239; illnesses, 223–24; 225; recreation, 201–02; temperance, 213; tobacco, 226; YMCA, 214–15. *See also* Durango; Sandwich; schools; women
Chinese, 12, 25
Christmas, 162, 236
Churches: buildings, 159; charity, 161–62; evangelists, 154–56; nationalism, 153; role, 151–53; sermons, 160–61; Sunday problems, 152. *See also* individual denominations
Circus, 239
Civil War, 8, 234; fades, 36; GAR, 206–07; significance, 206–07
Cleveland, Grover, 30, 33–34
Cliff Dwellers, xvii. *See also* Mesa Verde
Cody, Will "Buffalo Bill," xv–xvi
Coleman, Grace, 108
Coleman, Maude, 108
Colorado Equal Suffrage Association, 170
Colorado Springs, 11
Columbus Day, 235
Congregationalists, 156, 159
Converse, Ira, xvi, 21, 224
Conway, Capitola, 22
Conway, James and Mary, 22
Cook, Lillie, 225
Cook, Mattie, 89
Corlinsky, Charles and Annie, 21
Coxey, Jacob, 32
Cripple Creek, 129, 206
Culver, George, 6, 225
Culver, James, 6
Culver, Sherman and Louise, 21

David, Edwin, 224
Davis, Walter, 37
Day, David, 217, 246; career, 113–14; depression 1890s, 31; "Free Silver," 84, 86; observations, 51, 52, 55, 125, 184, 230; Ute rush, 127–28; women's football, 179

Deacon, William, xiii, 91, 115
Debs, Eugene, 33
Deibel, May, 23
Deibert, Fred, 155
De Kalb, 12
De Kalb County, 4
Democrats, 76, 77, 78. *See also* Durango, "Free Silver;" Sandwich
Dent, Joseph, 136
Dentistry, 223
Denver, 10, 128, 249
Denver & Rio Grande RR, 51, 248; coal mining, 53; Durango, 9–10, 11; street names, 46; tourist attraction, 246; Ute rush, 127
Depression: 1890s, 29–33
Dickens, Charles, 1, 12, 237
Dickson, Samuel, 91, 214
Dieterich, Lewis, 55
Diphtheria, 223–24
Dogs, 97, 230
Dommick, George and Belle, 19
Drugs: addiction, 212, 213, 222, 229
Durango: birth/growth, 9–12; city government, 89–95, 193, 228–29, 230; cost living, 59–61; depression 1890s, 29–33; economic hinterlands, 99–102, 247–49; politics (local), 75–79; promotion 121–25; Spanish-American War, 35–39; twentieth century, 245–49, 252
Durango Athletic Park, 198
Durango Brass Band, 235
Durango Club, 199
Durango Iron Works, 55
Durango Railway and Realty Company, 59
Durango Reading Club, 144
Durango Wheel Club, 137, 192
Dyas, Joseph and Mary, 21, 73

Easter, 162. *See also* churches
Education. *See* children; schools; teachers
El Moro Saloon, 134
Electricity, 57–58; lights, 96–97; railroad, 101
Enterprise Company, xvi, 6, 48; history, 33, 49, 50
Environment, 8; impact on, 250–51; pollution, 226–27, 239–40; smelter, 50. *See also* water

INDEX

Episcopalians, 156, 159
Eureka Flouring Mill, 55

Fairs, 126–27. *See also* Sandwich Fair
Families. *See* children; women
Farmington, New Mexico, 11
Fat Woman's Club, 185
Fire: threat, 94–96. *See also* Durango; Marcy Block; Sandwich
Firemen's Tournament, 198
Fishing, 149
Flag: fight about, 112
Fletcher, Baker and Mary, 22, 23–24
Fluelling, Mary, 22
Football, 236; high school, 196–97; women, 179
Fort Lewis, 12, 105; baseball, 195; Indian school, 99–100
Forsythe, Nellie, 23; courtship, 181–82; daily life, 173–74, 201; music, 234; World's Fair, xiii, xiv. *See also* William Woodbury
Freeland Corners, 5
"Free Silver": politics, 79–87
Frost, Charles and Harriet, 20

Gage, Almon, 6
Gallotti, Frank, 35
GAR. *See* Grand Army of the Republic
Geneva Lake, Sycamore & Southern Electric Railway, 101
Gill, William, 19
Glen Park, 57, 200
Gonner, Frank and Hattie, 65, 146
Goodman, Edna, 201
Goodman, George and Ida, 19, 140
Goodman, Gus 19
Gordon, John, 234
Graden, Thomas, 12, 217; mayor, 93; mill, 55
Graden Mercantile Company, 55
Grand Army of the Republic, 31–32, 34, 215, 234; campfires, 162; history, 206–07; history revision, 211, 212; patriotism, 208; Post, 510, 207, 209; Sedgwick Post, 207; Spanish-American War, 38
Graves, Mary, 110
Graves' Nursery, 55
Ground Hog Day, 239
Gunderson, Sarah, 225

Gypsies, 231
Hague, James, 86
Hall, Alfred and Testa, 20
Harris, Charles, 252
Hartman, Frank, 116
Hartman, Lillian, 116, 170
Hayden, Sophia, xv
Health, 4, 180, 221–22; death, 183. *See also* children; medicine; women
Helm, Wesley, 35
Henry, James and Allie, 19
Hesperus, 53, 54
Hills, Eden, 128–29
Hispanics, 18, 238; "Mexican Flats," 25
Holidays. *See* individual days
Holmes, Oliver Wendell, Jr., x, 8; Civil War, 207
Hospitals, 222
Houck, Ralph, 161, 162
Hudson, W. H., 208
Hummel, Bathsheba, 22

Immigration, 188
Irrigation, 13. *See also* agriculture
Isgar, George and Helen, 23
Ives, Harriet, 110

J. Kehl & Sons, 55
Jackson, Harry, 20, 55
Jews, 25
Johnson, Carl and Ida, 20
Johnson, Nelson, 20
Johnson, Otto, 54
July Fourth, 140, 234–35

Keeley Institute, 226
Kilborn, Nathaniel, 208
Kisel, William and Josephine, 20
Kleinsmid, George and Louise, 6, 21, 56
Klondike Gold Rush, 34–35
Kruschke, Ike and Hattie, 20, 21; baseball team, 194

Ladies Athletic Club, 178
Ladies Improvement Society, 172–73
Ladies Reading Club, 174
La Plata County, xvii, 13
Lawlessness, 230–31; image 249–50. *See also* Durango; Sandwich; Sandwich Fair

257

INDEX

Lease, Mary, 81, 177
Ledoyt, Ed, 21
Lewis, Mary, 6
Lincoln, Abraham, ix, 3, 216; birthday, 211, 237
Logan, John, 206, 207
Lowman, Frank, 115
Loyal Temperance Legion, 213
Lutherans, 156

Major, John, 155–56
Mancos, xvii
Marcy, Abram A., 59
Marcy Block, 70, 95
Marley, Effie, 115
Marley, Frank, 240
Martinez, Jennie, 107
Mays, Forrest and Harriet, 23
McCloskey, Reese and Mabel, 22
McCloud, Richard and Ellen, 20, 21; author, 116, 121, 122
McClurg, Virginia, 175, 176
McKinley, William, 36, 37, 84, 86
Mears, Otto, 123
Medicine: epidemics, 223–24, 225; health, 221–22; home remedies, 225; patent medicines, 226; physicians, 222–23; venereal diseases, 229. *See also* children; health; individual diseases; women
Memorial Day, 136; GAR, 207–08, 209–10, 212
Men: baseball, 193–96; business, 20–22, 46–48; education, 112–13; politics, 75–78; unions, 52–54; woman's suffrage, 171–72; workers, 59–60, 128, 139. *See also* children; Durango; red light district; Sandwich; women
Mercer, Margaret, 231, 232
Merchants: hours, 57; impact, 46–47; tokens, 56. *See also* business; Durango; Sandwich
Mesa Verde, 240; women save, 175–76. *See also* cliff dwellings
Methodists, 156, 159; cookbooks, 160; revival, 155–56; Sunday school orchestra, 148; women, 159
Mining: coal, 53–54, 138; contests, 198–99; declines, 248; gold, 35;

San Juans, 99. *See also* Cripple Creek; Klondike Gold Rush; San Juan Smelter
Mitten, John, 134
Modern Woodmen of America, 143
Monteith, Ogle and Christina, 19
Moody, Dwight, xvi
Morgan, Louise, 22
Mormons, 157
Mosher, Frederic and Julia, 20, 47
Music, 17, 40, 61; bands, 74, 232–33, 235; concert, 234. *See also* songs
National Guard, 206. *See also* football
Newark, 5
Newark Station, 6
Newman, Charles and Marian, 21, 217; building, 59
Newspapers, 37, 115–17. *See also* Miles Castle; David Day
Northrop, Henry, 181

Oglesby, Richard, 206
Old Settlers Association, 215
Old Settlers Union Picnic Association, 215

Palmer, William Jackson, 11, 53
Parks, 94
Parrott City, 12, 249
People's Press, 7
Peters, Theodore, 54
Phenix Theatre, 95–96
Philippine Islands, 39
Photography, 65
Plano, 5, 107. *See also* Reorganized Church . . . Saints
Populist Party, 30; "Free Silver," 81–87, trusts, 39; woman's suffrage, 171–72
Porter, 53, 54
Porter Fuel Company, 53–54
Porter, John, 12
Porter, Mary, 22
Porter, May, 229
Powell, Bint, 47
Potawatomi Indians, 3, 18
Preservation: history, 215–16
Presbyterians, 156, 160

258

INDEX

Price, Sarah, 110
Prohibition: churches support, 155–56; fight for, 76–77, 91–92. *See also* WCTU
Prostitution, 23, 229, 230. *See also* Durango; Red Light District
Pullman Strike, 33–34

Railroads, 4–5, 10, 30; danger, 71, 232; Pullman strike, 33–34. *See also* Chicago, Burlington & Quincy; Denver & Rio Grande
Recreation, 198–99, 200–01; vacations, 199–200
Red Light District, 21, 22–23, 89, 95–96; problems, 228–29, 230. *See also* prostitution; saloon
Religion, xiv, 7, 10; ministers, 153–56. *See also* churches; individual denominations
Reorganized Church of Jesus Christ of Latter Day Saints, 157–58
Republican Party; 10, dominance, 78–79. *See also* Durango; "Free Silver"; Populist Party; Sandwich
Rico, 31
Rivers, Bessie, 23
Rogers, Estella, 224
Roosevelt, Theodore, 38, 39; politics, 75
Russell, Lillian, 185

Salazar, Anton, 19
Saloon, 9, 48; fight to abolish, 76–77, 91–92, 212; social impact, 227–28. *See also* red light district; Sandwich
Sandwich: birth/growth, 3–9; city government, 89–98, 193, 230; cost of living, 59–61; depression 1890s, 29–33; economic hinterlands, 99–102; politics (local), 75–79; promotion, 121–25; Spanish-American War, 35–39; twentieth century, 245–49, 252
Sandwich Bank, 72
Sandwich Bicycle Club, 192
Sandwich Creamery, 55

Sandwich Fair, 126–27, 137, 138; crime, 231
Sandwich Fair Association, 126
Sandwich House, 73
Sandwich Manufacturing Company, 6, 69, 240; history, 48–49; workers, 139
Sandwich Opera House, 71, 142, 243n; apex, 234; history, 233; play, 150
San Juan & New York Smelter, 11
San Juan Pioneer's Association, 216
San Juan Smelter: history, 50–51; workers 139. *See also* environment
Sankey, Ira, xvi
Saxe, Grace, 155
Schools, 106–09; high schools, 107–09; problems, 111–12; students, 141, 142, 148, 150; textbooks, 111. *See also* children; teachers
Scoville, Jeanette, 175
Sedgwick, John, 207
Sedgwick, Wesley: banker, 47–48; Enterprise Company, 50
Sedgwick Post, 207–09
Sensabaugh, Oscar, 156
Sex, 180–81; venereal disease, 229. *See also* medicine; red light district; women
Shaw, James, 4
Shefler, Mattie, 23
Sherlock Holmes, 133
Sherman Silver Purchase Act, 30, 80
Silverton, 11, 31, 101
Skating, 142, 200–01
Skiing, 201
Sloan, Robert, 20
Smallpox, 224
Smelter City Brewing Association, 55
Smith, Georgie, 23
Smith, Louis, 201
Smith, Lucy, 225
Smith, Mabel, 201
Smith, William and Agnes, 145; career, 184; family, 201, 202
Somonauk, 5, 107, 198, 224; band, 235; rival, 8
Songs, 191, 202, 252; Civil War, 208; golden age, 202; hymns, 151, 163. *See also* music
Spanish-American War, 35–39

259

INDEX

Standard Smelter, 51
Starved Rock, 200
St. Mary's Academy, 106, 107, 158
"Stegosaurus ungulatus," 240
Stinson, Stephen B., 5, 8
Strater, Henry, 31
Strater Hotel, 136
Streetcars, 58–59, 68, 74
Strikes (labor): coal, 54; Pullman, 33–34; smelter, 52
Sunday, William "Billy," 151, 156; career, 153–54; saloons, 227
Susio, Antonio, 54
Suydam, Simon, 100
Sweeney, Daniel and Corthrise, 22, 129
Sycamore, 8

Tabor, Horace, 84, 233
Teachers, 105–06, 107, 109–10. See also children; schools
Telephone, 57; "central," 168
Temperance, 9. See also prohibition; saloon
Thanksgiving, 161, 237
Tiffany, George and Lillian, 21
Tobacco, 226. See also children; medicine
Tocqueville, Alexis, 186
Toi Gee, 25
Tourism, 125–26
Track (sport), 198
Transportation, 4. See also railroads
Trew, Sarah, 110
Trimble Springs, 192
Troeger, Jerry, 161
Turner, Frederick Jackson, xv, xviii, 250
Turner, Hope, 22
Twain, Mark (Samuel Clemens), xviii, 117, 133; politics, 75; recreation, 202; weather, 239, 240; women, 168–69

Underground Railroad, 8
Union Band, 74, 136, 233, 235
United Mine Workers, 52
United States government: impact, 99, 249
Utes, 18, 125; cede land, 100, 127–28, 147

Victorian Era, 1–2, 10; "Age of Innocence," 221–22; architecture, 43–44, 59, 68, 69; conformity, 106; church going, 151–52; election 1896, 86–87; ends, 251–52; joiners, 205; leisure, 202; memories, 240; racial, 23; society, 238; women, 179, 185–86
Vaile, William and Julia, 20
Valdez, Martin and Matilde, 19
VanScoy, Abraham T., 112

Walter, Gus, 55
Warren, Henry, 159
Water, 12; pollution, 227; settlement, 10; urban, 96. See also environment
Weather, 135, 239–40
Wentworth, John, 6
Wesson, Silas Dexter, 215, 216
Western Federation of Miners, 52
White, A. Gates: mayor, 77, 98, 217; prohibition fight, 91, 93
Wilder, Henry, 233
Williams, Milan, 155
Winne, Charles, 21
Woman's Christian Temperance Union (WCTU): goals, 212, 215; suffrage, 213
Woman's Literary and Study Club, 174
Woman's Relief Corps, 210–11, 212
Women: addiction, 12, 213, 229; athletics, 177–79; auxiliaries, 205; baseball, 179, 194; bicycling, 191–92; "central," 168; churches, 153, 159–60; clubs, 99, 144; courtship, 181–82; crime, 231; divorce, 182–83; editors, 115, 116; health, 179–80, 225; ideal, 147; nursing, 168; physicians, 47, 176; preachers, 177; principals, 110; relief corps, 210–11; role, 167; self improvement, 173–75; sex education, 180–81; teachers, 105–06, 110; typewriter, 168; vote, 78, 169–72; wife, 19, 22, 184–85; World's Fair, xiv–xv
Woodbury, William, 21, 111, 142, 245; career, 108–09, 110, 112–13; courtship, 181–82; Christmas, 236; football, 197; flu, 225; recreation, 201. See also Nellie Forsythe

260

Woodward, John, 134
World's Columbian Exposition, xiii–xviii
Worthington, Fanny, 177
Wright, Silas, 161

Wycoff, William and Maria, 21

Young Men's Christian Association, 214–15